111

Economics, Politics, and American Public Policy

Economics, Politics, and American Public Policy

James J. Gosling

M.E.Sharpe
Armonk, New York
London, England

Library of Congress Cataloging-in-Publication Data

Gosling, James J.
  Economics, politics, and American public policy / by James J. Gosling.
    p. cm.
  Includes index.
  ISBN 978-0-7656-1751-4 (pbk. : alk. paper)
  1. United States—Politics and government—2001– 2. United States—Economic
conditions—2001– 3. United States—Economic policy—2001– I. Title.

JK275.G68 2007
320.60973—dc22   2007003969

Printed in the United States of America

The paper used in this publication meets the minimum requirements of
American National Standard for Information Sciences
Permanence of Paper for Printed Library Materials,
ANSI Z 39.48-1984.

BM (p)   10   9   8   7   6   5   4   3   2

To Connie, my loving and supportive wife

Contents

List of Figures and Tables

Figures

Tables

Preface

Economic policy making involves political choice—choice that is value based. Should policy makers pursue economic policy that sacrifices jobs and personal income to control inflation, or should they tolerate higher inflation to maximize employment? Economists can describe and explain the trade-off between inflation and unemployment and its consequences, but policy makers decide where to set the balance. Economics and politics are inextricably linked in the fabric of American democracy. Economic conditions affect political decision making, and the political choices of economic policy makers affect the economy.

The market allocates value in a capitalistic economy. It cannot, however, adjust that allocation and its effects. Only government can. Using the tools of taxing and spending, policy makers decide the extent to which public policy should redistribute income and provide a social safety net. They can also provide financial incentives for business to increase its investment and for households to save more. Yet choices such as these have economic consequences to which policy makers are attentive. Moreover, globalization forces policy makers to consider the economic effects of their choices on foreign economies and on the international political relations that accompany them, as well as the reciprocal effects on the United States itself.

In exploring these relationships, this book is organized to parallel the development of a course I teach at the University of Utah. Like so many other authors, I decided to write this book because I could not find a core text that covers the subject matter the way I prefer to teach it. Although the interrelationship of economics and politics is intellectually challenging, I have made a special effort to make it understandable through clear writing and well-chosen examples, many of which students will find prominently covered by the media. Technical terms are set in bold type when first introduced and they are included in a glossary at the back of the book.

Instructors may wish to use this book as their primary text in courses on America's political economy. It would also work well as a key text in courses on American public policy. I wrote *Economics, Politics, and American Public Policy* to be accessible to undergraduates, including students majoring in something other than political science or economics, as well as to graduate students enrolled in master's programs in public policy and administration, who come to these programs with a wide variety of undergraduate degrees. This book could also serve as a supplementary text in American government courses.

A less comprehensive version of this book was published in 2000 by Addison Wesley Longman under the title *Politics and the American Economy*. Thanks go to Pearson Education for conveying the publishing rights to me.

James J. Gosling
Salt Lake City, Utah

Economics, Politics, and American Public Policy

An Introduction to America's Political Economy

Politics and economics are inextricably linked in the fabric of American democracy. The condition of the economy can affect political choice, and political decision making can influence the course of the economy. An economy in **recession**—a condition in which the real (**inflation**-adjusted) **gross domestic product** (GDP) declines for two consecutive quarters—affects both government revenues and spending. Personal income declines as a result of the increased unemployment that accompanies a sustained drop in the economy's output of goods and services. As aggregate personal income falls, so does aggregate consumption, and this lowered demand translates into reduced corporate profits. Thus both personal and corporate income tax revenues decline as a result of their shrinking tax bases, hitting the federal government the hardest, given its heavy reliance on income taxes. Although states also see their income tax revenues fall, they suffer an even bigger loss of sales tax revenues, because the sales tax remains their primary revenue source. Local governments that make sizable use of these tax instruments feel similar effects. Those that depend primarily on property taxes are less immediately affected, though a prolonged recession and slow recovery will typically drive down property values and correspondingly reduce the property tax base.

A recessionary economy packs a one-two punch. It depresses revenues and drives up public expenditures. As unemployment rises and personal income declines, more and more people become eligible for government programs that provide need-based public assistance. Welfare rolls and unemployment compensation claims rise, as do applications for publicly supported medical assistance. The latter, with medical care costs rising well in excess of general inflation, puts the greatest pressure on government budgets. The federal government and the states feel the fiscal pinch the most. All persons who meet eligibility standards for the joint federal- and state-supported Medicaid program have a legal (statutory) **entitlement** to receive the services it supports.

These fiscal pressures can wreak havoc on government budgets. Expenditures rise faster than revenues. The federal government can make do by incurring a **budget deficit** and using debt to finance costs over current revenues. In contrast, all states, except for Vermont, must balance their budgets; and a deficit leaves governors and legislatures little choice but to cut expenditures or raise additional revenues, both painful prospects politically.

Economic Performance Affects Political Relationships

Economic woes not only affect taxing and spending decisions, but they can also influence partisan political relations. The minority party is usually not shy about attributing a declining or flat economy to the leadership and policies of the majority party. Economic problems invite fanfare. The media, loving demonstrative controversy, zeros in on the escalating partisan attacks. That attention, in turn, crystallizes the popular association of economic troubles with the administration in power. As might be expected, the political conse- quences can be dramatic. Witness the experience of presidents Jimmy Carter and George H.W. Bush. President Carter had the misfortune of serving during a period of **stagflation**, in which high inflation accompanied slow economic growth and higher-than-expected unemployment. President Bush, basking in the afterglow of America's military successes in the Persian Gulf, soon found his popularity undermined by the politically ill-timed (at least from his perspective and that of his supporters) national recession of 1990–91. The recession's fiscal effects pushed the fiscal year (FY) 1992 deficit up above $290 billion, a level that Democratic candidate Bill Clinton exploited in the 1992 presidential campaign. The recession also all but wiped out the fiscal gains expected from the Budget Enforcement Act of 1990, a major deficit- reduction package that included a highly controversial tax increase. It was President Bush, not Congress, however, who soaked up most of the attention and blame for raising taxes, because he agreed to the tax increase not long after proclaiming on national television, "Read my lips, no new taxes."

The euphemism that "a rising tide lifts all boats" aptly applies to political economy. Political leaders of a national economy that experiences strong, sustained growth, with full employment but without excessive inflation, enjoy a veritable win-win situation. Favorable economic numbers are commonly associated with the high political popularity of elected public officials. Full employment with widely shared rising personal income provides the means for people to get ahead and improve their standard of living. It also swells public treasuries, giving governments the financial ability to meet the claims of groups and interests that would not be met in tight economic times. Even faced with a budget deficit, strong economic growth can allow policy makers to meet some claims for added spending while contributing to deficit reduction.

President Clinton, in his campaign for reelection, benefited from a sound economy. Taking full advantage of favorable economic reports preceding the 1996 election, he used almost every public forum to tie his administration's fiscal policies to the economy's strength. The litany commonly included the following evidence of success: a twelve-month, 3.4 percent increase in real (inflation-adjusted) GDP from the fourth quarter of FY 1995 to the fourth quarter of FY 1996, capped by a 4.7 percent increase from July through September 1996; the lowest combined rate of unemployment and inflation—the so-called **misery index**—since the administration of Lyndon Johnson; the creation of more than 11 million jobs since he took office; a reduction of more than 2 million recipients on the welfare rolls over the same period; and a national budget deficit at the end of FY 1996 that reached its lowest point since 1981 in **current dollars** and its lowest point since 1974 as a percentage of the GDP. With this economic record as a backdrop, President Clinton went on to handily defeat Republican challenger Bob Dole. Not surprisingly, national polls showed that the condition of the economy significantly influenced voter support for the president.

As the 2004 presidential election approached, President George W. Bush found himself with declining support (which had fallen steadily since mid-2003) for his handling of the war in Iraq. His popularity, however, got a lift from a strongly growing economy, for real GDP grew by 4.2 percent in 2004, up from 2.7 percent in 2003 and 1.6 percent in 2002. Fortunately for Bush, the strong GDP growth in 2004 was accompanied by strong job creation. In the ten months preceding the presidential election, the economy created slightly more than 1.8 million net new jobs. That performance was in marked contrast to a net loss of 1.7 million jobs from October 2001 through August 2003,[1] a period of economic recovery that opponents of the president labeled "a jobless recovery."

Policy Choice Affects Economic Relationships

Just as the economy can affect policy choice and its associated politics, political decisions can influence the performance of the economy. As discussed earlier, national political leaders see a healthy economy as advancing their political fortunes. Policy makers worldwide do what they can to support domestic economic prosperity. The tools they use may differ, but their goals are pointedly similar: economic growth, full employment, acceptably low levels of inflation, and adequate investment to foster capital development and innovation. The trick for policy makers pursuing economic growth is to expand the economy fully to its potential for production, being careful not to exceed that potential and run the risk of promoting accelerated inflation and the rising unemployment that follows. Chapter 2 provides an extended discussion of the most commonly used measures of national economic performance, and it applies those measures to evaluate how well the U.S. economy has performed over time.

Beyond national economic policy goals, governments also may want to pursue policies that extend economic development to underdeveloped regions of their nation. Directed regional growth, tapping resources and labor that had not previously been exploited to their potential, holds the promise of both enlarging the national economic pie and minimizing problems that result from a heavy concentration of industrial activity and population. In the United States, the federal government has largely been inactive in using policy tools to direct economic development geographically, in comparison to other national governments. Its closest venture has come in creating the Tennessee Valley Authority and the Appalachian Commission as investments in infrastructural support for regional economic development.

In addition to directing economic development geographically, governments can use their **regulatory authority**, taxing powers, and financial resources to prevent, discourage, or encourage certain *kinds* of economic development within their borders. Or they can take action into their own hands and develop and own the means of production themselves. In comparison to the rest of the industrial world, the U.S. federal government plays a limited role in shaping the composition of industrial production. It has, however, engaged in comparatively limited assistance to selected industries, employing a diverse and somewhat incoherent assortment of devices such as **tax expenditures** (special provisions in the tax code reducing liability), loans and loan guarantees, subsidies, financial support of basic and applied research, and job training assistance.

State and local governments have gone the farthest in supporting economic development. States have established agencies whose job it is to promote economic development, making special efforts to entice large manufacturing and service industries to open new plants and offices within their borders. States often compete against each other over economic development, using tax incentives, loans, subsidized labor training, relaxed regulations, and highway improvements and freeway access as their primary enticements.

Local governments also strive to attract new and expanded development within their jurisdictions, which puts communities in competition with one another. In that competition, local governments tend to employ some of the same tools used by the states, turning most often to **tax abatements**, which can consist of reduced tax rates, deferrals of tax liability, or outright exemption from taxation. Beyond tax considerations, local governments also can forgive corporations from their share of the costs of physical infrastructure needed to support an industrial plant or a large service enterprise, including the costs of curbs and gutters, street lighting, power sources, and extension of sewer lines. In addition, where permitted by their state, local governments can offer relaxed regulations to attract development, most commonly in the form of variances from planning requirements or land-use restrictions.

Corporations put these incentives in the larger context of a state's or a community's business climate and the quality of life it offers. Business climate includes the types of taxes a government employs and the tax effort it makes, prevailing wage rates and the extent of unionization in the area, the preparedness and cost of labor, and the overall regulatory climate. Quality of life refers to such considerations as quality of schools and higher educational institutions, crime rate, climate, neighborhoods and available housing, and recreational opportunities. Industries also consider other factors that bear on the soundness of business decisions, such as the ready availability of raw materials and energy resources, proximity to suppliers and transportation facilities, and access to key markets. In fact, research over the past three decades suggests that it is these elements of a sound business decision that most influence choice of location.[2] State and local government incentives appear to exercise only a marginal influence, primarily when the traditional elements of a sound business decision are essentially equal. Yet this knowledge has not dulled state and local officials' enthusiasm for development incentives. They have not been willing in a highly competitive environment to take the chance of losing ground because they fail to match or exceed the concessions offered by their competitors. This knowledge has, however, prompted state officials to redirect a good part of their efforts toward keeping industries within their state's borders and encouraging them to expand there. It also has increasingly prompted them to offer development incentives only after a corporation has narrowed its geographic search based on sound business considerations.

While these limited efforts to direct economic development geographically and the selective efforts to support industrial development of a certain kind have some effect on the economy, the real influence of government on the U.S. economy comes from the national government's efforts to influence the performance of the economy overall. Two macroeconomic policy instruments loom largest toward that end: monetary policy and fiscal policy.

Monetary policy, discussed in chapter 3, attempts to alter the money supply to influence the direction of the economy. Monetary policy works on the expectation that additions to the money supply get spent, fueling aggregate demand, while contractions of the money supply constrict aggregate demand. Changes in the money supply take place through the medium of a nation's credit system. Governments usually do not just print more currency to increase the money supply, a proven recipe for inflation; they influence the availability and cost of loanable funds. Restricted availability and the increasing cost of credit lowers aggregate demand, and liberal availability and the declining cost of credit raises it.

Unlike fiscal policy, monetary policy is not the direct responsibility of presidents or prime ministers. The responsibility for monetary policy lies with a nation's central bank; however, it would be naive to suggest that presidents and prime ministers do not influence monetary policy. Yet the degree of that influence varies with the relative political insulation of the central bank. In the United States, the Federal Reserve System functions as our central bank, and it is structurally insulated from presidential or congressional control.

Fiscal policy, which is covered in detail in chapter 4, deals with national governments' use of taxing and spending to affect aggregate demand and thereby influence the course of the economy in desired directions. Legislative bodies make taxing and spending decisions in most democratic industrial nations. Those choices, however, are typically shaped by presidents or prime ministers, who use the budgetary process to set their nation's fiscal agenda. Their budget recommendations suggest how much a nation should spend in a given fiscal period, how it should raise revenues to finance that spending, and how much debt should be incurred to support spending not covered by current revenues. In the United States, it is the president who initiates fiscal policy and prioritizes spending among the many federal government programs. The Congress then decides the extent to which it will follow the president's lead, but its decentralized decision-making structures and process mitigate Congress's ability to produce a coherent alternative to the president's agenda, despite its attempts to reform the budgetary process toward that end.

Although states and local governments engage in taxing and spending, national economic forces overwhelm the fiscal effects of those choices. Moreover, because nearly all states and local governments must balance their budgets, state and local decisions about taxing and spending usually run counter to national fiscal policy directions. When a national recession broadly depresses state economies, reducing revenues and increasing the costs of public assistance programs, state policy makers have little choice but to increase taxes or fees or to cut spending in certain programs and reallocate that **budget authority** to others. Both tacks reinforce the recession's dampening effects. In contrast, federal policy makers use fiscal policy in an economic downturn to stimulate the economy through increased national government spending or decreased taxes. Local governments' taxing and spending decisions have even less effect on the national economy than do those of states. Their heavy reliance on the property tax and the high percentage of their budget devoted to personnel costs give local government policy makers little flexibility to affect aggregate demand.

All governments, however, function as customers within a market economy, purchasing goods and services from private vendors. The federal government is the biggest single public customer in the United States and in the world. In addition, its financial aid to state and local governments helps them to finance their purchases of goods and services in the marketplace. At the state level, for example, federal aid expended by state agencies variously ends up in the bank accounts of engineering firms whose employees design, construct, and improve state highways; companies that produce and sell computer hardware and software; physicians and other health-care workers who provide medical care to the needy; and private-sector auditors who perform financial and performance audits commissioned by state legislatures.

Federal grants-in-aid have risen markedly over the years, from only $7 billion in FY 1960 to an estimated $454 billion in FY 2008. The Office of Management and Budget (OMB) estimates that federal aid for health-related programs will reach $219 billion in 2008, with the vast majority, nearly $202 billion, going to Medicaid. Another $53 billion is targeted for transportation, with $38 billion devoted to highways.[3]

The OMB projects that the federal government will directly spend $149 billion on capital investment in FY 2008. Most of that spending, about $107 billion, will go to defense-related procurement.[4] The federal government will spend an additional $127 billion in that same year on research and development, with $73 billion supporting defense applications.[5]

The Normative Inheritance of America's Political Economy in Comparative Perspective

Economic policy makers in the United States do not make decisions in a vacuum. Their options are limited by the structure and processes of America's political institutions, by competing political interests with different power bases and resources at their disposal, and by historical experience and ideology. Ideology influences whether conditions should be treated as problems, how problems are to be defined, and the standards of judgment to be used in evaluating competing alternatives.[6]

Classical Liberalism's Influence

Classical liberalism, with its roots largely in the writings of seventeenth- and eighteenth-century British economic and political theorists, provides an ideology that still influences the way American policy makers, and even the general public, look at government, think about their relationship to it, and hold expectations of it. In both economic and political affairs, liberalism draws a sharp line between the private and public spheres of citizens' lives.

The central organizing tenet of liberalism is that individuals are the best judge of what is in their self-interest. They should be free, therefore, to pursue their own interests as they see them, as long as that pursuit does not abridge the rights of others to exercise freedom.

Government exists to protect the rights of people. For John Locke, a contract exists between government and the people, under which government protects individuals from having their rights to personal freedom and property infringed upon by others, in exchange for citizens' support of limited government. As part of that contract, government action is legitimate only when it protects individual rights better than individuals can protect them alone.[7] Government's protection of civil liberty and the market's facilitation of economic choice serve as vehicles toward self-actualization. For John Stuart Mill[8] and other utilitarians, that pursuit of self-interest by individuals leads in the aggregate to the greatest collective good for the greatest number.

The market allows buyers and sellers to come together of their own volition to benefit themselves: buyers obtaining what they want, and sellers receiving payment for their goods or services that are wanted. In a competitive marketplace, both buyers and sellers look to prices as a gauge of whether it is in their self-interest to enter into a transaction. Buyers compare the price charged with their sense of the expected quality of the product or service, and sellers price their wares with a sense of how the quality of their product or service compares with others available. A transaction occurs when the buyer believes he or she has found something of acceptable quality at an acceptable price. Competition keeps prices down, because the buyer can usually find the same or a similar product or service in the marketplace; when that is the case, price tends to become the determining factor, though customers also may consider the quality of service that sellers provide. The market makes available goods and services that people want because someone believes that he or she can earn a profit by making or selling them. But the market turns on someone wanting something in the first place. Sellers use advertising to create wants and to entice consumers to identify with their products and services.

For Adam Smith[9] and other economic liberals, the striking thing about the market is that economic order can emerge as the unintended consequence of the actions of many people, each seeking his or her self-interest. The market itself sets priorities for private resource investment and expenditure, and the market exchange of supply and demand determines value. The important point here is that the market becomes a device for coordinating the economy, but without top-down, centralized command. It is the market, for Smith, and not government, that defines the substance of the economic product, the specific array of goods and services available, their quality, and their distribution.

Markets, however, are not naturally occurring phenomena. They are defined by laws and regulations. Capitalism is not the same the world over. Government itself shapes the nature of the relationship between the economic enterprise and government's involvement in it. In all nations, government imposes limits on market relationships, but the extent of those limits can vary considerably among political systems. On the one hand, government policy makers can elect to play a relatively restrained role: establishing the rules of economic competition among private interests, refereeing breaches of those rules and imposing sanctions, protecting the public from harms occasioned by business's pursuit of profits, and guarding against monopolies and unfair market practices. On the other hand, they can confer monopoly status on a private enterprise or can give government itself monopoly power. Classical liberalism's inheritance leans toward a relatively more restrained regulatory role for government in the United States; however, as we shall see in chapter 7, U.S. policy makers have not shied away from both regulating in the public interest and, less benignly, serving the interests of those regulated. Over the past thirty years or so, they have also actively pursued procompetitive **deregulation**, most prominently in the areas of trucking, rail, commercial aviation, telecommunications, natural gas, electricity, and financial services.

Government policy makers can choose to play a strong role in national economic planning, or they can tend to leave choices about strategic business directions to corporate officers. They can lever banks to provide credit in support of government-blessed enterprises, or they can leave those decisions, as business choices, to banks and other financial institutions.

Aversion to National Economic Planning and Neocorporatist Guiding

Despite America's wartime experience with industrial policy, policy makers have shown little interest in national economic planning and government-guided credit allocation, with the notable exception of military technology and weapons development. Nor have U.S. policy makers been enamored of Europe's embrace of **neocorporatism**, which voluntarily brings together representatives of government, business, and labor to shape national industrial strategy and manage conflict among the sectors' participants. As applied in several continental European nations and in the United Kingdom and Ireland, the policy has selectively focused on establishing production priorities, allocating capital, and negotiating agreements covering prices, production levels, and wages. Neocorporatism works most effectively where both unions and corporations are organized into so-called **peak associations**, to which individual unions and corporations are willing to yield significant authority to represent their interests, and where government policy makers are willing to make concessions regarding economic and social policy as part of the bargaining. As Graham Wilson put the latter, "increases in welfare state benefits were often the oil that lubricated the machinery of agreements on economic policy."[10]

For the most part, the overseas appeal of neocorporatism dulled after the mid-1980s. Taxpayer resistance to high and rising welfare spending, changes in the composition of the labor force that eroded organized labor's strength, a diminished political focus on class issues, and the competitive pressures induced by globalization all contributed to weakening the fabric of neocorporatism. The rising competitive imperative of globalization put a growing premium on labor market flexibility, including greater freedom to hire and fire, as well as to exact work from employees given constraints imposed by generous bargained agreements on vacations, on sick leave, on maternity and paternity leave, and on what constitutes a disability.[11] Moreover, the liberal reawakening embodied in the "Reagan Revolution" in the United States and "Thatcherism" in the United Kingdom exerted a gravitational pull felt even in the traditional centers of Social Democracy.

Neocorporatism never caught on in the United States. Structurally, corporations and labor unions never gave their associations and federations enough power to represent them authoritatively. Individual corporations, inclined to go it alone in advancing their relationships with labor and government, often stake out conflicting positions. Individual unions such as the United Automobile Workers and the Teamsters have chartered their own course in labor relations, and particularly in wage negotiations, not reliant upon positions taken by the peak federations. Organized labor in the United States failed to achieve the penetration and strength that it did in Europe. After reaching a high of 33 percent in the mid-1950s, union membership as a proportion of the nonagricultural workforce declined precipitously to only about 12 percent in 2006.[12] Having escaped feudalism and never mounting a viable Socialist movement, the United States has had no sharply divided class system, no aristocracy, and no self-conscious working class—factors that foster union membership.

In Asia, with the notable exceptions of Singapore and Hong Kong, East Asian governments have played a strong role in shaping the course of economic development. Government officials have not been averse to pressuring banks to lend to favored corporations best positioned to advance national economic goals. Mercantilist industrial policy launched Japan on its ascendant path to world leadership in electronics and automobile manufacturing. Japan's Ministry of International Trade and Industry and Ministry of Finance applied their influence to direct capital from the Industrial Bank of Japan and the Japanese Development Bank to favored industries. Just as strengthening globalization eroded the underpinnings of European neocorporatism, it also weakened the ability of the ministries to control industrial development.

Compared to Europe and Asia, the U.S. government's intervention in the economy has been relatively restrained. Both ideology and the checks and balances of constitutional architecture have underlaid that restraint. So has historical development. As David Vogel points out, big business developed in the United States before big government did, a relationship reversed in most other nations.[13] As the saying went, "What is good for General Motors is good for the country."

Irrespective of differences regarding government's selective intervention to improve the direction and performance of the economy, all governments use their taxing and spending powers to alter the effects of market outcomes. The market allocates economic value but has no ability to redistribute market allocation. Only government can do that. The extent to which government is disposed to engage in redistribution varies considerably among nations and is largely a product of political culture and patterns of historical experience. As we shall see in chapters 8 and 9, the United States is less inclined than the Euro-area nations to raise the revenue necessary to pay for a well-funded, extensive network of social support—a strong safety net, as some may call it. Compared to the European states, the United States offers less generous cash public assistance benefits, less support for public housing and housing subsidies, and no system of universal health care, even though the United States spends a larger share of its national income on health care than does any other industrial nation.

The Allure of Keynesianism

Governments have not been reticent about using macroeconomic policy tools to influence the course of the economy. John Maynard Keynes, a British economic theorist, writing during the Great Depression, accepted the tenets of classical economic theory but also promoted a broader, more activist role for government in the market economy.[14] For Keynes, government has an obligation to secure the reliable performance of the economy as a whole. Although he recognized the power of the market to function as an invisible hand to coordinate the economy, he also realized that the economy is subject to periods of expansion and contraction. In a slumping economy, consumers are more wary of satisfying their material wants and more inclined to save rather than to spend. The resulting downturn in aggregate demand induces businesses to reduce inventories and postpone orders for new products, thus prompting manufacturers to cut back on production and lay off unneeded workers. This snowballing effect further propels the economy into decline and increases unemployment.

The Great Depression thrust unemployment to record heights in both the

United Kingdom and the United States. Contrary to classical economic theory, the economy showed no signs of self-correcting. The high unemployment of the Great Depression appeared not to be transitional, as the classical theory of self-adjusting labor markets suggested. Keynes feared that the economy would remain in the doldrums as long as low demand persisted.

Increased saving was not the answer for Keynes. In fact, he viewed saving as the enemy of recovery. Spending was the answer—spending that would increase aggregate demand. The problem for him was how to achieve increased demand in an environment of sustained underemployment of resources. That is where government comes in. National governments can use debt to finance spending beyond their ability to cover the costs out of current revenues. Keynes saw major deficit-financed government spending as the spark that could ignite the economy, propelling aggregate demand that would revitalize markets and bring the unemployed back to work. For Keynes, a large pool of trained workers existed during the Depression, who were ready and willing to go back to work if only there were sufficient demand in the economy for the products they produced. Massive government spending could create that demand, and Keynes viewed government as having an obligation to step in and get the economic ball rolling in a depressed economy.

Keynes, however, also saw that obligation as not just limited to recessionary conditions. An activist government should work to manage aggregate demand whenever market forces prove insufficient to create enough demand to keep unemployment at acceptable levels. Although Keynes preferred increased government spending as government's foremost instrument to expand demand, he recognized that demand could be fostered through tax cuts as well. But for tax cuts to generate increased demand, those benefiting from them would have to spend their increased after-tax income rather than save it. In worrisome economic conditions, people might be more prone to save rather than to spend. Significantly increased government spending, on the other hand, obviates that uncertainty; it translates directly into higher aggregate demand.

Keynesian theory also gives national economic policy makers the expectations and tools to cool down an overheated, inflationary-prone economy. The recipe again lies with government action to influence demand, reducing it by decreasing spending or increasing taxes. Keynes's primary concern, however, was not how to slow down an overheating economy but how to stimulate an economy operating below capacity, bringing it to full employment and sustaining it there.

The major political contribution of Keynesian theory is its justification for government intervention in the economy. Remember that classical liberal theory prescribes a limited role for government and requires that government justify its intervention in society and the economy. Keynes not only legitimized government intervention to secure national economic prosperity; he also honored it. In doing so, his activist orientation has had lasting political implications. Those supporting activist government, believing that government has a highly constructive role to play in improving the quality of life and conditions of its citizens, broadened the agenda to include other forms of government intervention, including justification for a growing welfare state.

In focusing on government intervention in managing aggregate demand to achieve full employment, Keynes did not worry much about the inflationary effects of overstimulating the economy beyond its productive capacity, because his primary concern was how to mobilize underutilized resources. That concern fell to his intellectual successors. One prominent disciple, A.W. Phillips, identified an inverse relationship between unemployment and inflation.[15] He found that as unemployment falls, inflation rises, because the growing scarcity of labor drives up wage rates; and higher wage rates typically inflate the cost of the products or services provided—that is, unless they are accompanied by proportionally increased productivity. He found the converse also to be true: inflation drives up the cost of labor, inducing employers to attempt to get by with less of it. Thus governments face a dilemma. Their efforts to increase aggregate demand can lead to inflation that rises to unacceptable levels. Conversely, their efforts to control inflation can lead to growing unemployment.

The trade-off apparent in the so-called **Phillips curve** reinforced the interventionist inclinations of Keynesians. It became incumbent on economic policy makers to anticipate the effects of this trade-off and to use fiscal and monetary policy tools (with Keynesians preferring the fiscal policy variety) to mitigate its negative effects, striving for an acceptable balance between unemployment and inflation. In employing policy tools to achieve that objective, policy makers tend to err on one side or the other. They may be willing to accept a little more unemployment for a little less inflation, or the converse. That choice represents an inherently political judgment. The stagflation of the late Carter years, and the periods of strong economic growth with low unemployment *and* low inflation during the second half of the 1990s and the recovery from the 2001 recession, prompted both economists and policy makers to question the empirical validity of the postulated trade-off.

Capitalism and Democracy

Our classical liberal inheritance holds that individuals know best what is in their self-interest. America's capitalistic market economy and its democratic political system provide avenues for individuals to act in their own interest, whether they act individually or participate as members of enterprises or associations. In the market, individuals or collective enterprises participate as self-interested buyers or sellers. In democratic politics, individual participation takes a number of forms: expressing political opinions and policy preferences publicly, supporting candidates for office, voting, and contacting elected representatives and other public officials. Individuals also seek to further their personal interests by joining their forces in organized groups. As members of interest groups, individuals contribute to their organization's financial support and stand ready to add their voice to its collective voice when called upon.

Both markets and democratic politics distribute things that people value. Participants judge the extent to which these systems produce outcomes that are indeed in their interest and commensurate with what they believe they deserve. This sense of just deserts lies at the center of Robert Lane's important comparison of market justice and political justice.[16] Using a myriad of public opinion data, he argues that Americans regard the market as more just than democratic politics. The public readily recognizes the value they derive from market transactions. They feel that they deserve what they get, for they are putting either money or product on the line, and the competitive interaction of supply and demand is yielding a fair price for what they are getting in return. The relationship between cost and return is direct and evident. Such is not the case for politics. National taxpayers typically question the value they get from government in relation to what they pay in taxes. They typically recognize few tangible benefits that directly affect their lives, while they see their tax dollars supporting benefits received by others. Taxpayers also may question the amount of government spending in support of nondivisible goods, such as national defense and environmental protection, viewing it in excess of what they believe is needed to accomplish national objectives. At the same time, they may exclude collective goods altogether from any calculus of personal benefit, as Robert Lane suggests. In general, too, Americans share a sense that there is "fat" in government programs, that government agencies can operate more efficiently with fewer resources devoted to administrative overhead. This belief stems in part from how Americans view the public sector in relation to the private sector.

Recent poll data reinforce Lane's conclusion that a significant majority of Americans believe that the U.S. marketplace provides people with the opportunity to succeed and that hard work is the ticket to success. According to the Pew Research Center's trend study of American public opinion and values, four out of five respondents consistently agreed at different points between 1994 and 2004 with the statement that "everyone has it in their own power to succeed,"[17] and seven out of ten respondents consistently agreed at different points between 1994 and 2000 with the statement that "most people who want to get ahead can make it if they're willing to work hard."[18] A Gallup Organization survey found

81 percent of respondents agreeing that America affords "plenty of opportunity and anyone who works hard can go as far as they want."[19] In another Gallup poll, 76 percent were satisfied with the "opportunity for a person in this nation to get ahead by working hard."[20] Responding to a Washington Post–Harvard University–Kaiser Family Foundation poll, 78 percent agreed with the proposition that "people should take responsibility for their own lives and economic well-being and not expect other people to help."[21] Poll data also show that the public does not begrudge the success of those who achieve it. Nearly nine of ten Americans (89 percent) "admire people who get rich by working hard."[22] And of those who believe that they "are doing well financially," 86 percent attribute their success to their "own efforts and abilities."[23]

A Carnegie Corporation–funded survey of immigrant opinion shows that immigrants are attracted to the United States by the same values that Americans hold dear: freedom, opportunity, and economic return for personal effort. Almost nine in ten say that the United States is better than their country when it comes to "having more opportunity to earn a good living." Eight in ten agree that "a person has to work very hard in this country to make it—nobody gives you anything for free." Nor are immigrants looking for government assistance; they are seeking jobs. A large majority (73 percent) say that "it is extremely important to work and stay off welfare."[24]

In the private sector, individuals and enterprises assume risks in their pursuit of rewards. The quest for an acceptable profit margin motivates risk taking by business. Sole owners or partners invest their own resources in entrepreneurial ventures, commonly incurring debt to finance new businesses. Large corporations may turn to the broader public for financing, offering shares of stock for sale in the financial marketplace. Here corporate officers take risks with their and other people's money, and the return received depends on how well the corporation does financially, though corporate officers are often insulated personally from the consequences of underperformance, as their base level of compensation frequently remains intact nonetheless. Moreover, corporate contracts commonly provide executives with severance pay should they be terminated. With small businesses, it is the owners who directly suffer the consequences of underperformance or failure: their profits decline or their losses mount, potentially forcing them into bankruptcy. But risk is a recognized part of entrepreneurial activity. Investors put their money behind what they believe are good economic ventures—benefiting when right and losing when wrong. A certain direct responsiveness and accountability exist.

Even though Americans have faith in market capitalism, preferring market allocation to political distribution, they hold business corporations and their management in somewhat lower regard, and that difference has grown following the corporate scandals of the early to mid-2000s, in which several highly publicized exposés uncovered officers of several large corporations overstating sales, inflating revenues, and hiding debt to inflate their company's stock prices. The corporate names of Enron, Global Crossing, WorldCom, Tyco, and Adelphi Communications became synonymous with greed and corruption. Most surprisingly, public opinion surveys that followed reporting of the scandals found a majority of respondents perceived the uncovered behavior as not out of the ordinary, viewing it as "not isolated," "always like this," or "always been commonplace."[25]

In citizens' relationship with government, they may vote for elected officials to represent their interests and may use a number of avenues to influence their representatives' decisions, but it is the elected officials and their appointees who make the choices that shape public policies and allocate resources. Responsibility and accountability are far from direct. Individuals do not control their own destiny through their political participation. Their interests compete with the interests of others and get mediated through the politics of mutual partisan adjustment. Poll data consistently show that a sizable majority of the public believes that elected officials do not represent its interests. Only about a third of the respondents consistently agreed with the statement that "most elected officials care what people like me think" when asked by Pew pollsters in the 1990s and first half of the 2000s. And between 66 and 76 percent of respondents agreed with the statement that "elected officials in Washington lose touch with the people pretty quickly."[26]

Not only do people trust the market more than they trust politics, but the market itself inhibits efforts by policy makers to alter market allocations. As Charles Lindblom argues, the market "imprisons" policy making that attempts to move from market justice to greater distributive justice. The market possesses what Lindblom refers to as "an automatic punishing recoil." Policy makers who look to sizable tax increases to finance programs of redistribution must confront the anticipated dampened aggregate demand and its effects on employment. Market forces also stand ready to punish attempts to greatly strengthen government regulation in the public interest, such as efforts to toughen environmental protection standards that may include requiring industry to adopt expensive new technology. Calls for raising the minimum wage or establishing a "living wage" are met with estimates of the economic consequences of those initiatives.[27]

Government policy makers are fully aware of the aggregate consequences of business executives pursuing their own bottom-line interests, and they realize that the automatic punishing recoil of business disincentives can hit them as well. When the economy suffers, elected government officials know that they, too, could lose their jobs. As Lindblom puts it, "Government needs a strong economy just as much as business does, and the people need and demand it even more."[28]

The Problem of the Noncompetitive
and Growing Income Inequality

Americans, on the whole, reject the idea of an essentially equal distribution of material rewards. They prize equality of opportunity and display a healthy distaste for forms of discrimination that would keep anyone from his or her place at the starting line. Yet they distrust government advantaging anyone in that competition, particularly when government action benefits someone else. The problem remains how to deal with those who fail to succeed. What about those who "fall through the cracks" of capitalism? What obligation does government have to them? Further, if people regard redistributive programs suspiciously, how can people be expected to support or tolerate them politically?

If people generally believe that they get about what they deserve in the marketplace, as Lane argues and public opinion research continues to support, how can they be expected to treat those who get very little? In dealing with this issue, most Americans tend to differentiate conceptually between the "deserving needy" and the "not-so-deserving needy." Because the working presumption is that people want to get ahead and will act in their self-interest toward that end, those who find themselves in need through no fault of their own, such as those who have become disabled on the job, merit public assistance of some sort. Conversely, those who do not make substantial effort to compete, even if it may mean competing at the lowest rungs on the social ladder, are seen as less deserving of public assistance. Within this rigid characterization, people struggle most with questions about government's obligation to those who are gainfully employed but earn barely enough to keep them out of poverty or about those whose economic fortunes have fallen, who have lost well-paying jobs (for example, as a result of corporate downsizing), and who have exhausted their personal savings while waiting for comparable employment.

In putting these issues in perspective, Americans tend to fall back on the principle of market justice. If a person falls on hard times, he or she needs at least to get by as best as possible—if necessary, taking a job well below one's previous station in life. Even better, this American ethic calls upon that individual to regroup; seek retraining, if available; and start anew. Reality attests, however, to the many practical obstacles that thwart such a turnaround.

Conventional wisdom suggests that government does have an obligation to assist people caught in certain circumstances to help themselves. For instance, few question the value of unemployment compensation. Most see government as having a legitimate obligation to provide the means of support to those who find themselves temporarily out of work. Their approval may rest in part on the fact that they, as taxpayers, are not paying for unemployment compensation; employers are. Similar support exists for Social Security, for which the criterion of just deserts influences how people perceive the largely compulsory retirement program administered by the federal government. With Social Security, people who meet minimum employment requirements during their working years contribute, along with their employers, to their own retirement. Retirees are just getting back what they deserve—or at least that is how most Americans see it, despite the significant redistributive features of Social Security. But what about the longer-term needy who have been unemployed for a protracted period or those who work part- or full-time but who fail to earn enough to keep them out of poverty? That is the subject of discussion in chapter 8.

The debate preceding recent welfare reform in America addressed these questions and reinforced the notion of temporary assistance directed at getting the downtrodden back on their feet. Reformers decried welfare as an institution on which millions of recipients had become dependent. The challenge for reformers was how to get recipients off welfare and back into the economy as competitors. Work experience and job training became part of the formula for success. It was widely recognized, however, that a combination of insufficient jobs and budgetary constraints that limit training opportunities left a large number of chronically unemployed still dependent and without any improved means to compete. For them, government's admonition became: just do your best. Federal funds would no longer be available to support welfare benefits for those who exceed government-imposed time limits on aid. The questions persist nonetheless. What has happened, and will happen, to those who remain unemployed and needy? Whose obligation—if anyone's—is it to provide assistance? In reality, does that obligation pass from the federal government and the states to local communities and private charities? Or is that obligation reduced, in practice, to a minimum, as government policy squeezes dependency out of its system of public assistance? The verdict is still out, but we can expect that millions will continue to fall through capitalism's cracks.

Among those fortunate enough to have jobs and earned income, income inequality rose sharply over the past three decades. Not only did the market allocation of cash income become more unequal, but federal income tax policy exacerbated income inequality. Those at the top of the income spectrum increased their share of both pre-tax and after-tax income the most. Expansion of the Earned Income Tax Credit (EITC) and the child tax credit improved the after-tax position of low-income earners, but middle-income earners experienced the greatest loss of market-income share, and they received the smallest relative benefit from federal income tax cuts. Chapter 9 discusses rising income inequality and the associated middle-class squeeze.

Measuring Economic Performance

Before we turn to economic policy making, focusing specifically on monetary and fiscal policy, it makes sense to examine how economists measure a nation's economic performance. As we shall see, economists employ a number of different, but related, indicators of national economic performance. This chapter covers eight of them: output, income, saving, investment, worker productivity, employment, unemployment, and inflation. It discusses how these indicators are measured, their interrelationships, and the tradeoffs that exist among them.

Output, Income, Saving, and Investment

Every dollar of economic output creates a corresponding dollar of income. The earners of that income can either spend or save it. In a strongly growing economy, consumers satisfy more of their wants and needs, and businesses increase their productive capacity to meet higher consumer demand. As economic growth and the corresponding income it generates declines, consumers typically cut back on their purchases, reducing the very demand that entices businesses to manufacture products and provide services, though consumers may sustain their demand by cashing in some of their savings or by going into debt. Faced with lower demand, businesses will reduce their orders for new products and draw down their inventories. Needing fewer workers to produce products, businesses will likely reduce the size of their workforce. As employment growth falls, so does growth in personal income. As growth in personal income declines, so can demand for goods and services. A sliding rate of economic growth can reach the point when it turns negative. Yet before we discuss the concept of an economic recession, we need to explore how output and income are measured.

A country's economic output can be measured in one of two basic ways: its **gross domestic product** (GDP) or its **gross national product** (GNP). The GDP includes the aggregate value of goods and services *produced or provided domestically*—that is, within a nation's borders. It does not matter who produces or provides them. Thus products manufactured by foreign-owned firms count toward a nation's GDP, just as if they were produced by a domestic industry. The GNP adds the profits of a nation's business firms earned from foreign operations, along with the wages of that nation's residents employed abroad, and it excludes profits from foreign-owned firms earned within that nation's borders, together with the wages of foreign workers employed in that nation. Of the two, the GDP is the more commonly used measure in the United States and elsewhere. International comparisons of national economic output are invariably made using the GDP.

Both measures deal with the *sale* of goods and services in the marketplace. Neither captures the productive value of noncompensated labor, whether it takes the form of volunteer work, home improvement, or household chores. The GDP also excludes government **transfer payments** such as cash welfare assistance, unemployment compensation, veterans' benefits, or Social Security; nor does it count intergovernmental aid payments. Thus federal grants-in-aid to state and local governments, and state aid to local governments, are excluded. This fact does not mean that the economic activity financed by transfer payments and intergovernmental aid is lost forever from the calculation of national economic output. It is captured later when individuals and governments subsequently spend those governmental resources on goods and services.

In calculating the GDP, care must be taken to avoid double counting. The process of producing a product includes several stages. Take the automobile, for example. Its production process includes initial design, the purchase of raw materials, the production of some components and the acquisition of others, the assembly of components, and painting and other finishing. To avoid double counting, the GDP counts only the dollar *value added* at each stage of the process. Staying with the automobile example, double counting would also take place if the newly bought car were sold to another buyer right after its initial purchase. To avoid that potential pitfall, the GDP excludes the resale value if it occurs within the same fiscal quarter as the original purchase.

Similarly, the GDP does not include the value of **capital gains and losses** in assets, including real estate, financial securities, and collectibles. Economists put capital gains into two categories: realized and unrealized. Capital gains are realized when the owner of an asset sells it at a profit—when the gain is cashed out, so to speak. Although realized capital gains produce cash that can be spent, they do not change economic output. It is quite conceivable, though, that the party profiting from the transaction will spend the newfound return or use it to make an investment. At that point, should it occur, the cost of the purchase or investment would be included within the GDP. Unrealized capital gains can be thought of as "paper gains" that reflect increased market value but are not cashed in. They do, however, have economic value, because

Table 2.1

Annual Percentage Change in Real GDP, 1990–2006

1990	1.9
1991	−0.2
1992	3.3
1993	2.7
1994	4.0
1995	2.5
1996	3.7
1997	4.5
1998	4.2
1999	4.5
2000	3.7
2001	0.8
2002	1.6
2003	2.5
2004	3.9
2005	3.2
2006	3.3

Source: Bureau of Economic Analysis, U.S. Department of Commerce.

they can typically be used as collateral to support borrowing. The existence of unrealized gains can also make their owners feel wealthier and prompt them to save less than they otherwise might.

Getting a sense of a nation's economic well-being involves considering both the size of its economy (the value of its aggregate output) and the direction and rate of change of its output. Yet to validly compare change in value over time, it is necessary to control for the effects of inflation, to focus on *real* rather than nominal GDP. Table 2.1 shows the annual changes in real GDP from 1990 through 2006, and Figure 2.1 breaks down real GDP growth by the goods and services sectors.

To compare a nation's economic growth to that of other nations, two other considerations become relevant. First, because countries' populations vary greatly, it is necessary to compare GDP on a per-person, or per-capita, basis. Moreover, because currency values differ among nations, there must be a means of equating them. The most commonly accepted methods include **currency exchange rates** and measures of **purchasing power parity**. The former is the rate at which one currency can be exchanged for another. Governments can establish an official exchange rate for their currency, fixing its value vis-à-vis other currencies (typically done by *pegging* its exchange value to a major world currency, most often to the U.S. dollar), or they can allow their currency's value to *float* in currency markets, where demand and supply set value. An

Figure 2.1   **GDP by Industrial Sector: Percentage Change in Real Value Added, 1995–2005**

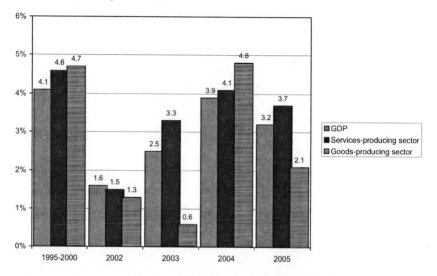

Source: Bureau of Economic Analysis, U.S. Department of Commerce.

intermediate approach involves a capped float, in which a nation allows its currency value to float within government-set limits. China has recently followed this tack, tying the allowed degree of float to a pegged exchange value with the U.S. dollar. The Chinese government decides the extent to which it will loosen or tighten the degree of float allowed.

The second method of comparing currency value, purchasing power parity (PPP), adjusts exchange rates to reflect differences in the purchasing power of currencies in their own countries. Although the exchange rate value of currency continues to be the most widely accepted standard for comparing national economic output, a school of thought exists that believes the PPP method provides a better comparative measure of a country's standard of living.

Thus far we have alluded to the actors whose economic transactions contribute to the GDP, namely households, businesses, and government, as they consume and invest. It is now time to discuss their contributions more systematically.

Components of the GDP

As introduced earlier, the GDP summarizes in a single number the dollar value of the output of the U.S. economy. That single number reported by the U.S. Department of Commerce is a highly complex amalgamation of consump-

Table 2.2

Components of the GDP: Dollar and Percentage Shares, 2006

	In $ Billions	Percentage Share
Consumption	9,269	70
Goods	3,785	29
Services	5,484	41
Private Investment	2,213	17
Government Spending	2,528	19
Federal	927	7
State and Local	1,601	12
Exports Minus Imports	−763	−6
	13,247	100

Source: Bureau of Economic Analysis, U.S. Department of Commerce (Final Revision for 2006).

tion and investment spending by households, businesses, and government, along with a summary measure of the United States' **trade balance** with the rest of the world (represented as net exports, or exports minus imports). The components of the GDP can be represented as follows:

GDP = c (for consumption), i (for private investment),
  g (for government spending, both consumption and investment),
  and x-n (for exports minus imports)

The sale of consumer goods and services accounted for 70 percent of the value of the GDP in 2006—more than four times the contribution of private domestic investment, at 17 percent. Government spending added another 19 percent. The sum of these components exceeds 100 percent because the U.S. trade balance constituted a negative 6 percent of the GDP, as imports exceeded exports by $762 billion in 2006. Within the consumption component, spending on goods contributed 29 percent of the GDP, while spending on services added 41 percent. Within the governmental component, state and local governments spent 1.7 times more on goods and services and investment than did the federal government. (See Table 2.2.)

In addition to the so-called product account side, the U.S. Department of Commerce also reports the corresponding income side.[1] Income takes the form of corporate profits, self-employed proprietors' income (profits of unincorporated businesses), capital depreciation allowances, compensation paid to employees (including wages and salaries, employer contributions to employee pension and insurance funds, and employer contributions to Social

Security and Medicare), rental income, and interest. Of these forms, employee compensation constitutes the largest share by far, accounting for close to two-thirds of national income in 2006. Corporate profits and proprietors' income, the next two largest categories, account for 14 percent and 9 percent of national income, respectively.[2] Regarding the former, corporations pay out a portion of their after-tax profits as **dividends** to stockholders, and the percentage can vary considerably from year to year.

Personal Income

A growing national economy increases national income, because every dollar of output yields a corresponding dollar of income. That income takes various forms, as already discussed, and goes to corporations, unincorporated businesses, and households. To get a sense of personal economic welfare, we want to focus on income that finds its way into the pockets of members of households—the primary end-use consumers of goods and services sold in the marketplace. For this measure, we turn to the Department of Commerce's data on personal income.

The measure of personal income includes employee compensation, proprietors' income, and rental income of persons—as does national income—but excludes corporate profits and capital depreciation allowances. It also replaces aggregate *net* interest with interest earned on the savings of households and adds dividend income derived from the investments of households. Personal income also importantly adds income from government transfer payments, while subtracting employee and employer contributions for Social Security. Employee compensation is by far the largest component of personal income, followed in order by government transfer payments, proprietors' income, interest, dividends, and rents. (See Table 2.3.)

Not all personal income is available to be spent. Members of households pay taxes on their income, which reduces their consumer power. **Disposable personal income**, which subtracts tax payments, is therefore a better measure of ability to pay. Household members need not spend all of their disposable personal income. By definition, that which is not spent is saved. They may, however, spend in excess of their personal income, going into debt to do so, as Table 2.3 shows to have been the case in 2006.

Figure 2.2 illustrates that personal saving as a percentage of disposable income has steadily declined since 1980, turning negative in 2005 for the first time since the Department of Commerce began reporting personal saving. Without access to savings, a nation cannot invest. The only way for a nation to invest more than it saves is for it to borrow the savings of other nations, and that borrowing entails both costs and risks.

Table 2.3

Personal Income, Disposable Personal Income, and Personal Saving, 2006

	In $ Billions	Percentage Share
Employee Compensation	7,477	68.7
Wages and Salaries	6,023	55.3
Fringe Benefits	1,454	13.4
Proprietors' Income	1,015	9.3
Rental Income of Persons	77	0.7
Personal Interest Income	1,017	9.3
Personal Dividend Income	640	5.9
Government Transfers	1,602	14.7
Less Social Security Contributions	−945	−8.7
Personal Income	10,883	100.0
Less Personal Taxes	−1,360	
Disposable Personal Income	9,523	
Personal Outlays	9,626	
Personal Saving	−103	
Personal Saving as a Percentage of Disposable Income	−1.1%	

Source: Bureau of Economic Analysis, U.S. Department of Commerce (Final Revision for 2006).

Figure 2.2 **Personal Saving as a Percentage of Disposable Income: Selected Years 1960–2006**

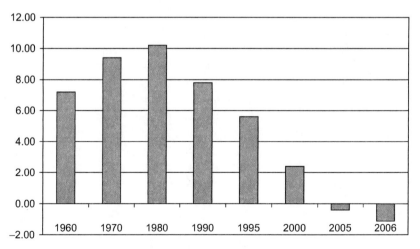

Source: Bureau of Economic Analysis, U.S. Department of Commerce.

Saving and Investment

Investment is important because it is used to increase or replace a nation's capital stock. Investment finances land development, industrial plants, buildings, machinery, and other capital items. It provides the financial resources to enhance a nation's ability to expand supply to meet rising demand and fuel economic growth. It also provides the financial wherewithal for industry to modernize its equipment and increase its productive efficiency.

There are three sources of national saving: households, businesses, and government. Household, or personal, saving was briefly introduced in the preceding section. By an important accounting convention, all saving in the household sector is equated with financial investment. It does not include any investment in nonfinancial assets. For instance, the purchase of durables such as automobiles and refrigerators is treated as personal consumption rather than investment. New housing construction falls within business investment, not household investment. Businesses invest by drawing on their savings, just as households do. Corporations earn profits from their enterprises, and they pay taxes on that income. They may distribute some of those profits in the form of dividends to stockholders. The remainder, the so-called undistributed profits, is available for investment. Finally, governments can save as well. They do that when they run an operating **budget surplus**—when revenues exceed expenditures. The accounting convention that businesses make all nonfinancial investment applies to government saving, just as it does to household saving. Budget surpluses, when they infrequently exist, contribute to the larger financial investment pool.

All three sectors—household, business, and government—can *dissave*, to use a nongrammatical convention of economists; that is, they can spend in excess of their income. They can do that by borrowing to fill the gap. Household members can take out loans from banks and credit unions, but more frequently they run up unpaid balances on their credit cards. Businesses can also borrow to finance overspending, but that behavior cannot continue indefinitely. At some point, they will no longer be able to get credit and will go out of business or declare bankruptcy. Unlike the federal government, the vast majority of state and local governments are required to balance their operating budgets. The federal government faces no such constraint; it can legally run a budget deficit, and it frequently does.

Table 2.4 illustrates the three sectors' respective contribution to national saving. Business saving far exceeds household saving, and the household share of saving has declined precipitously since the end of World War II, with its sharpest decline occurring since the early 1980s. Government's share of saving has also dropped significantly when compared with the period from 1947

Table 2.4

U.S. National Saving and Investment Rates: Selected Years, 1947–2006

	Average Shares of Gross Domestic Product					
	1947–82		1983–99		2000–2006	
Gross Domestic Investment	20.5		19.4		18.9	
National Saving	20.3		16.9		14.7	
Private	17.3		17.2		14.1	
Household		6.0		4.8		0.8
Business		11.3		12.4		13.3
Government	3.1		−0.3		0.6	
Federal		1.4		−1.7		−0.5
State and Local		1.6		1.4		1.1
Net Foreign Capital Inflows	−0.2		−2.6		−4.2	

Source: Kevin L. Kliesen, "Do We Have a Saving Crisis?" (St. Louis: The Federal Reserve Bank of St. Louis, July 2005), 3; Bureau of Economic Analysis, *National Income and Product Account Tables*, March 29, 2007, Table 5.1.
   Note: Shares do not add due to rounding.

through 1982. Business's increased share of saving has helped to offset the relative decline in government and household saving but not nearly enough to fill the growing gap between national saving and investment. To do that, the United States has tapped the savings of the rest of the world. As discussed in chapters 4 and 6, the question remains how long foreign nations will continue to be willing to plow their savings into the United States.

Worker Productivity

An economy grows by increasing the monetary value of the goods and services it produces. It can do that by adding new workers to increase production, when merited by demand, or by getting existing workers to produce more, by increasing **worker productivity** (defined as output per hour of work). Through increased worker productivity, an economy's output can conceivably grow without the addition of workers. When that happens, businesses benefit by expanding their output of goods and services without having to bear the salary and fringe benefit costs associated with adding new workers, and any salary increases paid to existing employees are justified by the rising output of those workers. In fact, higher worker productivity dampens the inflationary effects of those salary increases. As long as labor's share of the real dollar value of the increased output attributed to rising worker productivity remains constant or increases, the real median income of workers also rises, thus improving their standard of living. As will be discussed in chapter 9, however, the share

Table 2.5

Change in Worker Productivity, Nonfarm Business Sector, 1961–2006

Years	Average Percentage Change
1961–65	3.7
1966–70	2.0
1971–75	2.4
1976–80	1.2
1981–85	1.7
1986–90	1.3
1991–95	1.7
1996–2000	2.6
2001–6	3.0

Source: Bureau of Labor Statistics, U.S. Department of Labor.

of national income going to workers has shrunk since the recession of 2001. In the ensuing period of recovery and growth, corporate profits' rising share of national income has squeezed labor's share. As we will see later, wage and salary income generated by the post-2001 recovery grew more slowly than in any of the prior post–World War II recoveries. Business, not labor, reaped most of the fruits of economic expansion.

Table 2.5 shows changes in worker productivity in the nonfarm business sector from 1961 through 2006. Growth in worker productivity averaged 2.7 percent a year between 1961 and 1975 and then fell off sharply, averaging only 1.5 percent annually between 1976 and 1995. However, it reversed course sharply, averaging 2.8 percent annual growth between 1996 and 2005, even bettering its strong 1961–75 performance. Especially noteworthy is the 3.0 percent annual average rate of productivity growth from 2001 through 2006, which exceeded most economists' forecasts and almost doubled that of the Euro area and Japan. High worker productivity allowed the GDP to grow even though the U.S. economy experienced employment decline from early 2001 through mid-2003, and it augmented employment growth thereafter.

Accounting for change in worker productivity is not an easy task. Economist Paul Krugman calls productivity growth "the single most important factor affecting America's economic well-being" but admits that economists have difficulty explaining why it changes.[3] One common thread of explanation for the post-1995 surge in productivity points to technological progress and increased investment in new information and communications technology. Technological advances not only increased productivity in the high-tech industries themselves but made it possible for a wide range of industries to improve the efficiency of their supply and production processes.[4] Although business investment in information and communications technology slowed a little in

Figure 2.3 **Change in Nonfarm Employment, 1996–2006**

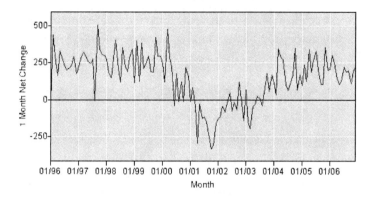

Source: Bureau of Labor Statistics, U.S. Department of Labor.

the first half of the 2000s while worker productivity increased, perhaps the seeming disparity can be explained by the proverbial learning curve. It takes a while for users of new technology to learn how best to apply it; contributions to improved quality and efficiency result from the learning process of application and adjustment.[5] Comparing the United States to Europe, it appears that U.S. firms not only increased their spending on technology in the late 1990s faster than did European firms, but they had the greatest success in applying information and communication advances to increase productivity.[6]

Employment and Unemployment

Economic growth is typically associated with rising employment, but it is possible for an economy to grow at a moderate pace and still lose jobs. The so-called jobless recovery from October 2001 through August 2003 provides just such an example. Real GDP grew by an average of almost 2 percent over that period, still a modest rate of growth by historical standards, but the U.S. economy netted a *loss* of 1.7 million jobs. Drawn-down inventories and high productivity growth help account for this apparent anomaly. With economic growth strengthening markedly in the second half of 2003, the economy added 7.3 million net jobs between July 2003 and the end of 2006.[7] (See Figure 2.3.) Solid employment growth and continued high worker productivity contributed the resources to meet the heightened demand commensurate with a quarterly rate of growth in real GDP that averaged a strong 3.6 percent during the period.[8]

Employment not only provides the human resources to produce products and deliver services and in the process generates income to meet the needs and wants of consuming households, but it also contributes to human dignity and social welfare. The work routine of jobs adds structure and regularity to life, replaces idleness with its potential attendant social dysfunctions, and enhances self-respect. For the most part, people appreciate the value of work, and they want jobs. Yet not everyone who wants a job is able to find one. Unemployment is a reality even in a good economy.

Measuring Employment and Unemployment

Two federal government agencies use different survey methods to measure employment in the United States. With the first, the Bureau of Labor Statistics in the Department of Labor coordinates monthly collection of employment data from employers. The bureau uses federal and state agents to count the number of jobs filled for a statistically valid sample of 400,000 places of work within the United States at a given point in time—for the payroll period that includes the twelfth day of every month. The establishment survey, also known as the current employment statistics (CES) survey, is drawn from both the private and governmental sectors. With the second method, the Census Bureau in the Department of Commerce surveys households, not employers. As part of its monthly current population survey (CPS) of about 60,000 households, census workers interview household members of working age about their employment status. Self-reporting therefore serves as the basis for the Census Bureau's report on employment and unemployment in the United States. An important difference between the two methods is that the establishment survey makes it possible for a person holding two jobs to have both jobs counted, whereas the CPS counts only the status of being employed or unemployed, irrespective of the number of jobs held. The CPS also includes reported self-employment, while the establishment survey does not. Largely because of this addition, the CPS measure of employment regularly yields higher employment figures.

Economists, business leaders, government policy makers, and the media tend to look to the establishment survey as the authoritative measure of employment, because it is based on payroll data, which are regarded as more objective than self-reports. Nonetheless, it is not uncommon for political figures to turn to the method that makes the employment case most favorable to their political interests. The Census Bureau's CPS is the sole source for monthly unemployment data.

To be considered unemployed by the Census Bureau, a person of working age must be out of work, actively looking for employment, and available to work. The bureau therefore excludes from its unemployment count those who are unemployed but not seeking work. If that policy were changed and these individuals were treated as unemployed, reported unemployment would rise. What about those who are employed part-time but actively looking for full-time work? They are counted as employed, though the bureau separates out part-time employment in its reports.

What is considered an acceptable level of unemployment? A certain level of unemployment exists even in the best economy. Economists characterize **structural unemployment** as an unemployment floor that is difficult to break through. Structural unemployment results from the following conditions: (1) changes in the composition and requirements of an economy that create a mismatch between workers looking for employment and the jobs that are available to them, (2) the unwillingness of workers to take jobs they view as beneath their qualifications or their unwillingness to accept job offers at the wages offered, and (3) the inability of some severely disadvantaged job seekers to find employment even in economic good times.

Historically, structural employment was thought to fall in the 5 to 6 percent range. That mind-set conditioned expectations about how low unemployment could feasibly go. Assuming that 5 to 6 percent unemployment is about the best that can be expected, unemployment that averaged 6.2 percent during the 1970s and 7.3 percent during the 1980s did not look all that bad, but it was still higher than policy makers preferred. As unemployment declined to 4.9 percent in 1997 and continued to fall through 2000, averaging 4 percent in that year, 5 to 6 percent structural unemployment appeared unduly pessimistic. Even with unemployment rising to an average of 5.3 percent over the next six years, few calls of alarm could be heard. After 2003, the attention of economic policy makers turned to fighting inflation. For them, unemployment a little higher than 5 percent did not seem out of line.

High unemployment, when it occurs, is symptomatic of an ailing economy in which demand falls far short of supply. In that environment, employers have an incentive to lay off workers and draw down inventories. High unemployment, with its negative effects on personal income, suppresses consumer purchasing power and thereby further dampens demand. The challenge, then, facing economic policy makers is how to spur demand so that employers will add back workers to produce products and deliver services that meet the rising demand. Chapters 3 and 4, which cover economic policy making, pursue that discussion. Those chapters also cover the risk that policy makers face of overstimulating the economy and inducing unacceptable levels of inflation.

Inflation

Inflation is a rise in the overall price structure. Simply put, it occurs when demand exceeds supply. When demand for goods and services exceeds the economy's capacity to produce them, sellers are able to get higher prices for what they are able to produce. Moreover, as employers have a more difficult time finding qualified employees to increase production and expand services, the cost of labor is bid up. But is inflation really a problem if wages rise in sync with prices, and they do so pretty much predictably? Under those conditions, it would not be theoretically problematic within the sole context of the domestic economy. However, unrestrained price increases, even if matched by corresponding wage increases, would make U.S. goods and services increasingly expensive to foreign buyers and likely lower the value of the dollar in world currency markets. The real-world prospect of predictable tandem increases in prices and wages is itself tenuous, because prices can surge, and efforts to win corresponding wage increases often lag behind. When the growth of personal income fails to keep pace with price increases, consumers lose purchasing power. When prices increase faster than does interest on savings, the value of savings erodes.

Inflation also has redistributive effects. It redistributes income from those on fixed incomes to those whose wages and earnings from investment keep pace with or exceed inflation. Inflation also benefits borrowers, who pay back their loans with "cheaper" dollars, and it correspondingly disadvantages lenders. It is no wonder that lending institutions are prime inflation fighters.

Measuring Inflation

Government uses several different methods to measure inflation, most prominently the consumer price index (CPI), the producer price index (PPI), and the GDP deflator. The CPI measures inflation as experienced by the consumer. The index includes the price change for a "basket" of goods and services, including imported goods, purchased by the typical consumer. The CPI is therefore the best measure of the impact of inflation on the purchasing power of households. The PPI is the best measure of inflation before it hits the consumer, because it measures price changes paid by businesses for finished products. Unlike the CPI, the PPI does not include services nor does it measure the price changes of imported goods. It does include change in prices of capital equipment, which the CPI excludes. The GDP deflator is the broadest measure of inflation of the three. It measures change in the *overall* level of prices for the goods and services that constitute the GDP. The Department of Commerce uses the GDP deflator to convert nominal GDP to inflation-adjusted real GDP. The Social Security Administration ties increases in its benefit checks to increases in the CPI.

In addition to inflation, it is also possible for a national economy to experience **deflation**, or a decline in the overall prices of goods and services. (Deflation needs to be distinguished from **disinflation**, with which it is often confused. Disinflation is a decline in inflation, not a drop in the overall price structure.) Extended periods of deflation have been rare in the United States, though two stand out with notoriety in U.S. history: the persistent deflation between 1879 and 1896 and during the Great Depression. Deflation constitutes a serious economic problem because it depresses demand. As prices fall, consumers put off spending, waiting for prices to drop further. Since the Great Depression, economic policy makers have worried little about deflation, with one recent exception. Faced with a comparatively slow recovery from the recession of 2001, which saw continued employment decline, the monetary policy makers of the Federal Reserve drove the bellwether **federal funds rate** down to a mere 1 percent in June 2003, in an effort to reduce the already low risk of deflation. (See chapter 3 for an extended discussion.) Yet as the pace of economic activity quickened and employment grew and the outside risk of deflation disappeared, the Federal Reserve embarked on a consistent course of interest rate hikes aimed at keeping inflation in check.

A Trade-off Between Unemployment and Inflation?

Does a trade-off exist between unemployment and inflation? Said differently, does an inverse relationship exist between the two? As unemployment falls significantly, can we expect a significant increase in the rate of inflation? And as unemployment rises significantly, can we expect the rate of inflation to decline significantly? A.W. Phillips, an economist at the London School of Economics, identified a systematic relationship between the two using historical data on the British economy,[9] a relationship that other economists were quick to label the Phillips curve. He found that as unemployment falls, employers are forced to pay higher wages to workers, reflecting the growing scarcity of available qualified labor; higher wage rates usually inflate the costs of the products or services provided—that is, unless they are accompanied by proportionally increased productivity. He found the converse also to be true: as unemployment rises, inflation falls, because rising unemployment slows income growth and reduces demand.

The regularity of the trade-off, as he found it, carries implications for policy makers. Should they anticipate the trade-off's negative effects and use monetary and fiscal policy tools to mitigate them, striving for an acceptable balance between unemployment and inflation in a growing economy? Today's conventional wisdom is that economic policy makers have an obligation to intervene to achieve that objective. But in doing so, they make choices about where to set the balance, about whether to accept somewhat more unemployment for somewhat less inflation, or vice versa. That choice is both an economic and political judgment.

Monetary policy has become the preferred instrument of national economic management. The public expects Federal Reserve policy makers to use monetary

Figure 2.4   **Change in the Misery Index, 1960–2006**

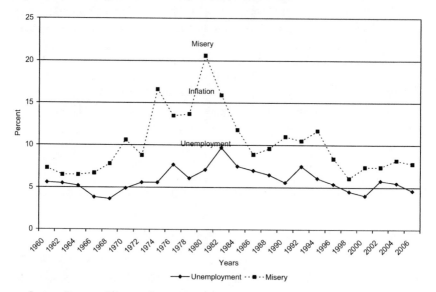

Source: Bureau of Economic Analysis, U.S. Department of Commerce; Census Bureau, U.S. Department of Commerce.

policy to keep inflation in check but also to stimulate demand when unemployment heads toward unacceptable levels. Through Alan Greenspan's leadership as chairman of the Federal Reserve Board, the public has come to expect that the Fed will engage in proactive management of the economy that keeps inflation or unemployment in line. In comparison, Congress, typically acting in response to presidential initiatives, has employed fiscal policy in more of a reactive mode. This contrast will become clear in the next two chapters.

What, however, are the implications for policy makers when the economy fails to behave as Phillips suggests it does? What about when inflation and unemployment both rise? The widespread acceptance of the perceived realities of the Phillips curve was first shaken by the experience of the mid- to late 1970s and into 1980. High inflation coexisted with high unemployment—that is, at least higher unemployment than occurred during the first part of the 1970s and particularly during the 1950s and 1960s. For 1978 inflation rose to almost 8 percent, while unemployment stood at a little higher than 6 percent, an unemployment level well in excess of the Carter administration's policy of 4 percent unemployment. By 1980 the unemployment rate rose to 7.1 percent, and inflation jumped to a staggering 13.5 percent. No trade-off between the two was apparent. As Figure 2.4 vividly illustrates, simultaneous high inflation and high unemployment conspired to drive the so-called misery index (the unemployment rate added to the inflation rate) in 1980 to a historically unmatched peak. The period from 1992 through 1998, a time of sustained economic growth, provided the second notable test of validity of Phillips's formulation. During that period of economic recovery followed by strong economic growth, both unemployment and inflation fell. The 1992–98 experience led many popular economic commentators to speak of an era of new economics brought about by the implementation of new technologies, higher productivity, and increased global competitiveness, all of which conspired to suppress inflation while employment rose sharply. These factors, along with proactively successful monetary policy, prompted economists to consider whether the economy had reached a point that could accommodate stable inflation at low levels of unemployment and how long that might continue. Even though economic growth continued strongly over the next two years, averaging 4 percent in 2000 and driving unemployment still lower, the annual inflation rate rose from 1.6 percent in 1998 to 3.4 percent in 2000, the highest annual average since 1991, showing renewed signs of the trade-off predicted by the Phillips curve. As Figure 2.4 illustrates, inflation and unemployment continued for the most part to move in moderately inverse directions for the remainder of the decade.

The Nonaccelerating Inflation Rate of Unemployment (NAIRU)

Economists have long been interested in the concept of a level of unemployment consistent with stable inflation, known as the nonaccelerating inflation rate of unemployment (NAIRU). In the words of a prominent economist, the NAIRU "represents the economy's sustainable unemployment rate when wages and prices have had sufficient time to adjust to demand and supply pressures."[10] When unemployment is below the NAIRU, inflation can be expected to rise; when unemployment is above it, inflation can be expected to fall.

The theoretical construct of the NAIRU is grounded in changes in production costs. Businesses pass on higher production costs to buyers and may reduce prices to reflect lower production costs. Production costs tend to rise when the economy grows robustly, because businesses make fuller use of their productive capacity and bring on line less efficient equipment to meet the demand. Businesses respond to rising demand by adding employees, and the growing scarcity of labor bids up wage rates. Price increases follow. In contrast, a slow-growing or stagnant economy constrains wage growth and prompts industry to turn away from its older, less-efficient plants and equipment in favor of more modern ones to meet lower demand.[11]

The operational problem, however, is that economists disagree over how to identify when the NAIRU balancing point has been reached, and they debate about how to explain changes in the NAIRU over time. Rising productivity, however, is the explanatory factor that economic researchers most commonly cite. Increased productivity helps to keep inflation at bay even as employment expands to meet higher demand.[12]

The importance of the quest for greater understanding is clear for economic policy, particularly monetary policy. With unemployment below the NAIRU and inflation expected to increase, the Fed can take proactive steps to keep it in check and avoid the painful consequences of unacceptably high inflation.

Economists talk about the **sacrifice ratio** required to bring inflation under control—that is, the extent to which unemployment has to increase to bring inflation down by one percentage point. The Federal Reserve Board now puts the sacrifice ratio at 4 : 1, meaning that it takes an increase of four percentage points in the unemployment rate to lower the inflation rate by one percentage point.[13] The consequences of that sacrifice are clear.

The Ideal Economy and a Reality Check

The ideal national economy enjoys both high worker productivity and reasonably full use of its available human and capital resources that produces strong economic growth with acceptably low inflation. The ideal economy also provides sufficient income growth to sustain demand in the marketplace, as well as to generate enough saving to meet the nation's investment needs.

The reality is that an economy's ability to sustain strong economic growth is limited. A national economy goes through cycles of growth and contraction as growth reaches a peak, drops to a trough, and then rises to the next peak. The trough should be understood as a low point, not necessarily a recession (at least two consecutive quarters of decline in the GDP), although some troughs constitute recessions. Economists refer to that movement from peak to trough to peak as a **business cycle**. The U.S. economy has experienced thirty-four business cycles since 1854, one about every four and a half years. Thus history teaches us that sustained strong economic growth has been illusive, though we have enjoyed more frequent longer periods of solid growth over the past twenty-five years or so, including 1983–89, 1993–2000, and 2003 through the time of this writing. It is true that the economy experienced recessions in 1990–91 and 2001, but they were relatively mild.

These periods of growth should not lead one to conclude that the business cycle is no longer part of economic reality. Nor should the United States' recent success at maintaining comparatively low unemployment together with acceptable rates of inflation be the basis for concluding that the trade-off between unemployment and inflation described by the Phillips curve is no longer operable. High worker productivity has helped to raise potential GDP and to contain inflation. But it is questionable whether productivity can be sustained without increased investment in human and physical capital.

Over the past twenty-five years, the United States has taken the path of spending itself into prosperity. Rising demand for goods and services has driven economic growth. Americans' zeal to consume has turned saving negative, forcing the United States to rely on the savings of foreigners to finance a growing slice of U.S. domestic investment. The question remains how long the rest of the world will be willing to send their savings our way.

Finally, focusing on the measures of national economic performance discussed earlier does not tell us much about who benefits from economic growth. It does not tell us how the shares of national income growth are distributed and with what effects. Chapter 9 picks up that discussion and also examines the future challenges that economic policy makers can be expected to face.

Monetary Policy Making

Unlike fiscal policy, for which Congress directly exercises its constitutional power to tax and spend (although the president typically sets the national agenda), Congress has vested the authority for monetary policy in an independent government agency, the Federal Reserve, commonly referred to as the Fed. The Fed sets national monetary policy by greatly influencing the availability and cost of credit in the United States, as it affects the level of reserves that thrift institutions have available to lend to willing borrowers and the interest rates charged. Monetary policy's objective is to promote economic growth and full employment, but within acceptable levels of inflation.

Monetary policy can be employed to stimulate the economy. It can be used effectively to jump-start the economy when aggregate demand is down and consumers lack confidence in the economy and in their personal futures. The pursuit of self-interest helps to account for monetary policy's efficacy. Individuals and businesses look to exploit situations to their advantage, as economic theory teaches. A stagnant or declining economy is not conducive to major new economic endeavors, all other things being equal. Flat or depressed demand tends to discourage increases in corporate spending. For corporations, why would it be in their best interest to expand productive resources or acquire new equipment when demand is insufficient to meet existing production? It would make more sense, instead, for them to draw down current inventories and lay off workers, or at least not add any, while postponing investment. The catch, however, lies in the caveat of all other things being equal. Can policy makers act in such a way that would-be spenders or investors will judge that the time is indeed right to act? That is where monetary policy can be used to bias the incentives of economic actors.

What if the cost to individuals and corporations of making major capital purchases can be lowered significantly? Might that influence their decision to go ahead, even in a poor economy? If loanable funds become available at an attractive rate, and if would-be consumers believe that they are more likely to go up rather than down later, that perceived lower cost of money might just be enough to get them to borrow and make the investment.

Monetary policy can also be an effective tool in an overheated economy, in which inflation exceeds acceptable levels. The objective in that condition is to lower aggregate demand, trading off reduced inflation for some increase in unemployment. Monetary policy makers act to tighten the availability of credit and increase its costs. A steep increase in the cost of loanable funds creates a disincentive for credit-financed spending. Consumers and businesses tend to wait for more favorable interest rates. If enough people behave that way, aggregate demand declines, unemployment rises, and inflation drops.

Monetary policy cannot control long-term interest rates. They are set in a highly competitive market in which borrowers bid for capital. But, as noted, monetary policy can influence short-term rates. Not only does the short-term cost of loanable funds affect the relative willingness of borrowers to take on debt, but short-term interest rates send important signals about what the future economy might portend. Investors who believe that a modest increase in short-term interest rates presages a series of future increases are less likely to purchase long-term securities than are those who see a solitary adjustment acting to nip inflationary tendencies in the bud. Thus interest rate changes, the way they are positioned by monetary policy makers, and the perspectives of would-be investors can all influence the behavior of participants in capital markets.

The Federal Reserve System

The Federal Reserve System is led by a seven-member Board of Governors, appointed by the president to serve staggered fourteen-year terms subject to confirmation by the Senate. The president also appoints the board's chair and vice-chair to renewable four-year terms, which also require Senate confirmation. The Board of Governors is augmented in its policy-making functions by the presidents of the twelve Federal Reserve banks, who are appointed by regional governing boards, subject to approval by the Board of Governors. (See Figure 3.1.) The twelve Federal Reserve banks and their twenty-five branches carry out a wide variety of financial and regulatory functions, including serving as a depository for the banks in their own district, distributing the nation's currency and coin, operating a nationwide payments system (involving interbank check clearing), and regulating member banks and bank holding companies. Federal Reserve banks also serve as fiscal agents of the U.S. government, performing several services for the Department of the Treasury, including maintaining the Treasury's funds account; clearing Treasury checks; and conducting auctions of Treasury securities, as well as issuing, servicing, and redeeming them.[1]

The presidents of the Federal Reserve banks, in addition to providing executive leadership for these functions, have representation on the highly important

Figure 3.1 **The Federal Reserve System**

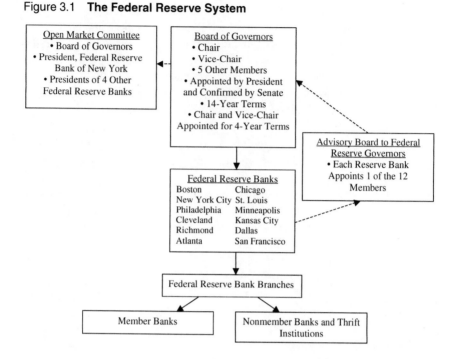

Federal Open Market Committee (FOMC). The FOMC is composed of the seven members of the Board of Governors and five of the twelve Reserve bank presidents. The president of the Federal Reserve Bank of New York is a permanent member, and the other presidents serve rotating one-year terms. The other Reserve bank presidents not serving on the board attend meetings and participate in the discussions but have no vote.

The Fed's Tools of Monetary Policy Making

The FOMC directs the buying and selling of government securities on the open market as the principal instrument of monetary policy. When the domestic trading desk at the Federal Reserve Bank of New York *sells* Treasury securities through about three dozen large-volume dealers to the highest bidding banks, it draws reserves from the banking system, thus shrinking the availability of loanable funds. Conversely, when it *buys* government securities at the lowest price the market will bear, it pays for them by adding reserves to the banking system, thus increasing the capacity of banks to make loans.

These market operations, in turn, affect short-term interest rates charged to borrowers. As the reserves of financial institutions decline, interest rates rise, reflecting the basic factors of supply and demand. Conversely, a rise in reserves decreases interest rates, reflecting the increased availability of loanable funds. Transactions of the FOMC importantly affect the **federal funds rate** (FFR), the rate of interest that depository institutions charge one another for overnight loans. Overnight borrowing allows the borrowing institution to acquire resources beyond its existing reserves to meet the immediate needs of its commercial customers and to meet **reserve requirements** (the percentage of deposits that depository institutions must keep in cash or as non-interest-bearing balances in Federal Reserve banks). When the FFR changes, short-term interest rates available to borrowers tend to move in the same direction, as commercial lenders typically follow the Fed's lead. However, that association has not been uniform over time.

It should be noted here that the Fed's open market transactions do not directly affect long-term interest rates. Long-term rates are a product of judgments made by market participants—both domestic and foreign—about what the condition of the economy and associated interest rates will be ten, twenty, and even thirty years in the future. While the Fed's actions might raise the FFR in the near term and make current borrowing more expensive, rates on long-term bonds might remain level, or even fall, if buyers believe that the long-term prospects are for lower interest rates (perhaps premised on the expectation that slower future economic growth will prompt the Fed to expand reserves and trigger lower interest rates, thus making yields on long-term bonds more attractive than expected yields in the long run).

During Alan Greenspan's nineteen years as Federal Reserve Board chairman, the FOMC elected to target the federal funds rate as opposed to controlling the money supply, technically referred to as monetary aggregates, as had been case with the Paul Volcker–led Board that preceded the Greenspan era. In targeting the FFR, the FOMC decides whether economic conditions merit raising or lowering the rate for commercial overnight borrowing and by how much. Meeting eight times a year, the FOMC reviews national economic indicators and considers regionally based input from officials of the twelve Reserve Banks. Drawing upon that analysis, the chair of the Board of Governors recommends any change in the FFR, and FOMC members vote on that recommendation. As we shall see later, the committee regularly follows the chair's prescribed course of action. Once the FOMC determines the FFR target, it instructs the trading desk of the New York Reserve Bank to buy or sell federal securities on the open market in quantities that will affect the FFR by the desired amount. The FOMC continues, as necessary, to fine-tune its buying or selling to come as close as possible to getting the day-to-day FFR to mirror the targeted rate.

In addition to the FOMC's actions, the Federal Reserve Board possesses two other policy instruments that it can use directly to effectuate its monetary policy. First, it can change the reserve requirement that it imposes on depository institutions, the requirement that they hold a certain percentage of their deposits—typically between 8 and 14 percent—in reserve, either in vault cash or as balances in Federal Reserve banks.[2] When the Fed raises the reserve requirement, banks have less money available to lend, exerting upward pressure on interest rates. Conversely, when the Fed lowers the reserve requirement, banks have more funds available to lend, depressing interest rates. In practice, the Fed has made increasingly infrequent use of changes in the reserve requirement as an instrument of monetary policy, preferring instead to rely on open market operations and their targeted effects on the FFR. Yet the very existence of the reserve requirement provides a stable base on which the Federal Reserve Board can use open market transactions to affect the price of reserves by adjusting their supply.

The Fed can also raise or lower the **discount rate**, the rate of interest charged to depository institutions that borrow directly from Federal Reserve banks. Any financial institution subject to reserve requirements is eligible to borrow from the Fed. The economic relationships parallel those of altering the reserve requirement. An increase in the discount rate raises the cost of credit and reduces demand for it. A decrease lowers cost and increases demand.

Discount borrowing accounts for only a small fraction of total reserves and is used far less as an instrument of monetary policy than it was in the 1950s and 1960s. The discount rate carries a higher rate of interest than the FFR, lately running a full percentage point higher. Moreover, depository institutions tend to borrow from the Federal Reserve only after they have drawn from all other available sources of funds, a practice encouraged by the Fed. Given its marginal effect on reserves, a change in the discount rate alone is unlikely to affect interest rates significantly, as open market operations and their effect on the FFR tend to overwhelm the discount rate's effect on commercial interest rates.

The Historical Foundation of the Current Federal Reserve System

The Federal Reserve System was established by Congress in 1913, following a protracted period of economic downturn, monetary instability, and bank failure. As banks became increasingly unstable and depositors increased their pace of withdrawal, banks had to liquidate assets and call in loans to cover the demand for cash. To make matters worse, a growing number of banks refused to clear checks drawn on the accounts of other banks, inhibiting commercial activity. A consensus formed both inside and outside of government that something had to be done about the mounting chaos. Agreement centered on the proposition that some authoritative entity needed to control the level of reserves that banks must keep on hand to meet depositors' demands for their money, to regulate and facilitate check clearing, to distribute currency, and to act as a last-resort source of loans when banks needed to increase their reserves.

Concurrence was much harder to reach on what the nature of this new institution should be. Should it be part of the Department of the Treasury, with that agency's cabinet ties to the presidency? Should it take the form of a loosely knit association of banks, within which the banking industry would be charged with regulating itself? Or should Congress create a hybrid institution that would have governmental status but still enjoy a substantial degree of operating independence from both the president and Congress, while also incorporating the expertise of the banking industry and reflecting its interests?

Following the outlines of a compromise reached among President Woodrow Wilson, key congressional leaders, and the banking community, Congress passed the Federal Reserve Act of 1913, which created a highly decentralized Federal Reserve System consisting of twelve Reserve banks and a seven-member Board of Governors. The act gave the president authority to appoint five of the members to staggered ten-year terms, subject to confirmation by the Senate. The secretary of the Treasury and the comptroller of the Currency served as ex officio members.

Under the legislation, however, real power resided with the Reserve banks. Each bank could set its own discount rate and conduct its own open market operations. The act gave the Federal Reserve Board no authority to mandate uniform discount rates throughout the system. Although it called upon the board to coordinate monetary policy, carrying out that charge proved illusive in practice, because initiative for open market operations lay with the various Reserve banks.

The backdrop of the Great Depression provided impetus for greater central-ization of the Federal Reserve System. Decentralization limited the ability of the Fed to speak with one voice on monetary policy. Both President Franklin Delano Roosevelt and the Democratic majority in Congress saw the need for uniform monetary policy that could substantially inject capital into the banking system and finance economic expansion. The resulting Banking Act of 1935 created the Federal Reserve System that we know today. It removed the Treasury secretary and the comptroller of the Currency from the Board of Governors, expanded the terms of presidential appointees to fourteen years, and, most importantly, created the FOMC, which combined presidential ap-pointees and Reserve bank presidents in charting open market operations. The Board of Governors retained authority to set the discount rate.[3]

The Evolving Goals of Monetary Policy

When Congress originally established the Federal Reserve System in 1913, effective monetary policy took a backseat to bank regulation. Ensuring adequate bank reserves and facilitating check clearing took precedence over influencing the availability and cost of loanable funds. The only reference in the original legislation touching on economic management was a charge to the Federal Reserve to provide an "elastic currency," one that would expand to meet the needs of a growing economy.[4] The Fed's use of monetary policy evolved over the twentieth century. It did not engage in open market transactions until the 1920s and then did so in a largely ad hoc manner.[5] During World War II and its near-term aftermath, the Fed acted to keep interest rates low: first, to reduce the cost to the federal government of financing the war effort and, subsequently, to provide relatively cheap capital to finance the industrial transition from a war economy to a domestic one.

The Employment Act of 1946 established the nation's economic policy goal of fostering "conditions under which there will be useful employment opportunities . . . for those able, willing, and seeking to work, and to promote maximum employment, production, and purchasing power."[6] Yet it did not refer explicitly to the Federal Reserve. In Congress's expression of intent, full employment became the privileged objective. However, the Fed took a more conservative view in the 1950s of the level of economic growth and employment that could be reached without triggering unacceptable inflation. Monetary policy, although somewhat erratic, was moderate and aimed at keeping inflation low.

The election of Democrat John F. Kennedy to the presidency in 1960 set the stage for a change in national economic policy. The Kennedy administration believed that the economy was positioned to sustain higher levels of employment without triggering an increase in inflation. Facing the prospect of a recession in 1962, President Kennedy proposed large cuts in both personal income tax and corporate income tax rates to stimulate economic growth. Although Congress did not approve the cuts until early 1964, following Kennedy's assassination, the cuts had their intended effect of markedly raising aggregate demand. That stimulant, along with the increased federal spending that accompanied the Great Society's War on Poverty and the United States' expanding military commitment in Vietnam, put increased pressure on prices, with inflation rising from less than 2 percent in 1962 to almost 5 percent six years later.

Monetary policy was overshadowed by fiscal policy for most of the 1960s, as is discussed in chapter 4. The Federal Reserve chose not to tighten available reserves and appeared to buy into the sentiment that the balance point should be tipped in favor of growth. The Fed maintained that posture for most of the 1970s. Despite some monetary tightening largely at mid-decade, partially in response to rapid and steep increases in the price of oil and petroleum products resulting from supply shocks, the Fed continued to tolerate historically high rates of inflation to lower unemployment. By the end of the decade, however, both inflation and unemployment had reached unacceptably high levels, defying the conventional wisdom that inflation and unemployment are inversely related (that is, as inflation rises, unemployment declines). In 1978 inflation rose to almost 8 percent, while unemployment stood at a little more than 6 percent—a level well in excess of the Carter administration's policy of 4 percent unemployment. It is not surprising that Congress, in the Full Employment and Balanced Growth Act of 1978, added the promotion of stable prices to the Fed's charge to promote maximum employment and moderate long-term interest rates.[7] By 1980 inflation had risen to almost 14 percent, and unemployment hovered above 7 percent. Inflation won out as the pressing economic and political problem. Opinion polls showed that the public, by a three-to-one margin, saw inflation as a more serious problem than unemployment.[8]

In 1980 Chairman Paul Volcker led the FOMC to approve a series of sharp increases in its sale of federal securities in the open market, designed to drastically shrink the money supply and reduce the capacity of banks to make loans, thereby driving up interest rates. The FFR reached 17 percent in 1980, the highest in modern history. For the Volcker-led Fed, the objective of monetary policy was to squeeze double-digit inflation out of the economy, even if it entailed steeply rising unemployment and the loss of jobs. By 1982 inflation fell to about 6 percent, but unemployment climbed to 10 percent—the result of highly restrictive monetary policy. By 1986, after the FOMC's subsequent actions to lower interest rates and stimulate demand, inflation stood at only 2 percent, a level reminiscent of that of the early 1960s. Unemployment, over the four years, came down to 7 percent, a level still higher than executive and legislative branch policy makers found tolerable.

The Mystique and Record of the Greenspan Era

Alan Greenspan served longer as chairman of the Federal Reserve Board than did any of his predecessors. Originally appointed to the board by President Ronald Reagan in 1987 to fill an unexpired term, Greenspan was reappointed in 1992 by President Bill Clinton to a full fourteen-year term that expired on January 31, 2006. All presidents, from Reagan through George W. Bush, designated him as chairman. Prior to serving on the board, Greenspan headed a prominent economic consulting firm and served on the boards of several major corporations. His prior government service notably included chairing the Council of Economic Advisers in the Ford administration and the National Commission on Social Security Reform during President Reagan's first term in office.

Under Chairman Greenspan, the Federal Reserve turned to targeting the federal funds rate as its principal tool of monetary policy making.[9] As inflation picked up steam early in his first term, Greenspan recommended a number of pitched increases in the FFR during 1988 and the first half of 1989. Over that period, the FFR rose from just below 7 percent to almost 10 percent. Then, with the inflation rate falling following the 1990–91 recession, Greenspan urged his colleagues on the FOMC to loosen the restraint and pursue a policy of targeting incremental reductions in the FFR as a means of fostering economic recovery. The FFR consequently fell to 3 percent by September 1992. To get it there, the FOMC reduced the targeted rate nineteen straight times, in increments of twenty-five to fifty basis points (with 25 basis points equating to a quarter of 1 percent). The strategy was to accommodate growth gradually, not precipitously.

With real GDP growing by 2.7 percent in 1992, up from a *negative* 0.2 percent one year earlier, the FOMC held pat, keeping the FFR at 3 percent throughout 1993. And even though inflation remained low, at 3 percent, in 1993, Chairman Greenspan encouraged a preemptive reversal of course beginning with the February 1994 FOMC meeting. The committee, in turn, raised the FFR to 3.25 percent and sent the signal that future increases should be expected. Its next two hikes, in March and April, suggested that the committee would continue its established pattern of incremental adjustments. However, the FOMC became more worried about the prospects of significantly higher inflation and shifted to a more aggressive preemptive stance, raising the targeted rate by fifty basis points in both May and August, followed by a hike of seventy-five basis points in November—the biggest one-time increase during Greenspan's tenure as chairman. The committee added another jump, this time of twenty-five basis points, in February 1995, putting the FFR at 6 percent, but also indicated that the series of increases had likely come to an end. After nudging the FFR down to 5.25 by January 1996, in response to leading economic indicators suggesting a slowing of economic activity, the Fed kept it fairly constant through 1999. Considering that real GDP growth averaged a strong 4.3 percent during those four years and unemployment fell from 5.6 percent to 4.2 percent, the Fed's restraint is especially noteworthy and somewhat surprising.

Greenspan's optimism about the prospect of growth with low inflation was rooted in what he believed to be the sound fundamentals of the U.S. economy. They included low inflation and unemployment, heightened global competition restraining wage growth and limiting companies' ability to pass along higher costs to consumers, corporate restructuring and downsizing that have improved business efficiency, rising worker productivity associated with new technological applications involving recent advances in computers, and a fiscal policy of deficit reduction embraced by President Clinton and the Congress.[10] As the chairman told Congress, "The Federal Reserve is intent on gearing its policy to facilitate the maximum sustainable growth of the economy, but it is not, as some commentators have suggested, involved in an experiment that deliberately prods the economy to see how fast it can grow."[11] While a number of his colleagues on the FOMC did not share their chairman's sanguine scenario, they have been willing to follow his lead because of the demonstrated success of his judgments.[12] In fact, there have not been more than two dissents on any FOMC monetary policy vote since 1992.[13] Between 1996 and 1999, years of remarkable growth of economic output and employment, inflation *fell* from 3 percent to 2.2 percent.

Public confidence in Greenspan's leadership soared. Popular publications such as *Business Week* and *U.S. News and World Report* recounted the nation's record of economic successes and were quick to attribute them to Federal Reserve Board policy under Greenspan's leadership. *Time* magazine put Greenspan on its cover. Articles and editorials raised the issue of whether economic prosperity could be extended indefinitely. Pundits wondered whether the United States had embarked on an era of "New Economics," in which there need not be a trade-off between unemployment and inflation. The triumphant among them mused over whether the grip of the traditional business cycle had been broken. Even President Clinton shared the optimism, stating, "I believe it's possible to have more sustained and higher growth without inflation than we previously thought."[14]

Most economists, however, were not prepared to embrace a new economics of indefinitely sustainable growth with price stability. They saw strong economic growth and falling unemployment as beckoning government-imposed restraint lest inflation once again become a problem. The trick comes in assessing the appropriate timing for restraint. Alan Blinder of Princeton University, and a former Federal Reserve vice-chair, was one who believed that growth must be managed if it is to be sustainable. For him and other mainline economists, much faster economic growth invariably leads to unacceptably high inflation and to the inevitable corrective policies that will cause unemployment to rise to unacceptable levels. Blinder relied on the historical relationship between inflation and unemployment, using unemployment as an indicator of aggregate pressure on capacity. He also questioned the premise that the U.S. economy could expect significant continued productivity gains that would keep inflation in check during high growth, asking why we now should expect information technology to raise worker productivity significantly when the trend line—which covers periods of vastly expanded computing power and technological innovation—points to continued marginal growth in worker productivity overall, despite gains in the manufacturing sector (which during the period of the FOMC's restraint accounted for only 20 percent of the GDP).[15]

This critique is not without irony. It was less than five years earlier that Greenspan was subjected to criticism for prematurely stifling economic growth as the FOMC sharply raised the FFR in 1994. Robert Eisner, Lester Thurow, James K. Galbraith, Barry Bluestone, and Bennett Harrison were among the economists who took this position in varying degrees.[16] Thurow led the assault, stating boldly that "rising inequality and falling wages are more important problems than the ghost of inflation."[17] Galbraith's prescription was to test the limits, for, like Bluestone and Harrison, he viewed the employment and income gains brought by growth as outweighing the risk of price-level increases. Bluestone and Harrison emphasized the social value of faster growth, arguing that, if used wisely, it holds the only realistic hope of raising living standards, reducing the gap between the rich and poor, and helping to solve many of America's social problems.

Greenspan's willingness to push the envelope of growth in the second half of the 1990s temporarily placated these critics. He did so because, as discussed earlier, he judged the risk to be low. Efficiency-generating corporate restructuring, heightened global competition, and improved worker productivity offered the promise that inflation could be held in check.

Yet the period of Greenspan-led forbearance in monetary policy was not without its challenges. Growing asset values—both in the stock market and in housing, but especially in the former—prompted concern that the associated rising wealth effect would inflame demand and push consumption higher, putting pressure on prices. Observers, including Greenspan himself, questioned how long asset values could be sustained. The chairman even branded the run-up in stock prices as the product of "irrational exuberance" on the part of investors, a characterization that sparked a marked short-term price correction on Wall Street. Yet Greenspan was leery about the Fed being in the business of bursting stock market bubbles; its job, as he saw it, was to facilitate growth to the economy's full potential without losing the fight against inflation. For Greenspan, concrete evidence that tied inflation to rising asset values was needed. In fact, inflation was on a downward track between 1996 and 1999, even though leading economic indicators suggested that a rebound in inflation could be right around the corner. As an insurance policy, the chairman urged the FOMC to ratchet up the FFR in three increments during the first five weeks of the new century, bringing the targeted rate to 6.5 percent in May 2000.

Recall that it was also about this time that both presidential candidates were arguing about what should be done with a federal budget surplus projected to exceed $4 trillion between the 2001 and 2010 fiscal years. It soon became evident that surpluses of that magnitude were no more than a pipedream. In fact, the $236 billion budget surplus at the end of FY 2000 declined to a surplus of $127 billion one year later and then gave way to a string of deficits.

Investors' exuberance, unsubstantiated by traditional investment criteria such as earnings per share and price-to-earnings ratios, created an asset bubble to be popped. And pop it did in the last half of 2000, a decline that was accelerated by the terrorist attacks of September 11, 2001, and that continued through September 2002. The economy officially fell into recession during the first three quarters of 2001, even though real GDP managed a meager 0.8 percentage-point gain during the calendar year. Unemployment rose from 4 percent in 2000 to 6 percent in 2003, an increase that would have arguably been steeper had the FOMC not reduced the FFR thirteen times between January 1, 2001, and June 25, 2003. During that period, the rate fell from 6.5 percent to a bare 1 percent, as the Fed injected the greatest monetary stimulus in history.

Setting the FFR at 1 percent gave the FOMC little room for further downward adjustment. Some economists worried that with inflation dropping from 2.8 percent in 2001 to only 1.6 percent in 2002 and with the FFR at a historically low level, the Fed might be painting itself into the proverbial corner, should economic recovery languish and inflation drop even further. Those most concerned even raised the prospect of deflation, in which the index of prices declines. For them, the nosedive in interest rates offered an insurance policy against the remote possibility of deflation, or at least a reduction of risk.[18]

Under Greenspan's urging, the Fed began its series of interest rate reductions just days before George W. Bush assumed the presidency. And the new president made good on his promise to cut taxes, as Congress passed legislation in June that would shrink tax revenues by $1.35 trillion through December 31, 2010, reinforcing the stimulus provided by monetary policy. Reductions in income taxes would account for about $875 billion of the total tax cut, while a phaseout of estate and gift tax liability would add another $138 billion. The remainder would come from changes in income tax deductions favoring married couples, child tax credits, pension and IRA liberalization, and favorable tax treatment for educational expenses.

As is discussed in greater detail in chapter 4, Bush justified the tax cut on two grounds: ideology and economic theory. On the former, he argued that taxpayers deserve to get back money they contributed to the surplus in the first place. Echoing classical liberal argument, he suggested that taxpayers would know better than the federal government how best to use the surplus dollars. On the latter ground, he justified the big tax cut as contributing to economic recovery, boosting aggregate demand when spent, and contributing to increased investment when saved.

Two years later, Congress enlarged the tax cut by $350 billion, providing additional stimulus aimed at spurring faster job-creating economic growth. At President Bush's urging, Congress further reduced individual income tax rates and moved up the dates on which rate reductions would take effect, along with lowering the maximum tax rate applied to dividends and long-term capital gains. Stimulative fiscal policy reinforced stimulative monetary policy—in contrast with the early 1980s, when a fiscal pedal was matched with a monetary brake.

By 2003 economic recovery was well under way, as real GDP rose by 2.7 percent in that year. Growth of 4.2 and 3.5 percent followed in 2004 and 2005, respectively, paralleling the average annual rate of growth during the miracle years from 1996 through the end of the decade. With fears of deflation put aside, the FOMC reinstituted a series of thirteen incremental rate hikes, which lifted the FFR from its low of 1 percent to 5.25 in late June 2006. Along the way, Chairman Greenspan carefully inserted language accompanying the announced targeted rate increases that signaled the Fed's commitment to further monetary loosening. Phrases such as "the Committee believes that policy accommodation can be maintained for a considerable period" or "the Committee believes that policy accommodation can be removed at a pace that is likely to be measured" shaped expectations in the securities market.[19]

Greenspan's service on the Federal Reserve Board ended on January 31, 2006. During his long tenure as chairman, the U.S. economy experienced the two longest expansions on record. Under his watch, the economy survived the October 1987 stock market crash, the comparatively mild recessions in 1990–91 and 2001, the 9/11 terrorist attacks on American soil, and a major decline in equity prices during 2000 and 2001. Chairman Greenspan became not only the personification of the Federal Reserve Board but the international model of the successful central bank leader. Honors poured in, including the U.S. Presidential Medal of Freedom, the French Legion of Honor, and British knighthood.[20]

The Beginning of the Bernanke Era

Greenspan's successor, Ben S. Bernanke, served as a member of the Board of Governors before being nominated to the chairmanship by President George W. Bush. From 2001 to early 2003, Bernanke served in the White House as chairman of the Council of Economic Advisers. He assumed the Fed chairmanship at a time of substantial job growth, correspondingly low unemployment (which had just fallen below 5 percent), high worker productivity, and low core inflation (despite the historically high price of oil and natural gas).

Unlike Greenspan, Bernanke served the majority of his professional career in academe. Having earned a doctorate in economics from the Massachusetts Institute of Technology, he served more than twenty years as a professor of economics at Stanford and Princeton universities, including stints as founding director of Princeton's Bendheim Center for Finance and as chairman of the economics department. He also served as founding editor of the *International Journal of Central Banking*.

Pledging to continue the Greenspan legacy, Bernanke nonetheless signaled that he might have greater interest than his predecessor in turning to the more transparent practice of **inflation targeting**, in which the Fed would announce inflation targets that it wished to achieve in the near term and then adjust interest rates to expected changes in inflation. The central banks of several industrial nations, including those of the United Kingdom, Australia, New Zealand, and our neighbors Canada and Mexico, employ some variant of inflation targeting. And these nations have been joined recently by the former Soviet-satellite states of Hungary and Poland. Bernanke's predecessor eschewed formal inflation targeting, despite its growing popularity abroad. Greenspan preferred throughout most of his tenure to offer only veiled hints about the likely course of future monetary policy, offering nuanced comments that hinted at the likely near-term direction of interest rates.

While Bernanke may influence the Fed to alter its course and adopt inflation targeting, he appears likely to share Greenspan's aversion to using monetary policy to respond to movements in asset prices. Despite urging from some of his colleagues on the FOMC, Greenspan failed to support using monetary policy to stem rapid increases in stock market and real estate prices. The run-up in equity prices was dealt powerful blows by the 2001 recession and the downturn in investor confidence wreaked by the terrorist attacks in September of that year. In response, the FOMC sharply reduced the FFR, as discussed earlier. In a sense, the Fed engaged in a sort of mop-up operation directed at minimizing the economic damage and stimulating recovery.

As one bubble burst, another continued to grow. Home sales in the United States began an almost consistent rise in 1995 and set four consecutive records from 2000 through 2004 before leveling off and then moderately declining in 2005.[21] Home sales in California topped the five-year rate of growth, rising 102 percent. Markets in other states experienced growth rates of more than 50 percent; among these were Nevada (79 percent), Florida (75 percent), Maryland and New Jersey (74 percent), New York (69 percent), and Virginia (63 percent). Nevada is a notable case, because it had the fastest one-year growth, at 32 percent in 2004 alone.

Speculators helped to fuel the inflationary flames: one-quarter of the sales nationally went to investors who did not intend to occupy their newly acquired properties. Buyers, too, increasingly made use of alternative financing, electing adjusted rate mortgages (ARMs) and the newer interest-only mortgages. The latter device offers lower monthly payments than does traditional financing but fails to reduce the principal balance owed over the first several years of a mortgage's life. Yet in a speculative environment, with fast-rising home prices, borrowers hedge their hopes on capital gains that return far more financial benefit than incremental principal reduction provides.[22]

Looking at hot housing markets, economists want to know whether price increases reflect economic fundamentals or irrational exuberance, to borrow Greenspan's famous phrase. Unlike the former, the latter is characterized by a mass psychology that if prospective buyers want a piece of the pie, they had better jump into the market before prices rise even further. When buying hysteria sets in, the bubble in asset markets, like real estate, is primed to burst. When it does and prices tumble, increased loan delinquency and default follow. More significantly, home owners feel less wealthy and are inclined to cut back on spending, just as, in rising markets, they tend to increase spending, feeling the so-called wealth effect.

Despite the economic cost of lowered aggregate demand that accompanies burst growing asset bubbles, Chairman Bernanke has consistently espoused the approach of not responding to asset price increases, except insofar as they affect forecast inflation.[23] For Bernanke, "Once the predictive content of asset prices for inflation has been accounted for, there should be no additional response of monetary policy to asset-price fluctuations."[24] Thus inflation targeting becomes the instrument to keep the inflationary effects of asset price increases in check.

The Fed's Relationship with the Executive Branch

Presidents are much better positioned to influence fiscal policy than monetary policy, as they set the fiscal policy agenda. And facing an upcoming election, many in Congress may see their own reelection prospects linked with the president's to the state of the economy, thus providing an incentive for Congress to support presidential efforts to use fiscal policy to improve economic conditions—that is, unless partisan opponents in Congress believe that they can successfully deflect blame to the president for the economy's woes. In comparison, the institutional influence of presidents on monetary policy is far less marked.

The president appoints members of the Federal Reserve Board, but the length and staggered nature of their terms makes it difficult for a president to appoint a majority of board members, even though high member turnover can at times enable a two-term president to do so. Moreover, as monetary policy making has shifted to the FOMC, the addition of Federal Reserve bank presidents to the FOMC, joining presidential appointees, further distances the president from the committee. Nevertheless, the fact of institutional separation should not lead to the conclusion that the president lacks influence on monetary policy. The president's "bully pulpit" is his greatest nonlegal resource. Presidential statements garner attention, and when presidents highlight their visibility, political actors and the media pay attention to both the message and the political forces behind it. Federal Reserve chairs want presidential support for their board's policies and do not relish presidential criticism.

As history has shown, however, that does not mean that the Fed does whatever the president wants. In a highly publicized standoff in 1965, the Fed raised the discount rate despite strong opposition from the Johnson administration. Not only did CEA Chairman Walter Heller press the administration's case, but President Lyndon Johnson also personally made the appeal.[25] Facing rising inflation, Federal Reserve Chair William McChesney Martin and his colleagues on the board stood their ground.

The 1980 election year provides another case in point. Two months after he took over as chairman in August 1979, Paul Volcker pledged to Congress that the Federal Reserve would significantly tighten the money supply as its primary weapon against inflation, which had hit double-digit proportions. Both Treasury Secretary Michael Blumenthal and CEA Chairman Charles Schultze signaled the Carter administration's support for restrictive monetary policy—a stance perhaps motivated by the desire to suffer the economic fallout of inflation containment as far away from the coming election as possible. Then, with inflation more in check, perhaps the Fed would loosen constraints in advance of the coming election.

The need for aggressive restraint was apparent to all observers. The inflation rate (CPI-U) approached 15 percent in March 1980, up from 11 percent just three months earlier. In response, the Fed's rapid and sharp tightening of the money supply pushed the FFR above 17 percent in March. With the election less than eight months away, the Carter administration reversed course and began promoting lower interest rates. As one study concludes, President Carter and his agents communicated eight separate ease signals to the Fed from April through October.[26]

The FOMC complied, or so it appears, almost halving the FFR by July, dropping it to 9 percent. The earlier tightening had brought inflation down two percentage points between March and July but had increased unemployment from 6.3 percent to 7.8 percent during that same period.

In midsummer it appeared that the economy had bottomed out and was growing again, and inflation looked to be rising anew. Fearing another wave of spiked inflation, the Fed returned to tightening the money supply, and the FFR rose from 11 percent in September to 14 percent on election day. President Carter publicly branded the rate hikes as "ill advised." Carter argued that the Fed was pushing interest rates higher "than economic circumstances warrant."[27]

The 1980 election not only gave Reagan a landslide victory but also swept conservatives into Congress, giving Republicans control of the Senate for the first time since the Eisenhower years. Political support clearly existed for a more restrictive monetary policy, as inflation stubbornly remained close to 13 percent at year's close. The FOMC followed suit, free of any compunction about jeopardizing the reelection of a sitting president who appointed many of its members.[28] By the time the new administration took office, the FOMC had raised the FFR to 19 percent.

The Reagan administration supported the tight money policy of the Volcker-led Federal Reserve Board as necessary to bring inflation under control. But as unemployment reached post-Depression record highs toward the middle of Reagan's first term, a number of his economic advisers grumbled that the Federal Reserve was too slow in easing credit restraints to help the economy grow out of the 1981–82 recession, a recession that was precipitated in good part by inflation-fighting monetary policy. Yet apart from a few media stories of presidential discontent, administration officials elected not to take on the Fed directly, probably due significantly to the president's own antipathy toward inflation, which was clearly reflected in his August 1983 message announcing Volcker's reappointment as chair. Reagan commented that Volcker "is as dedicated as I am to continuing the fight against inflation. And with him as Chairman of the Fed, I know we'll win that fight."[29]

Nearly a decade later, Richard Darman, George H.W. Bush's OMB director, and Nicholas Brady, Bush's Treasury secretary, took issue publicly with Alan Greenspan's unwillingness to urge the Federal Reserve to take actions that would lower interest rates and stimulate recovery to the extent the administration wanted. Both understood the political implications of slow recovery. Greenspan, however, voiced his determination to stay the course and support measured, sustainable, noninflationary recovery.[30] President Clinton and his administration reaped the economic fruits of that approach. In return, President Clinton reappointed Greenspan to another four-year term as chairman.

Given the Greenspan-led Board's record of success in guiding the economy's sustained boom through 2000, President George W. Bush deferred to the Fed chairman's calls on monetary policy. Both Greenspan and Bush saw the need for marked reductions in the FFR during the course of 2001, Bush's first year in the presidency. In fact, the president viewed the greatly loosened monetary policy as a welcomed complement to his expansive fiscal policy of large income tax cuts. As evidence, he, too, reappointed Greenspan to another, and his last, term as chairman. Then, with economic recovery strongly under way leading to the 2004 elections, the Bush administration voiced no concerns about the gradual tightening that followed. And the continued strong growth of the postelection economy, with well-contained core inflation, gave Bush and his economic advisers good reason to continue their support of Fed policy.

Over the course of executive-Fed relations, presidential administrations have created formal structures to advance communication between the executive branch and the Fed on economic policy. President Dwight Eisenhower established an Advisory Board on Economic Growth and Stabilization (ABEGS), which included the chair of the President's Council of Economic Advisers (CEA), the secretary of the Department of the Treasury, other selected cabinet agency heads, and the chair of the Federal Reserve Board. The advisory board served as an institutionalized forum for assessing the economy's performance and fostering communication about appropriate policy responses. However, the fact that the chair of the CEA chaired the advisory board's meetings conveyed the reality of fiscal policy's ascendancy over monetary policy as a tool of economic stabilization at that time. Although the ABEGS ceased to exist during the Kennedy administration, President Kennedy formally brought together his top fiscal officials—the CEA chair, the secretary of the Treasury, and the director of the Bureau of the Budget—joined by the Federal Reserve chair in what was referred to as the Quadriad, a structure continued by Kennedy's successor, Lyndon Johnson. Kennedy originally used the arrangement to ensure that the Fed would not use monetary policy to offset the growth-inducing effects of the administration's fiscal policy.[31]

As the balance tilted toward monetary policy as the preferred instrument of economic management from the 1980s to the present, Fed chairs have been less inclined to participate in formal efforts to coordinate fiscal and monetary policy. Representatives of presidential administrations, particularly since the Clinton years, have become more respectful of the independence of the Fed. According to former Federal Reserve governor Laurence Meyer, the Fed chair and the Treasury secretary meet at times for breakfast or lunch, and members of the CEA and the Federal Reserve Board meet monthly for lunch, but the discussions tend to focus more on technical issues related to the performance of the economy and to its outlook. Participants shy away from discussing the direction of monetary policy or its relationship to fiscal policy, in contrast to the earlier years.[32]

Congressional Oversight

Federal law not only provides the Federal Reserve with independence in monetary policy making but also shields it from traditional forms of congressional oversight. Unlike most federal agencies, the Federal Reserve System does not rely on congressional **appropriations** for its financial support. Instead, it derives its revenue primarily from the interest on U.S. government securities it has acquired through open market operations, along with the interest it earns from the discounted loans it makes to depository institutions. Federal Reserve banks also charge fees for the financial services they provide to banks and other thrift institutions. This financial independence from Congress removes the regularized oversight associated with the annual appropriations process and the scrutiny subcommittees give agencies, which is often linked to agency fulfillment of congressional expectations tied to appropriations. Federal law does, however, require the Federal Reserve chair to report twice a year to the congressional banking committees on the state of the economy and the course of monetary policy followed—occasions that can elicit hard questioning and heated exchanges when the economy is in trouble, especially when a congressional election is forthcoming.

Although Congress has given the Federal Reserve System freedom from the annual appropriations process and the oversight that goes with it, the Fed still is subject to Congress's power to amend the laws that give the Fed its authority and independence. Yet several factors mitigate Congress's inclination to alter present arrangements. First, the Federal Reserve enjoys a high degree of legitimacy in the American political system. Its widely perceived effective performance over the past two decades has strengthened its grip on favorable public opinion. Second, it has a solid foundation of constituency-based support in Congress, drawn from districts that represent major banking interests, traditionally strong supporters of Fed independence.[33] Third, the technical demands of monetary policy making, with its complex models and seemingly endless data, limit the feasibility of close congressional oversight. Fourth, the Federal Reserve provides a political shield for Congress. Poor economic performance can be blamed on Fed policies and their implementation. Conversely, members of Congress readily share the accolades that follow strong economic performance. Federal Reserve independence allows members of Congress to deflect negative fallout, while basking in economic success.

This does not mean that members of Congress are always shy about publicly sharing their opinions about what the Fed should do to address economic problems. In addition to establishing the goals of monetary policy by law, as discussed earlier, members of Congress can communicate their views on monetary policy in a number of ways, most typically through remarks in committee hearings and on the floor, as well as through public speeches. Although Congress can pass resolutions and enact legislation directed at the Fed, it has rarely done so.

Congress's most aggressive attempts to shape monetary policy occurred in the mid-1970s. The post-Watergate context of a weakened presidency, sizable Democratic gains in Congress as a result of the 1974 midterm elections, and a slumping economy combined to embolden Democratic leaders to use Congress's legislative powers to prod the Fed into expanding the money supply, thereby lowering interest rates. Senate Banking Committee Chairman William Proxmire (D-Wisconsin) led the charge. Proxmire's Senate-concurrent resolution directed the Federal Reserve to expand the money supply in the first half of 1975 and thereafter maintain growth in monetary aggregates commensurate with potential economic output in the long run. The Senate passed the resolution and the House adopted it but also inserted language in its substitute resolution (HCR 133) directing the Fed to lower long-term interest rates. Coming early out of a deep recession, Congress's direction echoed the Fed's own inclination. And the resolution's language gave the FOMC considerable latitude in deciding how much stimulus to apply.[34] In the words of a noted political historian of the Federal Reserve, "The Federal Reserve responded to HCR 133 overwhelmingly as a problem in congressional relations, not as a directive requiring a change in operating procedure."[35]

The Fed's monetary policy of the early 1980s also attracted substantial congressional attention. After greatly reducing monetary aggregates and driving the FFR as high as 20 percent, members of Congress, especially the Democrats, were anxious for the Fed to loosen restraint and replenish credit markets. Although members of Congress introduced a plethora of resolutions aimed at increasing the money supply and lowering interest rates, only one passed, and it was largely a token gesture.[36]

Since the early 1980s, Congress has demonstrated more of a willingness to let the Fed make monetary policy unencumbered by congressional intervention. Of course, protracted periods of strong economic growth have reinforced that inclination.

Issues of Interest and Distributive Benefit

Inflation and unemployment do not affect everyone the same. Inflation benefits borrowers, because it allows them to repay loans with cheapened dollars. Conversely, it hurts lenders, who not only receive payment in dollars that are worth less but must pay higher rates of interest to attract deposits. It is not surprising, therefore, that bankers want to keep inflation under control. Although unemployment most directly affects the pocketbooks of those without jobs, it is symptomatic of an economy in which demand falls short of productive capacity. Inadequate demand leaves employers with unsold goods and services, depressing their income and reducing their need for labor.

The cyclical nature of the economy, from which economic performance rises from trough to peak and then falls back to trough again, leaves hope that economic slumps will reverse themselves, returning unemployed workers to jobs once demand rebounds. Yet the rise from trough to peak does not mean that the unemployed will be called back to the jobs they have lost. The deep 1981–82 recession underscores this point. More than 2 million jobs were lost, many never to return, in the industrial Midwest and Northeast between 1980 and 1983 alone. Expanded application of technology, particularly robotics, increased productive efficiency at the expense of human labor. Michigan, Illinois, Ohio, and Pennsylvania accounted for almost 1.1 million lost jobs.[37]

The eight-month 2001 recession and its near-term recovery provide another case in point. In the thirty-one months between March 1, 2001 (the beginning of the recession), and September 30, 2003, well into the recovery, the U.S. economy suffered a net loss of nearly 2.5 million jobs.[38] About 1.1 million net job losses occurred after November 1, 2001, the official end of the recession, constituting what some observers have labeled a "jobless recovery."

Where to set the balance between inflation and unemployment is not just an economic issue but an important political one as well. Economic policy makers face the question of how much inflation we can tolerate in bringing down unemployment. Everyone's preference is to have both low inflation and low unemployment, and the U.S. economy has delivered both during most of the 1990s and in the first decade of the twenty-first century after the 2001 recession. But inflation and unemployment have moved in an inverse relationship for much of our economic history. Measures to stimulate economic growth and lower unemployment have had their inflationary consequences, and actions to dampen growth and fight inflation have resulted in higher unemployment.

Different interests have their own preferences as to how the balance should be set. As noted earlier, lending institutions want to set the balance on the side of stably combating inflation. Lenders are willing to pay higher rates of interest on deposits in order to protect the value of loan repayments. The construction and housing industries prefer low interest rates that encourage commercial building and new housing starts and are willing to accept higher inflation in return. Business wants low interest rates that facilitate consumer spending and that provide them with low-cost capital with which to expand their operations. They also are willing to live with moderately higher inflation, although business owners and executives understand that unacceptably high inflation erodes their real profits and leads the way to restrictive policies that constrain economic growth and personal income.

Among members of the general public, inflation most detrimentally affects those on a relatively fixed income. The degree to which price-level increases exceed the rate of return on savings and retirement benefits determines the extent to which their purchasing power is eroded. Workers whose wages are adjusted upward for inflation, as well as retirees whose income comes from investments in stocks, are far better protected against inflationary erosion over the long run than are those on relatively fixed incomes. However, economic downturns jeopardize investment returns and can cost jobs.

As monetary policy has become the nation's economic management tool of choice, the members of the Fed have assumed the weighty responsibility not only to guide the course of the national economy, but also to manage it in a way that protects the interests of all Americans. Yet Fed policy makers understand full well that their monetary policy choices to correct economic problems will have differential effects, distributing both benefit and hardship. The only way out of this dilemma is for them to be successful in proactively keeping the economy on a healthy and stable footing that widely spreads the benefits of sustained economic growth. We know, nevertheless, that the economy at times needs strong monetary medicine, and when the Fed administers it, it triggers effects that treat interests differently, as previously discussed.

Fiscal Policy Making

The benefits from a sound, growing economy are many and widespread, ranging from the financial to the political. A good economy increases personal income, generates resources for investment, creates favorable conditions for job growth, enhances citizen support for government, and advances the political standing of incumbents. Yet economic prosperity cannot be taken for granted. As discussed in chapter 3, history shows alternating periods of economic growth and decline. Workers, businesses, and elected public officials reap the benefits of growth and suffer the consequences of decline. In one sense, they are captive of the vagaries of economic cycles and fluctuations. In another sense, however, all share the conviction that government can and should act to stabilize the economy at desired levels of economic performance—our Keynesian intellectual inheritance. U.S. government policy makers rely primarily on monetary and fiscal policy-making tools to manage the economy. This chapter covers fiscal policy.

Although monetary and fiscal policy share the same objective of promoting economic growth and full employment, but within acceptable levels of inflation, fiscal and monetary policy makers go about that task differently. Fiscal policy deals with the tax and spending decisions of national governments and the relationship between them. In the United States, that means the tax and spending decisions of Congress, as affected by actions of the president. Tax and spending choices influence the national economy by affecting aggregate demand. Government taxes reduce aggregate demand because they take resources away from individuals and businesses that might otherwise be spent. Tax increases transfer additional resources from the private to the public sector and reduce the purchasing power of the former. Conversely, tax cuts transfer resources from the public to the private sector and increase after-tax disposable income that can be spent. Tax policy, depending on its structure, can also affect aggregate supply, to the extent that it provides strong incentives for individuals or firms to save rather than to spend.

Government spending adds to aggregate demand through the purchases that government makes directly or through those made by the recipients of government financial assistance, whether they be individuals or other governmental units. In the latter case, states and local governments in the United States spend federal aid directly or distribute it to individuals who, in turn, spend it. In either case, this added spending increases aggregate demand. Government spending can also influence the level and potential growth of a nation's economy, depending on the nature of that spending. Government spending on physical infrastructure, such as highways and bridges, and on education, technology development, and basic research, commonly referred to as human infrastructure, can provide the basis for increased productivity and the higher personal income that follows.

Spending must be financed. Governments can use current revenues to pay for their expenditures or, where permitted by law, can borrow to cover costs in excess of revenues. The U.S. federal government typically runs an annual deficit and sells Treasury securities to obtain the financial resources needed to cover expenditures in excess of current revenues. The resulting debt, then, must be paid off to security holders over the life of the bond or note. The federal government budgets that debt-service obligation as part of its operating budget, thus increasing pressure on the expenditure side of the budget. As debt obligation grows, either additional revenues must be found to pay the bill, or offsetting reductions must be made somewhere else in the budget.

The federal government faces no constitutional or statutory requirement to balance its budget. Most state and local governments are required to balance their operating budgets but are allowed to have separate **capital budgets**, within which they can incur debt to finance capital projects such as buildings and roads. Yet, as with the federal government, any resulting debt-service obligation must be met in the operating budget, which at the state and local level is subject to the balanced-budget requirement.

The federal government's license to run a deficit and finance it through debt constitutes an important tool of national fiscal policy, for if it had to close the fiscal year in balance, the president and Congress would have no way to expand spending beyond current revenue constraints. Lacking that ability, national policy makers would lose a powerful tool to increase aggregate demand in times of economic malaise. Without the federal government's ability to deficit-spend, economic policy makers would be without an important tool to fight unemployment.

What about cutting taxes to stimulate aggregate demand? Tax reductions can contribute toward increased aggregate demand, as long as the additional after-tax income is spent rather than saved. Facing a stagnant economy or sharp economic downturn, people tend to behave conservatively, putting off major purchases, largely restricting spending to meeting their basic needs, and saving for an uncertain future. In that environment, increased government spending becomes the only sure fiscal policy tool to stimulate demand.

Authority and Resources for Fiscal Policy Making

The U.S. Constitution gives Congress the authority to tax and spend on behalf of the national government. That power to tax and spend gives Congress the fiscal policy tools to influence the course of America's economy. The Constitution also gives Congress the authority to borrow and coin money and to regulate its value. This vesting of authority in Congress for economic policy making should not be interpreted to mean that Congress exercises sole, or even primary, influence in shaping U.S. fiscal policy. In fact, Congress has acted over time to delegate a great deal of operational authority over fiscal policy making to the president.

However, for the president to be successful in putting his distinctive stamp on America's fiscal policy, Congress must cooperate, approving the president's recommendations on taxing and spending. More often than not, Congress's choices represent an amalgam of compromises and accommodations that have presidential initiatives as their starting point. Congress has given the president responsibility for setting America's fiscal policy agenda, and presidents have expanded their own role.

The President and the Executive Branch

Among all of the tools available to the president to influence macroeconomic policy, it is the president's responsibility to submit a national budget to Congress that gives him an edge in fiscal policy making. Using his authority to develop an **executive budget**, the president recommends how much the federal government should tax, spend, and borrow in a given year. Working off the current year's budget, the president's recommendations set priorities that depart from that base. Those might include new programmatic initiatives, increases and cuts in funding for existing programs, and reallocations from some programs to others. The executive budget shapes the terms of the national budgetary debate and typically puts Congress in a reactive posture.

Even though the president's ascendant position in fiscal policy making has evolved over time, it is rooted in Congress's passage of the Budget and Accounting Act of 1921. That act created the vehicle of the executive budget and required that agencies submit their budget requests to the president instead of directly to Congress, as was done previously. The president could then decide whether to include, exclude, or modify agency requests. The executive budget was to become the president's budget, carrying the stamp of presidential priorities.

The Office of Management and Budget

To assist the president in carrying out budgetary responsibilities, Congress in 1921 created the Bureau of the Budget, which became the Office of Management and Budget (OMB) during the Nixon administration. Originally placed within the Department of the Treasury, the bureau was moved in 1939 to the newly created Executive Office of the President. The Great Depression, and President Franklin Roosevelt's activist New Deal initiatives in response to it, created the need for greater policy coordination and management oversight within the executive branch. The Executive Office of the President consolidated presidential staff assistants who were charged with those tasks. Although the number of presidential aides never exceeded twelve during FDR's years in office, the executive office's creation gave birth to the modern White House professional staff.[1]

In those early years, neither the Bureau of the Budget nor the Executive Office of the President played an explicit leadership role in shaping national fiscal policy. The bureau assisted the president in putting together the executive budget, but it played only a limited role in initiating policy development. Nor did it articulate an economic strategy that integrated its budgetary recommendations to the president. Before the Depression, the bureau followed the common inherited wisdom that the budget should be balanced except in times of war.

President Roosevelt remained a devotee of the **balanced budget** paradigm throughout his first term and early into his second term, even though he soon came to realize that governmental action was necessary to cut into the Depression's sustained high unemployment. To address the problem of high and rising unemployment, FDR followed a simple approach: use government to put unemployed people to work and give them income. Roosevelt put primary value on the benefits that gainful employment provided to people and not so much on the aggregate economic stimulus it provided. Government intervention was to be a temporary stop-gap measure, providing relief to a hurting populace. According to Herbert Stein, Keynesian theory provided a later "sophisticated rationale" for the increased government spending of the New Deal, without the president or his economic advisers having to worry about the theorized consequences of deficit-financed spending on aggregate demand or private-sector borrowing. It was not until midway into his second term that FDR came to appreciate the stimulative power of public expenditures to expand purchasing power, to raise recovery to a level at which it would run by itself.[2] Ultimately, the massive job-creating defense spending in support of U.S. involvement in World War II broke the back of unemployment. America did indeed spend itself into prosperity.

Keynes and his later disciples legitimized the New Deal's approach and provided the theoretical justification for demand-side expansionist policies of administrations to follow.[3] By the end of World War II, Keynesianism had won broad acceptance within the academic community and within the nation's capital. Government was widely seen as having a responsibility to use its fiscal policy tools to maintain full employment, and the institution of the president, in the wake of Roosevelt's political leadership, was acknowledged as the locus of governmental initiative. The public had come to expect presidential leadership in economic management, and it was ready to hold the president accountable for the economy's performance.

The Council of Economic Advisers

With Keynesian theory firmly in place, Congress acted in 1946 to institutionalize the national government's responsibilities for economic management by passing the Employment Act of 1946. A product of Keynesian-trained New Deal economists in the White House and their allies in Congress, the legislation formally strengthened the president's role in economic management—a role that Congress hoped would lead to an economy that could provide "maximum employment" and absorb the millions returning from military service. The act created the Council of Economic Advisers (CEA) to provide assistance to the president, and it required the president to report to each new Congress on the condition of the economy. That report, now called the annual *Economic Report of the President*, sets the stage for the president's executive budget recommendations that follow, which contain the tax and spending measures that embody the administration's fiscal policy.

Today, the OMB and the Department of the Treasury join the CEA in assisting the president to carry out his economic leadership. Of the three, the CEA operates at the broadest macro level. Its job is to apprise the president on the state of the U.S. economy and to offer advice about what measures can be taken to improve the nation's economic performance. In addition to its formal responsibility to prepare the president's economic report, the three-member council, and particularly its chair, advises the president on how the economy works, helping the president to sort out complicated economic relationships and be able to handle them in public discourse. Council members also assist in the preparation of presidential speeches on economic matters and help prepare the president for press conferences at which questions about the economy can be expected.

Council members have been drawn primarily from academe; usually they serve a few years in office and then return to their university appointments. Presidents appoint members for their economic expertise, but in doing so they look for candidates who share their views of the proper role for government in the economy. However, the CEA is not divorced from politics or partisanship.[4] Members and top-level staff assistants realize they have a duty to provide the president with sound analysis drawn from their academic and professional expertise, yet they are not disinterested in the president's political fortunes. They share an interest in making the president look as good as possible in the public arena. That combination can translate, on the one hand, into offering frank assessments of the state of the economy and how the administration's economic policies are working and, on the other, into putting a positive gloss on the administration's accomplishments. A careful reading of annual economic reports shows their public relations value to the president.

Compared to the CEA, the OMB is the operational arm of presidential fiscal policy. Fiscal policy must be translated into concrete tax and spending decisions. The OMB assists the president in developing and presenting the executive budget to Congress. At its inception, as the Bureau of the Budget, the office was charged with reacting to agency requests and recommending courses of action to the president on each. Over time, it has become a proactive force in policy initiation and budgetary development. Today, it not only analyzes agency requests but also articulates a policy and budgetary framework within which executive agencies are expected to work. That framework includes policy prioritization and fiscal limitations put on agency requests.

The director of the OMB is a member of the president's cabinet and a key policy architect within the president's small circle of top policy strategists. The director's role differs significantly from the other cabinet officers, however. Unlike department heads who have administrative authority over their agencies and are charged with both initiating and implementing policy in their respective areas, the OMB director is responsible for influencing and advancing presidential initiatives across agency jurisdictions. In exercising that responsibility, the director, because of the complexity and technical demands of the budget, is in a unique position among cabinet peers. The director sees the big budget picture and how the many pieces to the budgetary puzzle fit together and interrelate. He can suggest that a cabinet secretary does not fully understand the interprogram and interagency effects of a given budgetary recommendation or the overall fiscal constraints under which the executive budget is formulated. That comprehensive perspective not only enhances the influence of the director in budget development but also positions him to act as the administration's spokesman on the budget.[5]

The Department of the Treasury

The third executive branch institution that can influence national fiscal policy is the Department of the Treasury. Its influence on fiscal policy has been more a product of the broad-reaching role of the Treasury secretary and the stature of the individuals appointed to the post than of the administrative functions the department performs. Its primary functions are operational—collecting federal taxes and other revenues, managing cash flow and paying the federal government's bills, borrowing money and managing the **national debt**, printing and coining currency, and administering the U.S. **balance of payments** with other nations. The Treasury secretary also serves as U.S. governor of the International Monetary Fund, the World Bank, the Inter-American Development Bank, the Asian Development Bank, and the African Development Bank.

One of the oldest cabinet departments, the Treasury was established in 1789. Alexander Hamilton served as its first secretary. As officially the second-ranking cabinet officer, the Treasury secretary serves as the chief financial officer of the U.S. government and as a key presidential adviser on tax policy. The secretary's domestic economic influence comes not from overseeing departmental operations but from the ways in which presidents have chosen to use the incumbents as economic policy advisers. In most administrations, presidents have accorded their Treasury secretary a prominent role and strong voice in economic policy making, one that has often been built on a close personal relationship between the two. Recent examples include Ronald Reagan's appointment of James Baker and Bill Clinton's appointment of Robert Rubin.

Presidents have differed in how they have institutionalized economic counsel within their administrations. President Nixon chose to centralize macroeconomic policy advice under Treasury Secretary George Shultz, who was also designated as assistant to the president for economic affairs. Nixon's predecessors, Presidents Kennedy and Johnson, preferred to chair an informal economic advisory committee composed of the Treasury secretary, the chair of the CEA, and the director of the OMB. Presidents Reagan and Bush formalized this collective approach and broadened the membership to include a number of additional cabinet officers, including those from the Departments of Labor, Transportation, Commerce, and State, along with the president's U.S. trade representative. President Clinton enlarged the membership even further—adding the vice president; presidential assistants for economic and domestic policy; the secretaries of the Departments of Agriculture, Energy, and Housing and Urban Development; and the director of the Environmental Protection Agency (EPA)—as he established the new National Economic Council (NEC). Chaired by the president, the NEC was created "(1) to coordinate policy advice to the president, (2) to coordinate the economic policy making process with regard to domestic and international economic issues, (3) to ensure that economic policy making decisions and programs are consistent with the president's stated goals and to ensure that those goals are being effectively pursued, and (4) to monitor implementation of the president's economic policy agenda."[6]

Clinton's first presidential assistant for economic policy, Robert Rubin, played a significant role in guiding the council's agenda. As a result of his effective staff work and Clinton's growing confidence in his ability and advice, Rubin was named as Treasury secretary, replacing Lloyd Bentsen. In that position, the new secretary emerged not only as the administration's key spokesperson on economic affairs but as a key political strategist as well.

Across presidential administrations, it is clear that even though personal relationships between presidents and key administration officers and aides have a bearing on policy influence, institutional role still is the best indicator of influence. When the focus is narrowed from economic affairs—defined broadly—to fiscal policy, presidents have turned most often to their secretary of the Treasury and OMB director for counsel, putting their advice in the context of the CEA's analysis of the nation's economic condition and likely future, as well as in the context of the political realities as viewed by the president's chief of staff. Among the three economic advisers, however, it is the OMB director, whose task it is to put together the tax and spending plan, who most directly shapes the president's budgetary choices.

Congress's Role in Fiscal Policy Making

Although the U.S. Constitution gives Congress the power to tax and spend, Congress is not well positioned to set the nation's fiscal policy agenda. That continues to be true even after congressional reform of the federal budgetary process. Before the budget reform of 1974, Congress possessed little institutionalized ability to substitute its collective vision of national fiscal policy and budgetary priorities for that of the president's. Congressional decisions on taxing and spending were decentralized and fragmented, built on a foundation of "contained specialization."[7] Congressional subcommittee and committee leaders enjoyed considerable autonomy in their decision making. Mutual adjustment and reciprocity characterized the politics of aggregating committee recommendations within each chamber. No plan of congressional action informed committee choices. Congress's imprint on taxing and spending became the aggregate product of numerous discrete and often disconnected decisions.

While Congress lacked a collectively endorsed plan for its tax and spending actions, entitlement spending grew rapidly without Congress needing to make annual decisions on appropriations. With this automatic spending feature, largely a creation of Great Society legislation, entitlement spending grew three times faster than **discretionary spending** between 1960 and 1974 alone.[8] Spending seemed to be out of control, and Congress appeared to have no agreed-on strategy to deal with it.

Congress turned in 1974 to budgetary reform, to be used both to bring coherence to congressional budget making and to limit the president's ability to impound funds appropriated by Congress. Facing a president weakened by the Watergate crisis, Congress passed the ambitious Congressional Budget and **Impoundment** Control Act of 1974 by overwhelming margins, 80 to 0 in the Senate and 401 to 6 in the House. Congressional leaders hailed the act's passage as a "historic legislative development," providing a "new process by which Congress determines national spending priorities."[9] Congress was to set these priorities within the backdrop of its own fiscal policies, not those of the president's administration. It would start out by deciding how much the federal government should spend in the coming year and the extent to which it would cover that spending through taxes, fees, and debt.

The act altered the federal budgetary process and created structures to give Congress the ability to map out its fiscal direction. It created new budget committees in both the House and the Senate, each with its own staff, along with a new congressional staff agency named the Congressional Budget Office (CBO). Congressional leaders conceived of the CBO as Congress's alternative to the CEA and the OMB. The CBO would be responsible for developing its own, independent economic projections and estimates of revenues and spending, freeing Congress from its dependence on executive branch numbers.

The act also modified the federal budgetary process, changing the fiscal year and creating the procedural devices of **concurrent budget resolutions** and **reconciliation**. Concurrent budget resolutions, which do not require presidential approval, must be passed in identical form by both chambers of Congress. The budget act provided for two distinct resolutions. The first had to be adopted before either chamber could act on legislation that provides new spending authority, appropriates budget authority, or results in changes in revenues or in the public debt. It represented Congress's fiscal game plan for the session, establishing aggregate-level ceilings on budget authority and **outlays** (actual expenditures) and projecting revenues to be generated based on the CBO's economic forecasts and the resolution's assumptions about tax law, including any planned changes in current law. Comparing planned expenditures and anticipated revenues, the resolution yielded a projected level of deficit or surplus. Macro choices were to precede micro choices.

Following passage of the first resolution, the Senate and House budget committees, aided by staff assistants, parceled out budget authority and outlay targets to their chamber's committees and subcommittees to guide them in their budgetary decision making. When the resolution called for changes in entitlements, the budget committees instructed the substantive committees having jurisdiction over those entitlement programs to report legislation out that implemented the resolution's provisions. Similarly, the tax-writing committees—Ways and Means in the House and Finance in the Senate—were charged with acting on any tax changes called for in the budget resolution. The new budgetary timetable created by the act gave committees less than four months to complete action on all spending and tax bills. If the committees reported bills out that were not in line with the resolution's limits and intent, Congress had the opportunity to pass a second concurrent resolution—adjusting the first resolution's targets to conform to committee actions, making selective modifications in the resolution while retaining other provisions, or reaffirming the first resolution's targets and including reconciliation instructions to bring committee actions in line with the recommendations of the budget committees. If committees failed to comply, the budget committee could then roll the changes into a single bill, called the reconciliation bill, which would then be reported to the floor for a vote, bypassing the recalcitrant standing committees.

Congress has since done away with the second resolution, retaining a single resolution and the process of reconciliation. Congress today still uses reconciliation to bring committee actions into accord with the concurrent resolution's provisions, yet it also uses reconciliation to make last-minute changes that commonly emerge out of budgetary negotiations with the president or key presidential aides. Thus reconciliation cannot be viewed solely as a procedural tool internal to Congress, one that Congress uses to put the final touches on its own budgetary alternative to the president's. Instead, presidents and their key aides have used reconciliation as an eleventh-hour device to bring congressional budgetary decisions closer in line with presidential priorities, in a sense co-opting a process originally designed to serve Congress's own internal decision-making needs.

David Stockman, Reagan's first OMB director, set the precedent for using Congress's reconciliation process to advance an administration's policy goals. Working with a supportive Republican majority in the Senate and a sizable coalition of Republicans and conservative Democrats in the House, Stockman and other OMB officials hurriedly crafted omnibus reconciliation legislation late in the 1981 session that contained reductions in entitlement spending. These reductions, together with separate legislation that greatly cut individual income taxes, demonstrably launched the promised "Reagan Revolution"—a policy campaign that lost much of its steam during the remainder of the Reagan administration.

Subsequent OMB directors followed Stockman's early lead in working with Congress to fashion omnibus reconciliation bills that advanced presidential policy agendas. The Omnibus Budget Reconciliation Act of 1993 provides a salient illustration of strong executive-led reconciliation, as OMB Director Leon Panetta fashioned a major deficit-reduction package of tax increases and spending cuts that Congress passed with the exclusive support of Democrats, who were then in the majority in both chambers of Congress. Four years later, during President Clinton's second term in office, even though congressional Republican leaders played the lead role in structuring deficit-reduction reconciliation bills, one for tax law changes and another for spending adjustments, presidential negotiators significantly influenced the nature of that legislation. And the administration's contribution was the product of a team effort—composed of the president's chief of staff, OMB director, and Treasury secretary—rather than the work of a chief of staff or a budget director acting as the president's principal negotiator.

Presidential Leadership in Fiscal Policy Making

Presidents have largely set America's fiscal policy agenda; nonetheless, sentiments in Congress have influenced presidential postures. Presidents know that they need Congress's cooperation to get their policies enacted into law. Congress, in turn, looks for presidential leadership in steering the U.S. economy toward growth with price stability. That is not to suggest that economic policy making is free of partisan overtones. Yet both individual members of Congress and the president share a common interest in promoting the nation's economic health. Beyond their desire to secure what is good for the country, they realize that a strong economy enhances their chances of reelection. At the same time, political partisans are not averse to casting aspersions when others can be blamed for poor economic conditions. This tension between promoting the greater good and advantaging oneself and one's partisan colleagues has been variously played out over time. This section examines that connection as it traces presidential leadership in fiscal policy making, starting with the Great Depression.

The Great Depression, World War II, and the Postwar Economic Transformation

Herbert Hoover, when faced with a rapidly declining economy in 1931, supported a tax increase to replenish shrinking revenues. He chose to honor the widely accepted principle of budget balance, even if it risked further dampening demand and exacerbating recessionary conditions. His successor, Franklin Roosevelt, also found the allure of a balanced budget appealing but at the same time agonized over what government should do to assist the fast-growing ranks of the unemployed. The answer for Roosevelt was to support public works and employment programs, even if that entailed **deficit spending**. Yet he did not abandon his attachment to a balanced budget. Temporary deficits could be justified, in Roosevelt's eyes, as long as the deficit resulted from emergency expenditures. Conceptually, for Roosevelt, government still had an obligation to balance its "normal" budget while it incurred debt to address pressing human needs. Roosevelt and his administration used this distinction to justify deficit-financed support of financial assistance provided by the Federal Emergency Relief Administration and of work-relief programs such as the Works Projects Administration and the Civilian Conservation Corps.[10] It was not until well into 1938, following a seemingly intractable recession, that FDR came to accept the mounting advice of Keynesians, including the personal entreaties of John Maynard Keynes himself, that the president and Congress turn to increased federal spending "for its own sake" as a means of generating increased purchasing power. In doing so, FDR and his administration raised the indirect, multiplier effects of increased aggregate demand over the palliative effects of direct federal assistance. At the same time, he eschewed tax cuts as a fiscal policy tool.

America's entrance into World War II soon precipitated an increase in federal spending that dwarfed New Deal expenditures. Federal government expenditures more than doubled between 1932 and 1940, but they increased nearly ninefold between 1940 and 1945, rising from $9.4 billion to $92.7 billion. World War II sparked increased aggregate demand well beyond what New Deal programs could have hoped to achieve. It put people back to work, in military uniforms or in industries supporting the war effort. In doing so, it demonstrated the economic fruits of full employment. Aggregate personal income and savings increased markedly during the war years. Savings rose because patriotic citizens bought Treasury bonds to support the war effort and because the conversion from a peacetime to a wartime economy presented them with reduced spending options. Nonetheless, this increased pool of savings provided a financial reservoir for the postwar increases in aggregate consumption that followed.[11]

The war also left a legacy of record budget deficits and government debt. With the transition from a wartime to a peacetime economy, federal government expenditures declined precipitously, dropping from $92.7 billion in 1945 to $42.6 billion in 1950. By war's end, the U.S. Treasury had amassed a sizable base level of revenues that, barring a tax cut, could be used to support federal domestic programs aimed at expanding and improving the nation's infrastructure, assisting veterans in their return to civilian life, and accommodating the needs for government services of a growing postwar, "baby-boom" population. Although President Harry S. Truman successfully led the charge for immediate postwar tax cuts, as a Keynesian he was leery of the potential inflationary effects of subsequent reductions. Like Roosevelt before him, Truman believed in the virtue of a balanced budget, even though he realized the value of debt financing under certain circumstances. Truman, perhaps best described as a guarded Keynesian, preferred to finance current expenditures out of current revenues, if at all possible.

For Truman, inflation posed America's major postwar economic problem. He worried that growing civilian demand in the postwar economic transformation would outstrip supply and run up prices. For that reason, he steadfastly opposed Republican calls for postwar tax cuts, believing that consumers, whose demands had been suppressed by the austerity associated with war mobilization, would spend, not save, their additional disposable income. Truman, accordingly, vetoed three tax cuts approved by Congress, although Congress overrode the last of Truman's vetoes, in April 1948. He saw a balanced budget, combined with private-sector productivity improvements, as the best way for America's economy to grow without undue inflation. To dampen inflationary impulses in the short run, Truman called for a tax increase in 1948—an initiative that Congress rejected. An unexpected recession in early 1949 reduced concerns about inflation and replaced them with worries about rising unemployment. The onset of the Korean War in June 1950 energized demand but soon precipitated renewed fears of inflation. Within a year, inflation approached 8 percent. In that setting, the president and Congress turned to short-lived wartime price controls as a tool of inflationary restraint, which succeeded in dropping inflation below 1 percent during 1952 and 1953.[12]

In the aftermath of the Korean War, the U.S. economy embarked on a period of growth, spurred by domestic, not war-driven, demand. It also provided the beginning of a sustained test of national policy makers' resolve to employ Keynesian tools to manage the American economy, at a time when deficit-financed spending kept an upward pressure on prices. It was also a time when the Republicans, the party of Herbert Hoover, had regained control of both the presidency and the Congress.

Dwight Eisenhower, Truman's successor, shared his predecessor's affinity for a balanced budget. Like Truman, Eisenhower viewed inflation to be the most serious potential problem facing the nation's economy. In comparison, however, Eisenhower appeared more ready than Truman to accept somewhat higher unemployment in order to keep inflation at low levels when prices were not subject to control. The Eisenhower presidency's dogged pursuit of a balanced budget in an environment of inherited deficits helped to reduce inflation during most of its first term. At the same time, higher-than-expected revenues associated with unexpectedly strong economic growth provided a cushion for expanded spending while still allowing for a balanced budget. By early in his second term, President Eisenhower once again turned his attention to a fledgling reinflation. In January 1957 his budget message highlighted the importance of attaining a budget surplus, particularly as a tool with which to restrain inflation.[13] That stance ruled out any initiative to reduce taxes.

The Eisenhower administration's policy of turning an inherited deficit into a balanced budget, or even a small surplus, was tested by two recessions. The first, in 1954, was of moderate proportions and in large part the product of decreased defense expenditures. The OMB, without much fanfare, ordered the speedup of expenditures as a modest fiscal stimulus late in the 1954 fiscal year. President Eisenhower vowed to provide greater stimulus if necessary but chose instead a relatively conservative course, as the recession proved to be of short duration.[14] The second recession, in late 1957 and into 1958, was much deeper—pushing unemployment close to 7 percent and testing the administration's stable policy course.

As the recession deepened, calls for a tax cut intensified. The nation found itself in the midst of a recession, even as President Eisenhower and his top advisers continued to view inflation as the major long-term problem facing the U.S. economy. The dilemma for them was how to deal successfully with the recession they believed to be a short-term problem without creating the groundwork for later sustained inflation, a condition fostered by spending pressures brought by steep population growth and cold war competition. It was those pressures that kept the Eisenhower administration from enthusiastically supporting an economic stimulus package of increased federal spending on public infrastructure, as championed by economist John Kenneth Galbraith and demanded by some in Congress. They argued that the federal government should use increased spending to stimulate the economy and then resort to a tax cut if additional measures were necessary.

Without the president leading the charge, however, Congress approved only a modest package of additional spending, largely including increased highway spending and an acceleration of defense contract obligations, altogether amounting only to a $1 billion increase in annualized spending.[15] Tax cuts never materialized. Inflation remained the administration's privileged economic problem for the remainder of Eisenhower's term. With the revenue growth that accompanied economic recovery in 1959, not only could the 1960 fiscal year budget be balanced, but it even yielded a modest surplus. However, unemployment remained relatively high, at 5.6 percent, although that was down from a recession-high of 7.6 percent two years earlier—the political implications of which were not lost on Republican presidential candidate Richard Nixon, Eisenhower's vice president.

Critics, among them economist Paul Samuelson, viewed the Eisenhower presidency's conservative approach to fiscal policy as sacrificing higher potential economic growth to the shibboleth of a budget in balance or in surplus.[16] For Samuelson and others, Eisenhower's fiscal stance allowed economic recovery to lag far short of its possibilities. As a consequence, Americans had to contend with an unemployment rate that was higher than it could have been with greater fiscal stimulus. But for Eisenhower the question remained, Fiscal stimulus at what economic costs?

Priming Growth, Financing the Great Society and the Vietnam War, and Fighting Inflation

John F. Kennedy, the Democrats' presidential candidate, promised to improve America's rate of economic growth and lower unemployment while closing the so-called missile gap with the Soviet Union. Kennedy came into office predisposed to use the power of the presidency and Keynesian fiscal policy tools to realize his economic agenda. He took the position of those who argued that the Eisenhower administration had passed up an interventionist opportunity to extend economic opportunity and broaden its benefits by not tapping the unused potential in the American economy. The goal for the Kennedy administration was to get back to a full-employment economy and stay there.[17]

Faced with sluggish recovery from the mild 1960 recession and confronting the prospect of still another recession in 1962, Kennedy at first leaned toward accepting the advice of his adviser, John Kenneth Galbraith, to mount a large program of expansive federal spending. Many in Congress, however, remained wedded to the proposition that a budget surplus would allow for orderly growth while restraining inflation and providing the investment capital to finance sustainable growth. Business leaders added their political weight to that perspective. Although the signals were mixed on inflation, Kennedy calculated that the attractiveness of faster economic growth and reduced unemployment resulting from government intervention outweighed the political risks of any accompanying inflation. Yet faced with opposition in Congress and from the business community to significantly increased federal spending, Kennedy turned his sights on a tax cut as his means of economic pump priming, acceding to the advice of CEA Chairman Walter Heller and economist Paul Samuelson. For Kennedy, however, it was a second-best alternative, compared to the stimulus of significantly increased federal spending.

Both Kennedy and his advisers saw an opportunity to use tax cuts to close the gap between the economy's actual performance and its potential performance with full employment. In Kennedy's words, "Tax reduction will remove an obstacle to the full development of the forces of growth in a free economy."[18] Not only would tax cuts provide individuals with greater after-tax income that could be spent in the marketplace, they would also leave corporations with increased resources for investment. At the same time, Kennedy recognized that tax cuts would reduce federal revenues in the short run, but he held out the expectation that the economic stimulus resulting from them would increase national income and associated income tax revenues. Thus, he argued, it could be possible to stimulate the economy through tax cuts without jeopardizing a balanced budget, foreshadowing the arguments of supply-siders nearly two decades later. In his 1963 economic report to Congress, Kennedy argued that "tax revision, involving both reduction and reform, cannot only provide stimulus for growth and prosperity, but can even, as a result, balance the budget or produce surpluses."[19]

The tax cut proposed by the Kennedy administration was not a small one, a departure from the measured fiscal policy initiatives of the Truman and Eisenhower administrations. It called for sizable personal income tax reductions estimated to cost the Treasury about $14 billion a year, once fully phased in, notwithstanding any offsetting revenue increases resulting from greater economic activity triggered by the cuts.[20] The proposed legislation included across-the-board personal income tax rate reductions averaging about 25 percent. It also reduced the rate of corporate profits taxation and included liberalized capital depreciation schedules. Although Kennedy proposed the tax-cut package late in 1962, Congress, after considerable debate, did not approve it until early 1964, following his death.

The economy responded in the expected direction. Aggregate spending and real output rose, and unemployment fell. The GDP increased by a record $47 billion in FY 1965, well above the CEA's optimistic projection. Federal revenues rose, rather than declined, as economic growth generated tax revenues in excess of the amount foregone by tax cuts.[21] Yet scholars agree that it is problematic to determine how much of the economic growth and resulting revenue increases can be attributed to the stimulative effects of the tax cuts and how much should be associated with a normal upswing in the business cycle. One student of America's political economy attributes the strong economic performance to the larger collection of government policies. Marc Allan Eisner writes:

> At the same time that the economy was being pushed to full employment by the tax reductions, the increase in social spending via the War on Poverty and the increase in military demands via the war in Vietnam were sufficient to push the demand for goods and services beyond capacity. The result was an unemployment rate that associated with full employment and a growing problem of inflation. This inflation would become one of the major issues of the next fifteen years as successive administrations would promote price stability, whatever the cost.[22]

The Johnson administration was quick to take credit for the economic growth of the mid-1960s, but President Johnson himself appeared most interested in leaving his mark on American social policy. With economic growth, Johnson saw an opportunity to finance a major program of increased social spending targeted at improving the lot of America's disadvantaged population. For Johnson, a country's true greatness should be judged on how well it provides for its less fortunate citizens. The War on Poverty would be Johnson's legacy, and its pursuit, along with the United States' growing entanglement in Vietnam, became his preoccupation. Keynesian theory achieved a certain paradigmatic status among policy practitioners and academics alike following its widely perceived successful application in the mid-1960s. President Johnson, however, appeared to be far less motivated by fiscal policy objectives than by social policy goals and his own desire for a treasured place in history.[23]

Greatly expanded social spending and the rising costs of military action in Vietnam led to a growing budget deficit and rising inflation. In response, Johnson's advisers, drawing on the Keynesian recipe, urged him to consider a corrective tax increase. The large Democratic majority in Congress, however, showed no appetite for a tax increase, still basking in the glow of the 1964 tax cut. Johnson demurred, and the job of fighting inflation was left to the Federal Reserve Board's monetary policy, as discussed later in this chapter.

With inflation rising above 4 percent in 1967, up from 1.7 percent in 1965, and with the budget deficit topping $25 billion, compared to less than $2 billion just two years earlier, Johnson felt that he had no choice but to propose a tax increase. After all, America's widening involvement in Vietnam provided little opportunity for expenditure cuts in defense, and Johnson had little enthusiasm for cutting support for his Great Society programs, the biggest part of which received automatic funding given their entitlement status. Accepting the advice of his CEA chairman and OMB director, Johnson proposed a 6 percent personal and corporate income tax surcharge in 1967 as an instrument of economic restraint. Congress balked at raising taxes, following House Ways and Means Chairman Wilbur Mills's insistence that a tax surcharge be accompanied by spending cuts.[24] But facing intensified inflationary pressures nearing the 1968 election, Congress agreed to the surcharge, upping the ante to 10 percent—an action that political observers believe cost the Democratic majority seats in the presidential election year.

The surcharge's injection of additional revenues erased the deficit in 1969 but did little to lower inflation. By the time Richard Nixon assumed the presidency, inflation stood at 5 percent, the highest since the Korean War. Spending pressures, driven by growing entitlement programs, would keep inflation squarely on the policy-making agenda for another decade to come.

Although Richard Nixon proclaimed himself a Keynesian early in his presidency, he relied on the imposition of wage and price controls as inflation-suppressing policy instruments after Congress refused to accept his recommended spending cuts intended to produce an inflation-suppressing balanced budget. The controls once again worked temporarily, and inflation declined, without a corresponding increase in unemployment. An improved economy influenced Nixon to relax price controls, and it contributed to his reelection victory. Yet shortly following the relaxation of controls, the Arab oil cartel's restraint of supply sent the prices of oil and petroleum-based products climbing. Almost simultaneously, a U.S. and international decline in agricultural production drove up food prices. Inflation in 1974 reached post–World War II double-digit highs. Weakened by the Watergate scandal that would force him to resign the presidency, Nixon found himself in a tenuous position to function as the nation's chief economic policy maker.

Shortly after Nixon's resignation, the Ford administration launched a public relations campaign calling for voluntary restraint against inflation. The centerpiece of that campaign was the WIN button, for Whip Inflation Now, worn prominently by the president and his top officials and aides. The symbolic campaign failed to catch on, and it soon became an ineffectual embarrassment to the administration.

What the WIN campaign could not accomplish, a severe recession did. Brought on by oil shortages, related production slowdowns, and restrictive monetary policy, the gathering recession resulted in rising unemployment that coexisted for a while with still-high inflation. Soon, however, the restraining forces of recession prevailed, subduing inflation, but at the price of increased unemployment. The Ford administration continued to view inflation as the greatest threat to the country's long-term economic health, but both the president and Congress underestimated the recession's depth. Facing rising unemployment that threatened to reach double-digit levels, just as inflation was falling back into single-digit range, President Ford succumbed to his economic advisers' counsel and sent to Congress a stimulus package consisting primarily of temporary tax cuts, including an $8 billion tax rebate and a modest personal income tax reduction of $12 billion. Congressional leaders called for greater stimulus, but Ford demurred, fearing that significant permanent cuts would soon trade employment gains for a renewal of inflation. In May 1975 the unemployment rate rose to 9.2 percent, and it remained at about 8 percent by year's end. In response, Congress approved Ford's proposed extension of the temporary tax cuts. By the end of 1976, the economic numbers had improved. The unemployment rate dropped below 8 percent, still high compared to the 1950s and 1960s, and inflation fell below 6 percent. The recession's dampening of demand cut inflation about in half, even with the modest fiscal stimulus aimed at reducing unemployment.

Shifting the Battle to Unemployment and Stagflation

In contrast with his predecessors, Jimmy Carter defined unemployment, not inflation, as America's privileged economic problem. He found ready support among the Democratic majority in Congress, which had difficulty accepting that unemployment appeared to be leveling off in excess of 7 percent, well above the level traditionally associated with full employment. In fact, Democrats had been working since the mid-decade recession on legislation that would require the federal government to use fiscal policy to keep unemployment low. The original legislation required the federal government to create public service jobs to the extent necessary to bring unemployment within a 3 percent floor. After three years of debate, Congress finally passed a watered-down version in the form of the Full Employment and Balanced Growth Act of 1978, also known as the Humphrey-Hawkins Act. The amended version raised the floor to 4 percent and eliminated the public-sector job-creation provisions, essentially leaving 4 percent unemployment as a hopeful goal but without any accompanying enforcement mechanisms or sanctions. What remained was a largely symbolic statement made in a congressional election year.

Although unemployment stood at a little more than 6 percent by the end of 1978, still well above the legislated 4 percent unemployment rate, prices climbed precipitously. For 1979 inflation rose to 11 percent, up from 8 percent in the prior year, while unemployment remained essentially flat. The Carter administration found itself confronting both high unemployment and high inflation but with inflation looking the most menacing. Carter's heart remained with the unemployed, yet he realized that double-digit inflation posed the greater systemic problem for the economy. At the same time, he shared the growing concern that fiscal policy instruments as tools of economic management had met with checkered success, at best, during the 1970s. With the so-called misery index (the sum of inflation and unemployment rates) rising, Carter essentially punted, passing the baton of economic leadership to the Federal Reserve Board and, in particular, to its chairman, with the hope that at least a more restrictive monetary policy could bring down inflation enough to improve his reelection chances—but without triggering even greater unemployment, an outcome that would not be helpful politically. That tightening came too late to rescue Carter from electoral defeat at the hands of an inflation-weary electorate. With the election of Ronald Reagan in 1980, the Federal Reserve was freed of any compunction about greatly tightening the money supply at the very time that an incumbent president was seeking reelection. The highly restrictive monetary policies of the Volcker-led board that followed did indeed squeeze inflation out of the economy but at a cost of the steepest recession since the Great Depression. Double-digit inflation gave way to near double-digit unemployment—to an extent unexpected by the president, Congress, or the Federal Reserve Board.

The Shift to Supply-Side Fiscal Policy (or Was It Really Keynesianism at Work?)

Carter's successor, Ronald Reagan, promised to spur economic recovery by leading the nation away from the federal government's excesses of the 1970s, which he viewed as rooted, to a significant extent, in Johnson's Great Society. Reagan's campaign message was straightforward: reduce government's reach in the economy and in society by cutting taxes, reducing the growth rate of domestic spending, and paring back government regulation. The tax cut lay at the center of the Reagan agenda. And with broad public support, Congress in 1981 reduced individual income tax rates by 25 percent across the board. Although a small cadre of presidential advisers—most notably Jude Wanniski, Arthur Laffer, and Robert Mundel—cast the tax cut as an instrument of supply-side economics, aimed at inducing a wellspring of savings to provide the investment capital necessary to sustain economic recovery while keeping inflation in check, for Reagan it primarily served as a means of reducing the federal government's penetration, allowing taxpayers to keep more of their hard-earned income. At the same time, supply-side theory gave Reagan a justification for avoiding the draconian cuts in domestic spending that would otherwise have been necessary to balance the budget, especially since President Reagan also successfully convinced Congress to increase defense spending by 5 to 6 percent a year above inflation.

Contrary to the theory's expectations, personal saving declined, rather than rose, as a percentage of disposable income.[25] Recipients of the tax cut appear to have spent their higher after-tax income instead of saving it. In fact, it appears that people behaved as Keynesian demand-side theory would have predicted. They spent the nation's economy into recovery, a stimulus reinforced by large real-dollar increases in defense spending.

Scholars disagree, and the evidence is mixed, about whether the sizable cuts in personal and corporate income taxes contributed significantly to economic recovery and the seven years of growth that followed the early 1980s recession. In contrast, there is wide agreement that the tax cut, coupled with major increases in inflation-adjusted defense spending, led to a ballooning federal budget deficit. Rapid increases in uncontrollable spending—most notably on public assistance entitlement programs and in the form of interest on the public debt—added to the fiscal burden imposed by the conscious policy choices already outlined. Economic recovery carried with it the legacy of record post–World War II budget deficits, even though both inflation and unemployment fell within an acceptable range by the decade's end.

President George H.W. Bush inherited a growing economy with both inflation and unemployment in check, but right before the 1991 fiscal year, the economy fell into recession—an economic downturn that all but wiped out the deficit-reducing power of the compromise package of tax hikes and budget cuts approved by Congress shortly thereafter. The recession also proved untimely, occurring just as the Bush camp turned its attention to the president's reelection campaign. Economic recovery came too late to help Bush's electoral fortunes, and the recession's timing afforded Bush and his top aides little opportunity to work stimulus legislation through a Congress led by a politically unsympathetic opposition party. Bill Clinton, the Democrats' nominee, wasted little time in making the economy his number one campaign issue.

Deficit Reduction, Deference to Monetary Policy, and Extended Economic Growth with Low Inflation

It was Clinton who got the chance to offer Congress a package of fiscal stimulus. But with Republicans labeling much of the legislation as "pork," and the CBO warning that it could prove inflationary in a recovering economy, the newly elected president could not marshal sufficient votes from within his own party to win passage. He was later successful, however, in convincing enough Democrats in Congress to support reconciliation legislation containing a combination of tax increases and budget reductions aimed at reducing a recession-swelled federal budget deficit. Congress passed the deficit-reduction package without any Republican support. In fact, Vice President Al Gore cast the tie-breaking vote in the Senate.

The omnibus budget reconciliation act reduced the deficit by $433 billion over five years, and $240 billion of that amount came from tax increases. The biggest revenue boost came from increasing the top individual income tax rate from 31 percent to 36 percent, along with an accompanying 10 percent surcharge on taxes due on incomes greater than $250,000. By doing so, Congress took away some of the tax cut enjoyed by upper-income earners that the supply-side tax cut of the early Reagan years had produced.

In leading the way, Clinton was motivated by what he viewed to be the political imperative of deficit reduction, not by fiscal policy designs. He intended the tax increases as instruments to raise revenue and thereby reduce the deficit, as well as a means to restore some lost equity between high-income and other taxpayers, rather than as a tool of fiscal restraint.

The upturn in the business cycle started out slowly but accelerated quickly by mid-decade. Growth became strong, and the misery index dropped to its lowest point since the mid-1960s, creating a hospitable climate for the president's reelection bid. That strong growth continued throughout Clinton's second term, generating unexpectedly high revenues and greatly shrinking the federal budget deficit.

The real story of economic management in the 1990s, however, was not one of presidential leadership employing fiscal policy tools but of the Federal Reserve's use of preemptive monetary policy to keep inflation under control in a growing economy. That policy continuity created an environment of confidence and security, spurring investment, creating new jobs in record numbers, and sending U.S. stock markets to a series of new highs in the mid- and late 1990s.

Projected Surpluses, Tax Cuts, External Shocks, and Monetary Policy's Steady Hand

The vibrant economic growth of the late 1990s continued into the election year of 2000, causing the federal budget surplus to grow to $236 billion at the end of FY 2000—the third straight year of budget surplus. Heady economic scenarios projected growing future budget surpluses. Presidential candidates Bush and Gore debated what to do with the surplus revenues, which the Congressional Budget Office projected would cumulatively exceed $5 trillion over ten years.

Both candidates proposed packages of tax cuts, spending initiatives, debt reduction, and reserved revenues for Social Security. While both candidates pledged to set aside 52 percent of the projected surplus to ensure the future solvency of Social Security, Bush called for $1.32 trillion in tax cuts compared to Gore's proposed cuts of $480 billion.[26] Following the election, Congress upped President Bush's ante, passing legislation on June 7, 2001, that cut taxes by $1.35 trillion through December 31, 2010. In signing the legislation, President Bush put it in historical perspective, remarking:

> Across-the-board tax relief does not happen often in Washington, D.C. In fact, since World War II, it has happened only twice: President Kennedy's tax cut in the 1960s and President Reagan's cuts in the 1980s. And now it's happening for a third time, and it's about time.[27]

He continued, providing a rationale for the tax cut:

> Tax relief expands individual freedom. The money we return, or don't take in the first place, can be saved for a child's education, spent on family needs, invested in a home or in a business or mutual fund, or used to

reduce personal debt. The message we send today, it's up to the American people; it's the American people's choice. We recognize loud and clear the surplus is not the government's money, and we ought to trust them with their own money.[28]

The president did not justify the tax cut in Keynesian terms, as a fiscal stimulus, nor did he present it as a supply-side measure to encourage saving and the resulting investment. For President Bush, the tax cut represented both a just return and an instrument of individual freedom.

The promised string of surpluses, intended to finance the tax cut, failed to materialize, however. Although the federal budget did close the 2001 fiscal year with a surplus of $127 billion, it fell well short of estimates for that year. The budget fell once again into deficit in FY 2002, and annual deficits averaged $303 billion between the 2002 and 2006 fiscal years. A recession, military engagements in Afghanistan and Iraq, continued marked increases in publicly financed health care, and more tax cuts conspired to create budget deficits.

In response to comparatively slow recovery in employment following the recession in 2001, President Bush urged Congress to reduce individual income tax rates further and move up the dates on which rate reductions would take effect, increase the standard deduction for married couples filing jointly and the per-child tax credit, and lower the maximum tax rate applied to dividends and capital gains. These changes, among others approved by Congress in May 2003, added another $350 billion to the cost of forgone revenues through 2010.

This time around, the president offered his initiative as a means to accelerate economic recovery and create jobs, in part responding to critics' complaints of a "jobless recovery." Signing the Jobs and Growth Tax Reconciliation Act of 2003 (note the symbolic significance of the title), President Bush commented:

Today we are taking essential action to strengthen the economy. We have taken aggressive action to strengthen the foundation of our economy so that every American who wants to work will be able to find a job.[29]

In justifying the added stimulus, Bush sounded more like John F. Kennedy than like Ronald Reagan.

Deficits and Debt

Governments incur deficits because they spend more in a given fiscal year than they collect in revenues from taxes and other receipts. When that occurs, governments must borrow to make up the difference. However, governments' authority to borrow can be constrained by constitutional prohibitions or by statutory law. Budgets must be balanced in virtually all state and local governments in the United States. They are prohibited from running operating budget deficits and borrowing to obtain the resources to pay for spending in excess of revenues. Yet a qualification is in order here. States and most local governments possess the authority to use borrowing to finance capital acquisitions, such as the construction of courthouses and schools or highways and bridges. Following a separate capital budgeting process, state and local governments finance these projects by selling bonds to the public, paying back the amount of indebtedness over the lives of the bonds. In that way, future users of these capital projects contribute to their financing over time.

In contrast, no separate capital budget exists at the federal level. Capital expenses are budgeted within the operating budget. When revenues fall short of budgeted expenditures (called outlays in federal budgetary terminology) during any fiscal year, the federal government borrows to fill in the gap, irrespective of the capital expenses that exist in the mix. The federal government borrows money by selling Treasury securities of varying denominations and durations of maturity to willing buyers. The Federal Reserve acts as the Department of the Treasury's agent, auctioning the securities to the highest bidders. The bidders are financial intermediaries typically acting on behalf of large purchasers such as banks, corporations, and pension funds, both domestic and foreign. In auctions, buyers seek the highest rate of return possible, while the Treasury tries to acquire capital at the lowest obtainable interest costs. Once buyers acquire the securities, they can resell them on the secondary market, and it is not unusual for the same security to be traded many times prior to its maturity.

The federal government even borrows from itself. Several large federal programs draw their financial support from trust funds—into which revenues are deposited, and from which expenditures are debited. They include trust funds for civil service retirement, highway and bridge construction, airport construction, Medicare, and Social Security, among the largest. Federal law requires that any surpluses in trust funds be invested in Treasury securities, providing resources that can be used to help finance any annual deficit that exists. In addition to trust fund holdings, the Federal Reserve maintains a reservoir of Treasury securities that it uses to effect monetary policy—buying securities on the open market when it wants to expand the money supply and lower interest rates, and selling them when it wishes to contract the money supply and raise interest rates.

Economic conditions affect governments' revenues. Income and sales taxes are most responsive to changes in the economy. Property taxes are affected less broadly and less immediately. Changes in property tax revenues accompany changes in assessed value, which tend to reflect conditions in local, and even regional, real estate markets. Thus changed economic conditions most directly affect the revenues of the federal government and state governments, because approximately 77 percent of federal revenues comes from the individual income tax, and another 12 percent comes from the corporate income tax. The individual income tax generates about 37 percent of state revenues, the corporate income tax adds another 6 percent, and the sales tax yields approximately 41 percent. Local governments, in contrast, are heavily reliant on the property tax, which contributes almost three-fourths of their revenues.[1]

As the economy slows, the rate of growth in its output of goods and services falls. In a worst-case scenario, output can decline in absolute terms. When that happens for at least two consecutive quarters, the economy has officially fallen into recession. As the growth of output slows or turns negative, so does personal income. As personal income falls, so does prospective consumption. This lowered demand soon translates into smaller corporate profits. Thus both individual and corporate income taxes fall as a result of shrinking tax bases. Sales tax revenues decline as well, following the drop in personal income.

A recessionary economy also drives up economically sensitive public expenditures. As unemployment rises, so do welfare rolls, the ranks of Medicaid and food stamp recipients, and unemployment compensation claims. Because the federal government and the states share the costs of financing the most costly public assistance programs, Temporary Assistance for Needy Families (TANF) and Medicaid, they bear the brunt of the associated cost increases. The federal government finances food stamps, and the states largely cover the costs of unemployment compensation, except when Congress extends the duration of unemployment benefits and the federal government picks up the tab. To make matters more pressing, Congress created both Medicaid and food stamps as entitlements, meaning that people who meet eligibility standards have a legal right to services, whatever the cost. Many states did the same with their part of Medicaid, creating so-called **sum-sufficient appropriations** paralleling the federal entitlements.

With revenues down and recessionary-sensitive spending up, governments face revenue shortfalls. Balanced-budget requirements at the state level force budget makers to bring budgets into balance by increasing taxes and fees, cutting the costs of other programs, or employing a combination of the two approaches. Unlike all states except Vermont, the federal government can run a deficit.

Just as economic effects can boost spending above available revenues, so can policy choice. Tax cuts forego revenues that would otherwise flow into government treasuries, regardless of the motivation underlying the cuts. Decisions to expand discretionary spending—whether to meet increased workload or in support of newly created programs—add pressure to the spending side of the budget. External shocks generated by foreign military campaigns or terrorism or by natural disasters prompt responses that often entail major spending increases. Deficit pressures are at their height when the economy is in recession, taxes are cut, and policy choice increases discretionary spending. All three of these factors have contributed to the federal government's post–World War II deficit peaks.

As Table 5.1 illustrates, budget deficits were at their highest, both in current dollars and as a percentage of the GDP, following the national recessions of 1981–82, 1990–91, and 2001. Beyond the recessionary effects, discretionary policy choice in the early 1980s and early 2000 especially helped to enlarge the postrecession deficits. As we shall see later in this chapter, big individual income tax cuts and greatly increased defense spending expanded federal budget deficits and swelled federal debt.

Trends in Federal Debt

Before examining trends in federal debt, we must decide what federal debt to focus on. Do we want to look at gross federal debt, or does it make more sense to limit our analysis to debt held by the public? A strong argument can be made for following the latter approach. True, it excludes debt held in government accounts, but should that debt be treated the same as debt held by the public? The Treasury pays no *net* interest on debt held in government accounts, because interest earnings are repaid to the Treasury by law.

An argument can also be made that debt service payments to state and local governments, treated as part of the repayment of publicly held debt, represent a wash of sorts if we are concerned most with the condition of total government debt in the United States, including that of state and local governments. However, the traditional focus looks at federal debt alone and treats it and the national debt as synonymous.

Table 5.1

Federal Budget Deficit: Selected Years, 1970–2008 (in $ billions)

Fiscal Year	Deficit/Surplus	As a Percentage of GDP
1970	−2.8	−0.3
1972	−23.4	−2.0
1974	−6.1	−0.4
1976	−73.7	−4.2
1978	−59.2	−2.7
1980	−73.8	−2.7
1982	−128.0	−4.0
1983	−207.8	−6.0
1984	−185.4	−4.8
1985	−212.3	−5.1
1986	−221.2	−5.1
1988	−155.2	−3.1
1990	−221.0	−3.9
1992	−290.3	−4.7
1994	−203.2	−2.9
1996	−107.4	−1.4
1997	−22.0	−0.3
1998	69.3	0.8
1999	125.6	1.4
2000	236.2	2.4
2001	128.2	1.3
2002	−157.8	−1.5
2003	−377.6	−3.5
2004	−412.7	−3.6
2005	−318.3	−2.6
2006	−248.2	−1.9
2007*	−244.2	−1.8
2008e*	−239.4	−1.6

*= estimate

Source: Office of Management and Budget, *Budget of the United States Government, FY 2008, Historical Tables,* 23–6.

With debt held outside the federal government, interest payments flow out of the Treasury, to be held and used by others. Interest payments on domestically held federal debt remain within the economy and become part of the aggregate income from which government gets its own revenues, whether through taxes or borrowing. Moreover, a portion of the interest paid on foreign-held federal debt also finds its way into national income flows, as some of the dollar-denominated interest payments are reinvested or spent in the United States and are subject to federal tax. Even some of the earnings that leave the country will return in exchange for U.S. exports and assets such as financial securities and real estate.

Table 5.2

Who Holds the Federal Debt? (2006)

Debt Holder	Amount (in $ billions)	Percentage of Total
Federal Government Accounts	3,622	42.9
The Federal Reserve	769	9.1
Outside the Federal Government	4,060	48.0
	8,451	100.0
Debt Held by the Public: Domestic and Foreign		
Domestic Holders	2,695	55.8
Foreign Holders	2,134	44.2
	4,829	100.0

Source: U.S. Office of Management and Budget, *Budget of the United States Government*, FY 2008, *Analytical Perspectives*, 235; *Historical Tables*, 126–27.
Note: Debt held by the public includes debt held by the Federal Reserve but excludes debt held in other government accounts.

As Table 5.2 shows, approximately 43 percent of the gross debt of the federal government is held in federal government accounts. The Federal Reserve holds Treasury securities equal to another 9 percent. The remaining 48 percent is owned by a broad assortment of financial institutions, corporations, state and local government investment funds, foreign governments, and individuals, among others. In accounting terms, all debt not held in federal government accounts, including debt held temporarily by the Federal Reserve, is considered debt held by the public. Of publicly held debt, about 44 percent is owned by foreign institutions and individuals, a consideration discussed below.

Putting Debt in Perspective

To help put debt levels in perspective, it is useful to compare them to historical debt patterns and to the debt obligations of other industrial nations. Table 5.3 shows trends in federal debt dating back to World War II. At the end of World War II, debt held by the public exceeded 100 percent of the GDP. In other words, in 1946 it amounted to more than the dollar value of the U.S. economy's entire output for that year. As should be expected based on historical experience, America's debt load declined significantly in the postwar years, as defense spending's share of the federal budget shrank during peacetime, despite cold war tensions with the Soviet Union. A string of balanced or near-balanced budgets and solid economic growth during the late 1940s and a good part of the 1950s and 1960s allowed the publicly held federal debt to drop precipitously as a percentage of America's economic output, falling to

Table 5.3

Federal Debt Held by the Public: Selected Years, 1946–2008

	Debt Held by the Public	
End of Fiscal Year	In $ Billions	Percentage of GDP
1946	241.9	108.6
1950	219.0	80.2
1955	226.6	57.4
1960	236.8	45.7
1965	260.8	38.0
1970	283.2	28.0
1975	394.7	25.3
1980	711.9	26.1
1985	1,507.3	36.4
1990	2,411.6	42.0
1995	3,604.4	49.2
2000	3,409.8	35.1
2001	3,319.6	33.0
2003	3,913.4	36.2
2005	4,592.2	37.4
2006	4,829.0	37.0
2007*	5,083.3	36.9
2008*	5,345.4	36.8

*= estimate

Source: U.S. Office of Management and Budget, *Budget of the United States Government*, FY 2008, *Analytical Perspectives*, 223.
Note: Debt held by the public includes debt held by the Federal Reserve.

29 percent of the GDP in 1969, the last year of federal budget surplus before 1998. It continued to fall but at a much slower rate during the 1970s, sharply reversed course in the early and mid-1980s, and rose steeply in the early 1990s, reaching a post-1956 peak of 49.4 percent in 1993.

By 2001 debt held by the public as a percentage of the GDP had fallen sixteen percentage points from its 1993 level, thanks to deficit reduction followed by four years of budget surplus from 1998 through 2001. But a return to federal budget deficits beginning in FY 2002 began another upswing in the federal debt as a percentage of the GDP, climbing four percentage points between the 2001 and 2006 fiscal years. The OMB estimates that a continued strong economy and reduced federal budget deficits will keep the publicly held debt as a percentage of the GDP relatively flat through 2008.

Although debt held by the public in 2006 was at about the same percentage of the GDP as it was in 1965, the federal government's reliance on foreign borrowing, as a component of that debt, has increased greatly. In 1965 foreign holdings counted for almost 5 percent of publicly held debt. They rose to 44 percent in 2006.[2] Despite that seemingly dramatic increase, it should be recognized that foreign purchases of federal debt are only a modest part of the annual gross capital inflow from abroad. They are overwhelmed by foreign purchases of assets in the United States and by foreign investments in U.S. corporations. Moreover, because foreign buyers of Treasury securities are paid interest in dollars, the vast majority of that income makes its way into dollar-dominated accounts in U.S. financial institutions and is subsequently used to finance investments in U.S.-held assets or the purchase of American goods and services.

It is nonetheless true that the federal government has become increasingly dependent on foreign institutions and individuals to finance its debt. Historically, the federal government has not been nearly as reliant on foreign capital to finance its debt. During most of American history, individuals and institutions within the United States held nearly all the federal debt.

Another way of putting America's debt load in perspective is to compare the federal government's debt with that of other advanced industrial nations. The trick here is to make valid comparisons—comparing apples to apples, as the adage goes—comparing publicly held debt issued by the central government and not including debt issued by subnational governments. Table 5.4 shows the results of that comparison for 2003, the most recent year for which comparable data are available. Clearly, the national debt burden of the United States falls below that of most of the industrial nations with which it is usually compared. It is probable that the United States' comparative position has worsened somewhat since 2003, given that the federal government ran substantial budget deficits in the succeeding years—although their effect has likely been mitigated by the United States' comparatively strong economic growth.

Interest Obligation on the Debt

The fiscal implications of the federal government's debt hit home in the federal budget. Net interest payments on the debt have constituted a growing share of federal budget outlays. Although net interest on the debt is not treated as an entitlement program, per se, budget makers treat it as a form of uncontrollable spending, given that it is highly unlikely that the U.S. government would fail to honor its interest obligations. Rising net interest costs tend to crowd out other federal discretionary spending, particularly in the constrained environment of deficit reduction.

Beyond crediting interest to the holders of Treasury securities, the federal

Table 5.4

Comparative National Government Public Debt as a Percentage of GDP

Nation	Debt/GDP
Japan	139
Greece	119
Belgium	98
France	53
Sweden	50
Poland	47
Spain	43
United Kingdom	40
Germany	38
Canada	36
United States	35*
Mexico	25
Australia	8

Source: Organization for Economic Cooperation and Development, *Central Government Debt, International Comparisons*, 2003.

Note: OECD's reported percentage differs by one percentage point from that reported by OMB in Table 5.3.

government also has the obligation to pay back principal when securities are redeemed. Congress, however, does not appropriate funds for principal repayment. Instead, the Federal Reserve uses the proceeds of new borrowing to repay principal in a continuous process of selling and redeeming securities, borrowing enough to plug the deficit gap and honor redemptions.

Table 5.5 illustrates the changing claim that interest has made on the federal budget. Net interest outlays increased from $4.1 billion in 1946 to $227 billion in 2006. Although the cost of net interest payments in 1946 looks small in relation to the price tag sixty years later, their respective shares of federal outlays are fairly close. In fact, net interest's share of federal spending remained pretty stable throughout the period from the mid-1950s to the late 1970s, after having risen in the late 1940s and fallen in the early 1950s.

That stability at about a little more than 7 percent of federal spending changed dramatically from the late 1970s through the mid-1990s, as accumulated interest obligation on a string of large budget deficits markedly pushed up interest costs. Net interest's share of federal budget outlays increased from 7.3 percent in 1977 to 15.4 percent in 1996. Deficit reduction, followed by budget surpluses, dropped net interest's share of outlays to 7.1 percent in 2003, back again to the historical norm. Current forecasts point to a 9 percent share in 2008, reflecting the post-2001 return to deficits.

Table 5.5

Net Interest: Selected Years, 1946–2008

Fiscal Year	In $ Billions	Percentage of Outlays	Percentage of GDP
1946	4.1	7.4	1.8
1950	4.8	11.3	1.8
1955	4.9	7.1	1.2
1960	6.9	7.5	1.3
1965	8.6	7.3	1.3
1970	14.4	7.4	1.4
1975	23.2	7.0	1.5
1980	52.5	8.9	1.9
1985	129.5	13.7	3.1
1990	184.3	14.7	3.2
1995	232.1	15.3	3.2
2000	222.9	12.5	2.3
2003	153.0	7.1	1.4
2005	184.0	7.4	1.5
2006	226.6	8.5	1.7
2007*	239.2	8.6	1.7
2008*	261.3	9.0	1.8

*=estimate

Source: U.S. Office of Management and Budget, *Budget of the United States Government*, FY 2008, *Historical Tables*, 118–25.

Why the Deficit Rose So Steeply in the 1980s and 2000s, Putting the Federal Government Deeper in Debt

As discussed earlier, the federal government runs a deficit in a given fiscal year when revenues fall short of outlays. That can happen for two reasons: one under Congress's direct control and the other a product of economic forces. First, let's look at the part that Congress can control.

Congress authorizes federal agencies to spend money for public purposes. In some cases, that **authorization** allows agencies to spend whatever is necessary to accomplish the purpose of a particular federal program. Typically, such open-ended authority is tied to statutory requirements that an agency make payments or provide services to anyone who meets the program's eligibility criteria, as set by law. So, in a very real sense, it does not matter what estimates of outlays appear in the budget; the Treasury must cover the actual costs of the cash payments or services provided. Spending on Social Security, Medicare, Medicaid, and civilian and military retirement constitutes the bulk of federal entitlement expenditures. It is true that Congress can change an entitlement and reduce related spending by amending the statutory authorization itself—for example, toughening the eligibility requirements for federally funded medical assistance. In other cases, Congress must appropriate funding in order for agencies to spend it for authorized purposes. That provision not only gives Congress the flexibility to change the amounts appropriated from year to year but also places a lid on how much can be spent during the fiscal year. With so-called discretionary spending, agencies have no authority to overspend the amounts appropriated. It does not matter, for example, how many people qualify for services.

Congress, then, can exercise choice with both entitlement and discretionary spending. With entitlement programs, Congress can restrict or broaden eligibility for entitlements, and it can increase or decrease benefits. With discretionary spending, Congress can increase or decrease appropriations. It has the authority to act in both cases, but it may choose not to do so or it may not be able to muster enough votes to override a presidential veto.

Altering entitlements presents the greatest political obstacles. It is one thing to get a majority in Congress to cut a program's annual appropriation and quite a different matter to change an entitlement significantly or to eliminate it altogether. The political consequences of the latter may be far greater, and congressional leaders and rank-and-file members may not be willing to take the risk; nor may presidents be willing to take the lead. Congress's caution may be accentuated when the president's position on the proposed entitlement change is at odds with its own. The credible threat of a presidential veto can be enough to prevent majority support from developing.

Beyond considerations of political choice, the condition of the economy can affect relative budget balance. A strong, growing economy increases national income, which is subject to taxation. Rising revenues make it easier for budget makers to balance the budget; that is, unless spending follows apace. Significant revenue growth gives them leeway to meet political needs and keep spending at a level that reduces the budget deficit or attains balance or even a surplus.

On the political downside, a recessionary economy pushes up the aggregate costs of government programs, hitting entitlement-based social welfare programs the hardest. As unemployment rises, so do the costs of providing cash benefits or services to the growing ranks of the needy. Rising unemployment also reduces personal income, resulting in lower tax revenues. Those very conditions, in turn, can affect fiscal policy, prompting policy makers, perhaps, to increase government spending as a fiscal policy tool to raise aggregate demand and reduce unemployment.

Both economic downturns and conscious policy choice contributed to the large budget deficits of the 1980s and early 2000s. In contrast, most large changes in the federal deficit and debt before the 1980s, and in the early 1990s, were products of the business cycle. In the 1980s the Reagan policy agenda and inflation-fighting actions of the Volcker-led Federal Reserve combined to set the deficit on its upward spiral.

The Volcker and Reagan Legacies

As discussed in chapter 3, the Federal Reserve's Open Market Committee (FOMC) engaged in a monetary policy in the early 1980s that substantially constricted the money supply and drove up interest rates to rid the economy of historically high inflation. The shock monetary policy worked, as the inflation rate dropped to 6 percent in 1982 and then fell to 4 percent in the following year, but at the cost of reduced economic output, increased unemployment, and lowered federal revenues. But while the FOMC applied the monetary policy brake, the Reagan administration pushed down hard on the fiscal policy pedal, supporting a major income tax cut and sizable inflation-adjusted increases in defense spending, as chapter 4 details. Congress's concurrence significantly further depressed revenues and increased spending. Revenues remained essentially flat between 1981 and 1982 and actually declined from 1982 to 1983. Outlays rose by 16 percent between 1981 and 1983 alone, generating a deficit topping $207.8 billion by the end of the 1983 fiscal year.[3]

The economic growth that began in 1983 strengthened in 1984, as real GDP grew by a staggering 7 percent from a solid 4 percent gain the year before—both years in sharp contrast to a real decline of 2.1 percent in 1982. Real GDP continued to grow steadily at an average annual rate of 3.4 percent during the following five years, before dropping in parts of 1990 and 1991, the victim of yet another recession.[4] This one, however, could primarily be attributed to the business cycle, being far less a product of policy choice than was the recession of the early 1980s.

With the economy's strong performance between 1983 and 1989, a period Robert Bartley refers to as the seven fat years,[5] one could have reasonably expected to see the federal budget deficit decline significantly and the national debt shrink. Yet that did not happen. As Table 5.1 shows, the deficit actually rose in current dollars between 1983 and 1986, the years of steepest economic growth. It fell the following year and then pretty much leveled out through the remainder of the decade.

Why didn't America's economic growth cut into the deficit more sharply? The answer lies in policy choice. True to his campaign promises, Reagan championed major income tax relief and large increases in defense spending. Congress, for the most part, followed his lead in these areas. The Economic Recovery Tax Act of 1981, passed during Reagan's first year in office, cut income tax rates across the board by 25 percent. And although Congress

Table 5.6

National Defense Spending: Selected Years, 1946–2008

Year	Actual (in $ billions)	Constant 2000 (in $ billions)	As Percentage of Outlays
1946	42.7	405.7	77.3
1950	13.7	129.6	32.2
1955	42.7	320.1	62.4
1960	48.1	300.2	52.2
1965	50.6	291.8	42.8
1970	81.7	375.1	41.8
1975	86.5	262.7	26.0
1980	134.0	267.1	22.7
1985	252.7	356.5	26.7
1990	299.3	382.7	24.0
1995	272.1	305.9	17.9
2000	294.5	294.5	16.5
2003	404.9	365.3	18.7
2005	495.3	407.8	20.0
2006	521.8	417.2	19.7
2007*	571.9	446.7	20.5
2008*	606.5	461.3	20.9

*= estimate

Source: U.S. Office of Management and Budget, *Budget of the United States Government*, FY 2008, *Historical Tables*, 118–25.

subsequently enacted a dozen tax increases between the 1982 and 1990 fiscal years, largely through increased Social Security taxes, motor fuel taxes, and other nonincome taxes, those increases were not large enough to offset the amount of revenue lost due to the 1981 rate reductions.[6]

At the same time that Reagan set out to reduce the income tax bite, he also sought to return real-dollar defense spending to its 1970 level. Reagan believed that defense's purchasing power had dropped during the 1970s to a dangerous low, even though it began a modest climb in the late Carter years. For Reagan, the Soviet Union remained a threat that could only be countered by military strength, and he saw America's military capability falling short of the mark—in military personnel, equipment, and weapons development. A turnaround would be costly, and Reagan called for budget increases of 5 to 6 percent in excess of inflation. Here, again, Congress complied, at least through the 1986 fiscal year, as constant-dollar defense spending grew by 40 percent between 1980 and 1986. Constant-dollar defense spending flattened out for the remainder of the decade, although

Table 5.7

Domestic Spending: Selected Years, 1962–2008

Fiscal Year	Discretionary Spending		Means-Tested Entitlement Spending	
	Constant 2000 (in $ billions)	Percentage of Outlays	Constant 2000 (in $ billions)	Percentage of Outlays
1962	115.4	18.3	20.5	4.1
1965	140.0	22.6	23.7	4.4
1970	165.9	19.6	38.8	5.2
1975	218.0	21.2	73.5	7.7
1980	295.1	24.0	88.1	7.6
1985	254.7	17.2	94.2	6.6
1990	288.5	16.0	119.6	7.6
1995	301.7	17.9	201.6	12.2
2000	319.9	17.9	232.6	13.0
2003	389.1	19.5	290.1	14.2
2005	405.1	19.2	315.2	14.2
2006	407.8	18.7	306.6	13.3
2007*	410.1	18.4	311.3	13.2
2008*	399.2	17.6	318.6	13.3

*= estimate

Source: U.S. Office of Management and Budget, *Budget of the United States Government*, FY 2008, *Historical Tables*, 134–35.

defense spending's share of total federal spending actually fell during the last two years of Reagan's second term and continued to do so during the Bush administration. That slide accelerated during the 1990s following the breakup of the Soviet Union and the thawing of cold war tensions in Eastern Europe. (See Table 5.6.)

To offset the added costs associated with net tax cuts and defense buildup, Reagan sought to decrease domestic spending. Here he had mixed success. As Table 5.7 shows, discretionary domestic spending declined both in **constant dollars** and as a share of outlays during Reagan's presidency, although the rate of decline slowed during his second term. In contrast, constant-dollar, means-tested entitlement spending rose during all of his administration yet constituted a fairly consistent share of federal outlays over that period. Its relative share would have been larger had net interest not increased its share as starkly as it did during the Reagan years.

Given that the growth of defense and entitlement spending outstripped inflation and reductions in domestic discretionary spending were insufficient to offset any more than a small part of those spending increases, spending pressures alone were enough to produce a rising budget deficit. Add to the mix revenue loss from net tax cuts, and the ingredients were in place for mounting deficits—that is, unless economic growth would have generated sufficient other revenue gain to replace the foregone revenue and cover the costs of higher spending. That did not happen, despite supply-siders' most fervent hopes. Revenues did rise with economic recovery and growth but not enough to finance spending increases *and* fill the revenue hole created by the deep income tax cut of 1981.

The recession of 1990–91 made matters worse, producing a deficit of $290 billion by the end of FY 1992, the deficit's high point in current dollars, although the deficit was higher at the end of FY 1982 as a percentage of the GDP. It took a substantial 1993 deficit-reduction package, which contained both tax increases and spending cuts that did not rely on gimmicks, to begin to turn the budget picture around. An improving economy, leading to solid growth after mid-decade, brought the deficit steadily down. With Congress approving further, but more modest, deficit-reduction legislation in 1997, and with economic growth exceeding earlier expectations, the deficit turned into surplus at the end of FY 1998—a condition that continued through FY 2001.

The Greenspan and Bush Era

After hiking the federal funds rate (FFR) seven times between February 1994 and February 1995 as a preemptive hedge against inflation, the Alan Greenspan–led FOMC kept interest rates fairly stable until it notched them up modestly in mid-2000 to keep inflation in check. However, as leading economic indicators pointed to an economic slowdown, the FOMC began a series of marked rate reductions in January 2001. Between January 3 and May 15, the FOMC pursued a tightened monetary policy that reduced the FFR from 6 percent to 4 percent, employing five consecutive cuts of fifty basis points (half of 1 percent). By December the FFR had fallen to 1.75 percent, a dramatic decline. The U.S. economy officially fell into a relatively mild recession during the first three quarters of 2001, which conceivably could have been longer and deeper had the Fed not acted as aggressively as it did to spur demand.

During the recession and its near-term aftermath, the unemployment rate rose from an average of just below 4 percent in 2000 to an average of 6 percent in 2003, hitting a peak of 6.3 percent in June 2003—not exceptionally high by historical standards. As recovery progressed, the average annual unemployment rate fell further in 2004 and reached an average of 5.1 percent in 2005.

Just as loose monetary policy likely softened the effects of economic downturn, so did stimulative fiscal policy. At President George W. Bush's strong urging, Congress approved legislation in June 2001 and again in May 2003 that together cut taxes by $1.7 trillion through December 31, 2010. Major spending increases for defense, homeland security, and means-tested entitlements provided substantial fiscal stimulus. As Table 5.6 shows, defense spending grew by more than $227 billion between the 2000 and 2006 fiscal years, increasing its share of federal outlays from 16.5 percent to 19.7 percent during that period. Discretionary *domestic* spending increased by $88 billion over those years, enlarging its share of outlays from 17.9 percent to 18.7 percent, with nearly all of that increase attributable to spending on programs related to homeland security. Finally, although means-tested entitlement spending grew by $74 billion between FY 2000 and FY 2006, its share of outlays rose only marginally, from 13 percent to 13.3 percent.

It should not come as a surprise that the combination of revenue loss and higher spending produced sizable budget deficits. Though not as big as a percentage of the GDP, the resulting deficits from FY 2002 to FY 2006 averaged $303 billion over the five years, adding $1.3 trillion to the debt held by the public.

Historians may come to look at the turn of the century as the calm before the storm. The 2001 recession, the increased spending on homeland security following the 9/11 terrorist attacks, and the cost of military campaigns in Afghanistan and Iraq conspired to shift the federal budget balance from surplus to deficit beginning in FY 2002, with both presidential and congressional budget offices forecasting deficits throughout the first decade of the twenty-first century.

Moreover, demography provides little hope for an improved fiscal picture in the second decade of the twenty-first century. The front edge of the baby-boom generation will become eligible for full Social Security benefits and Medicare coverage in 2012. And while the number of retirees and their percentage of the population will grow, the number of workers supporting each retiree will shrink. The Social Security trustees project that the ratio of workers per beneficiary will decline to 3 : 1 in 2012 from 3.3 : 1 just ten years earlier and then fall to 2.6 : 1 in 2020 and to 2 : 2 in 2030. They forecast that by 2017 the annual cost of benefits will exceed tax revenues. That has already become the case with Medicare, as the Hospital Insurance (HI) trust fund began using interest earnings in 2004 to fill the revenue gap. The Medicare trustees project that by 2010 the trust fund will have to begin cashing in the Treasury securities it holds as assets. The Social Security trustees estimate that the same thing will happen to their fund by 2027.[7] The CBO sees Social Security and Medicare's claim on federal revenues growing significantly in the future. By its forecasts, Social Security and Medicare's share of federal spending will increase from 34.6 percent in 2006 to 46.6 percent in 2017, rising from 7.1 percent of the GDP in 2006 to 8.8 percent in 2015, putting heightened pressure on the deficit and debt.[8]

Why Worry About Deficits and Debt?

The effects of a slumping economy are obvious, but why worry about deficits and debt? That question evokes considerable debate and argument. Popular opinion pieces in magazines and newspapers typically paint both as serious problems that the American public should be greatly concerned about. In comparison, economists differ on the extent to which they view deficits and debt as problematic. This section reviews and evaluates the most widely held concerns, ranging from the unduly alarmist to those having the most substantive merit.

America's Path to Insolvency

Some people worry that a long string of budget deficits and the need to finance them through debt accumulation will lead the federal government on a path toward fiscal insolvency. They reason that the rising burden of deficit finance will so strain the government's ability to honor its interest and principal repayment obligations that investors, both domestic and foreign, will shy away from acquiring Treasury securities, threatening the U.S. government's ability to raise the capital it needs to make fiscal ends meet. However, that concern is more visceral than substantively grounded.

Because America's debt is denominated in dollars, any fear that the federal government would default on its obligations is groundless. As a last resort, the Federal Reserve could "monetize" the debt by selling Treasury bonds to the public, using the proceeds to finance the debt. Any reluctance to invest in U.S. securities would be offset by the higher rates of return that buyers could expect from the market. Moreover, prospective buyers recognize that the full faith and credit of the U.S. government stands behind its obligations, including its ability to raise tax revenue, in addition to its ability to create money. Thus concerns about insolvency are misplaced, although they make for good rhetoric.

Net Interest's Budgetary Squeeze

Net interest's claim on federal spending skyrocketed during the 1980s and continued largely unchecked until deficit reduction and subsequent budget surpluses drove down its share of federal outlays from a post–World War II high of 15.4 percent in FY 1996 to 7 percent in FY 2004.[9] However, the accumulated interest obligations arising from a return to budget deficits that began at the close of FY 2002 set net interest's share of federal spending on an upward course once again, but at a percentage more reminiscent of the 1950s through the 1970s, as Table 5.5 shows.

Should we be concerned about net interest's claim on federal revenues? Yes, we should, but not because interest obligations are pushing the country to the brink of bankruptcy. We should be concerned, instead, because interest payments on the debt represent forgone opportunity. The Treasury, through the Federal Reserve's sale of securities, has already captured the funds it needs to cover the spending commitments it has already made. Now it is simply paying off that indebtedness. It gets nothing new for that spending. In fact, that spending squeezes other potential spending, because interest payments exert a priority claim on federal budgeting. To the extent that federal budgetary outlays go to pay interest on the debt, they are not available for other important purposes, such as reducing the deficit or investing in America's physical and human infrastructure. Although it is true that borrowing may have provided the wherewithal to make those investments in prior years by financing spending that outstripped available revenues, the interest obligation incurred by that borrowing crowds out current spending. Reduced borrowing is the only way to pare down net interest's share of budgeted outlays.

Mortgaging Our Children's Future

Critics point to high interest obligations as mortgaging our children's future. As their argument goes, America's budget makers, by regularly allowing spending to exceed revenues, have been throwing a continuous party and leaving the bill for future generations to pay. Although it is true that net interest's future claims will fall with a balanced budget, they will still constitute a sizable share of federal spending—an obligation that will extend well into the future. If the economy does not perform as well as projected and a slowdown pushes the federal budget back into deficit, interest obligations will again rise rather than fall.

It is true that future taxpayers will annually have to foot the interest bill. Many of them, however, will also receive those interest payments. Because over half of the debt held outside the federal government is owned by Americans, the vast majority of interest paid augments their income. Part of the interest income paid to foreign institutions and individuals even makes its way back into the U.S. economy in the form of investments or the purchase of American goods and services, thereby increasing national income.

Obviously, not all who contribute their taxes to pay interest on the debt receive interest income in return. Some redistribution of income does occur. Yet even though upper-income individuals disproportionately receive that interest income, while all taxpayers pay the bill, many middle- and lower-income taxpayers benefit via pension funds, insurance, and small savings bond holdings.[10] Moreover, those at the lowest end of the income spectrum pay no federal income taxes at all and therefore incur no burden.

Crowding Out Credit

The federal government competes with private interests in credit markets. Some economists worry that government borrowing will crowd out or displace private borrowing or at least result in marked increases in interest rates charged private borrowers. Their thesis is that deficit spending adds a government demand for credit to an existing private demand, thus forcing up the interest rates that both government and private interests must pay. In that competition for scarce savings, government has the advantage. Not only must it borrow to fill the gap between revenues and expenditures, but it has the fiscal and monetary resources to meet the higher interest costs. The private sector, in contrast, is more likely to withdraw from the market, awaiting more favorable conditions.

Practice has failed to follow theory for most of the past three decades. Mid- and long-term interest rate movements have not been closely correlated with federal debt.[11] Given the size of the global debt market and the cross-national competition that occurs within it, changes in U.S. national debt exert little near-term effect over mid- and long-term interest rates. The larger factors of national economic growth and expectations of future inflation appear to overwhelm movements of debt ratios (debt as a percentage of the GDP). Research by Eric Engen and Glenn Hubbard (former chairman of the CEA) suggests that a one percentage point increase in the U.S. debt ratio increases long-term interest rates by only 0.35 percent.[12]

For short-term interest rates, the key factor has been not the extent of borrowing by the federal government but the monetary policy employed by the Federal Reserve. Investment demand strengthened with postrecessionary recovery, and interest rates proved acceptable enough to attract investors into domestic capital markets, despite competition from the federal government. At the same time, high federal budget deficits reduced national savings, which accompanied a growing decline in the saving of households. These parallel forces alone could have been expected to push interest rates up, had not the United States had access to foreign savings. Foreign savings filled the gap between available U.S. national savings and investment demand, as the United States sold increasingly large quantities of its assets to foreigners, thus moderating what would have been much stronger upward pressure on interest rates.[13]

The Deficit, National Saving, and America's Reliance on Foreign Capital

The federal government's borrowing to finance deficit spending drains off part of national savings that would otherwise be available to support domestic investment. National saving is the product of both private and government saving. But when the federal government runs a deficit, it dissaves (in the language of economics) rather than saves. The federal government's dissaving has been only marginally offset by budget surpluses existing at the state and local levels. The large deficits experienced in the 1980s and the early 1990s, as well as for most of the 2000s, have taken a big bite out of national savings. For instance, Benjamin Friedman shows that the federal government's borrowing in the 1980s absorbed an amount equal to nearly three-fourths of all net saving done by households and businesses in this country (that is, the percentage of the nation's income that households and businesses manage to save after spending for consumption and the replacement of physical assets that reach their useful lives).[14] Friedman likens that outcome to a society eating its seed corn instead of planting it. Once done, its people have no recourse but to turn to other societies for some of theirs.

National saving (also referred to as U.S. gross saving) as a percentage of the GDP has been on a downward-trending line since the end of World War II. It plunged during the 1980s and early 1990s and again in the 2000s, a product of plummeting household saving and federal budget deficits. The fall in national saving would have been greater had not business savings and state and local government budget surpluses offset some of the decline.

Saving is important because it finances investment. The only way a national economy can invest more than it saves is to tap the savings of foreigners, and that is what the U.S. economy has done. As national saving declined, the United States turned to the savings of foreigners to finance its investments, increasing their net claims on American assets. Fortunately for the United States, the higher saving rates of most other industrial nations have put them in a favorable position to pick up the slack. And the U.S. economy's reasonably strong fundamentals and record of growth provided an attractive lure for foreign capital. Given that the flip side of saving is spending, it should not be surprising that aggregate spending grew faster than national income; that is significant because the only way for an economy to spend more than it earns is to import more than it exports, to run a trade deficit. Thus, as Paul Krugman reminds us, "it was inevitable that the United States would develop a large trade deficit."[15] Chapter 6 explores that relationship in greater detail.

It is readily apparent that a key to improving America's **current account** deficit, the broadest statement of the trade deficit, is to increase national saving. By increasing its rate of saving, the United States becomes less dependent on foreign capital to finance its investment. As saving grows as a percentage of income, the trick becomes to switch the relatively reduced spending from imported goods to American-made products. Yet American consumer behavior overall shows few signs of altering its appetite or tastes.

The surest way, therefore, to increase national saving is to reduce the federal budget deficit and turn it into surplus. Of course, the federal government could attempt to use policy inducements, such as tax deductions and credits, to encourage its citizens to save more of their income, but prior attempts have fallen far short of expectations.[16]

Is There a Benign Side of Deficits and Debt?

Not all economists and critical observers worry much about deficits and debt. Some see them as far less problematic than do their colleagues in the mainstream; still others view deficits and debt, within limits, to be functional rather than dysfunctional for the economy. Those in the first camp argue that deficits and debt look different when put in the proper perspective or that their magnitude is far less ominous when they are measured differently. Those in the second, putting on their Keynesian spectacles, emphasize the contribution of deficits to economic growth, focusing on what they add to aggregate demand. This section explores both schools of thought.

One way of putting deficits and debt in perspective is to look at them in relation to the size of the economy—that is, as a percentage of the GDP. A large economy that generates a high national income has more room to run deficits and incur debt than does a much smaller economy. A rapidly growing economy is better positioned to take on rising deficit and debt levels than is a static or declining economy. Deficits and debt that take a declining share of the GDP place a lessening burden on the economy's ability to support them.

Tables 5.1 and 5.3, respectively, show changes in the federal budget deficit and in debt held by the public as percentages of the GDP over time. Deficit levels in the mid-2000s, while high, were still below those of the mid-1980s as a percentage of the GDP. The relative gap was even wider for publicly held debt as a percentage of the GDP, when comparing the mid-2000s to both the second half of the 1980s and the first half of the 1990s.

Beyond viewing deficits and debt in relation to the size of the economy and its relative growth, several prominent economists suggest that we should rethink the way in which the deficit, and its contribution to debt, is measured. Robert Eisner, a past president of the American Economic Association, argues that several adjustments should be made to the gross deficit.

The first adjustment takes into account the surpluses or deficits of state and local governments in the United States. Because laws require nearly all state and local governments to balance their budgets, both tend to underestimate revenues and build some leeway into budgeted expenditures, commonly leading to year-end surpluses. State and local budget surpluses either can offset a federal budget deficit when that deficit exceeds their aggregate level or can contribute to a national budget surplus. Eisner argues that if we are interested in the total impact of government on the economy, it makes the most sense to figure in the year-end conditions of state and local governments, together with that of the federal government.[17]

The second adjustment separates out the amount of federal outlays devoted to capital investment, treating them the way state and local governments budget and account for them, to arrive at the federal equivalent of state and local government operating budget balances. Recall that state and local governments enact capital budgets, distinct from their operating budgets, which provide them the authority to borrow up to approved levels to finance capital projects. The federal government has no such discretion. Capital expenditures are financed by operating revenues just as are all other expenditures. Yet it makes good economic sense to finance those projects using debt and requiring future users to contribute to debt retirement. This adjustment, then, relieves the federal operating budget from meeting the costs of capital investment.

The third adjustment corrects for the decrease in the real value of the debt due to inflation, on which a reduced amount of interest must be paid. Subtracting real interest savings, Eisner refers to this adjustment as an "inflation tax," one he argues that is just as real in its impact on people's behavior as is a revenue-generating tax increase.[18]

Although Eisner's colleagues such as Robert Heilbroner and Peter Bernstein[19] embrace these adjustments, the vast majority of economists prefer the traditional way of measuring the deficit. Paul Krugman is one of them. The deficit, for Krugman, is no statistical illusion. He is not interested in making the deficit appear less imposing. For him, the important fact is that the borrowing occasioned by deficits contributes to a decline in national savings and helps to cause a trade deficit.[20]

Should the Federal Government Do Whatever Is Necessary to Balance the Budget?

Because deficits sap national savings, contribute to trade deficits, and create interest obligations that squeeze other would-be spending, should the president and Congress do whatever is necessary to balance the budget? While there are many who maintain that they should, others are far less sanguine about the idea. Critics voice both political and economic concerns.

On the political side, detractors worry that a political climate that greatly constrains tax increases or rewards tax cuts will prompt policy makers to reach a balanced budget exclusively through spending cuts. Such a tack, critics argue, plays right into the hands of those who want to use deficit reduction as a means of reducing the size of the federal government. For them, the primary problem is big government, not the economic consequences of the deficit. In contrast, those who are concerned about following the path of spending cuts toward budget balance point out the programmatic implications of budget cuts—reductions that can erode government's ability to provide assistance to the needy, support education and training, modernize the highway system, and protect the environment. Here is where critics of balancing the budget connect the political and the economic. They remind us that all spending is not the same. Some government spending improves and expands our nation's physical infrastructure; other spending advances human capital. Broad-based spending cuts can jeopardize these forms of public investment. Although it is true that savings finance investment, so too can public borrowing; and borrowing that improves and expands infrastructure can also help to improve productivity.[21] Some evidence exists that nonmilitary *public* investment contributes more to productivity than does private investment.[22]

Of course, the most commonly voiced reservation about reaching a balanced budget concerns its effects on aggregate demand. Deficit spending adds to aggregate demand—demand for goods and services that will raise national output as long as some slack exists in the economy. Take that increment of demand away, and economic growth can suffer. As Robert Eisner is fond of saying, "The public deficit is the private sector's surplus."[23] Eliminate the public deficit, and you will wipe out the private sector's surplus, potentially threatening prosperity.

To minimize this dampening effect and still make progress toward reducing the deficit's contribution to debt, some critics of a balanced budget suggest that the president and Congress need only keep the deficit's annual contribution to debt below the rate of real economic growth and thereby reduce debt as a percentage of the GDP over time. Yet until the budget is balanced, the fact is that debt continues to build, squeezing national savings and requiring foreign capital to fill the gap, even though the debt takes a declining share of national income.[24]

Constitutionally Requiring a Balanced Budget

With a sound economy growing America out of its budget deficit in the late 1990s, calls for amending the U.S. Constitution to require a balanced budget subsided after fifteen years of nearly continuous legislative initiatives and congressional debate. The most recent attempt failed in 1997, as the Senate came up one vote short of the two-thirds majority required for passage. President Clinton's energetic last-minute lobbying proved to be the deciding factor in the amendment's defeat, despite the efforts of Senate Majority Leader Trent Lott (R-Mississippi), who actively used the prerogatives of his office in hopes of eking out a narrow victory. The legislation required the budget to be balanced starting in 2002 or two years after the amendment's ratification by the states, unless three-fifths of both chambers vote to allow a deficit in a given year. The bill also provided that deficits could be legally incurred in times of war or serious military threats. The amendment's defeat marked the sixth time since the first election of Ronald Reagan as president that a proposed constitutional amendment made it to the floor and was voted down.

Public opinion polls indicate that the American public has consistently supported requiring budget balance by constitutional amendment. Most people support the concept of the federal government living within its means, even though they, as individuals, may resort to deficit finance in their own lives. Support for a balanced budget amendment dissipates, however, when pollsters tell citizens that cuts in Social Security, Medicaid, and education might be required. In one poll conducted for CBS News and the *New York Times*, support fell from 80 percent to 30 percent when poll designers attached those conditions.[25]

Putting Effective Spending Limits Back in Place

Facing high and rising federal budget deficits, Congress passed the Budget Enforcement Act of 1990. The legislation placed caps on budget authority and outlays in each of three categories of discretionary federal spending—defense, foreign aid, and domestic—and collapsed the separate limits into a single cap beginning in the 1994. The Omnibus Budget Reconciliation Act of 1993 subsequently froze discretionary spending through FY 1998 at the 1993 fiscal year level. Spending could be exempted from the cap only if the president and Congress determined that an emergency existed, such as military conflict or a natural disaster. In the Balanced Budget Act of 1997, Congress extended and tightened the caps, setting them through the end of FY 2002 at levels 10 percent less than required to maintain spending adjusted for forecasted levels of inflation.

Congress's choice to place caps on spending represented a departure from its earlier practice of establishing budget reduction targets in the second half of the 1980s. The Balanced Budget and Emergency Deficit Control Act (commonly referred to as the Gramm-Rudman-Hollings Act), enacted in 1985, established *targets* for deficit reduction, which, if met, would have eliminated the federal budget deficit by the end of FY 1991. Two years later, Congress pushed back the expected date for budget balance to the end of FY 1993.

Under the law's provisions, if Congress proved unable to pass a budget that met the targeted deficit reduction, the president was to order automatic spending cuts, called **sequestrations**, apportioned equally between domestic and defense discretionary spending. Congress learned quickly how to "game" the system, by building optimistic revenue and conservative budget projections into their estimates of the year-end deficit. They also became adept at employing accounting gimmicks, such as shifting expenditures from one year into the next and using one-time revenues to plug spending gaps. In other words, they employed "rosy scenarios" that made it appear on paper that deficit-reduction targets would be met, thereby evading automatic spending cuts. Unlike the provisions of the Gramm-Rudman-Hollings Act, the spending cuts, discussed earlier, had real teeth.

In addition to capping spending, Congress also placed controls on entitlement spending in the Budget Enforcement Act of 1990, provisions that were continued in the subsequent legislation previously noted. Congress required that any increase in the deficit due to the creation of new entitlements or the expansion of existing ones be offset by corresponding reductions of entitlement spending elsewhere or paid for by new revenues. These so-called PAYGO requirements did not apply to spending increases caused by the growth of eligible clientele under existing entitlement law.

As the federal budget swung from deficit to surplus, members of Congress increasingly perceived the spending caps and PAYGO provisions as hemming in their ability to spend the surplus revenues. After years of deficit reduction and spending constraint, members were ready to be unhampered in their choices of what to do with budget surpluses. And projections of large surpluses to come whetted Congress's appetite for renewed spending. Both Republicans and Democrats joined in allowing the spending caps and PAYGO requirements to expire.

With the deficit well on the upswing by mid-2000, House Republican leaders proposed reintroducing caps on domestic discretionary spending but not on defense spending. They also called for the return of PAYGO offsets, though in a significantly modified form—requiring that expansions of entitlements be offset only by reductions in other entitlement spending and not by tax increases. House Democrats objected, arguing primarily that the Republican proposal would limit Congress's ability to respond to the needs of the disadvantaged. House Democrats also demanded that any reconstitution of PAYGO provisions apply to tax cuts as well as entitlement-driven spending increases—a position opposed by Republicans, who saw it as a prospective roadblock to making the Bush tax cuts permanent.

Following the 2006 elections, the new Democratic majorities in Congress were quick to adopt new PAYGO rules for each chamber early in 2007, and they applied them to both tax cuts and changes in entitlement law that result in increased spending. So, just as Republicans feared, any extension of the Bush tax cuts under the new rules would have to be paid for by other revenue increases or offset by spending reductions derived from changing the provisions of existing entitlements.

In reviving PAYGO constraints, Congress elected to employ rules of procedure rather than create them as statutory law, as was done in 1990 and continued through 2002. Under the adopted rules, any member of either chamber who believes that legislation that has come to the floor violates the PAYGO rules can raise a point of order. A ruling by the presiding officer sustaining the point of order effectively kills the legislative initiative. Both chambers, however, can waive the rules. In the House, it takes majority approval of a special order endorsed by the Rules Committee (which has a decided majority party advantage). The Senate can waive the rules by unanimous consent at any time in the process, or with a minimum of sixty votes after the point of order has been raised.[26]

If Congress applies the PAYGO rules consistently, fighting off waivers, it will have reestablished a tool to restore fiscal discipline and reduce deficit spending. But politics will determine how Congress uses that tool. PAYGO rules give Democrats a potentially effective procedural lever in negotiations with Republicans over the extent to which the Bush tax cuts should be reconstituted or allowed to expire.

While PAYGO provisions once again have teeth, Congress has been left with largely ineffectual limits on federal discretionary spending. In the absence of statutory caps, only the spending guidelines included in congressional budget resolutions remain to potentially restrain discretionary spending. Yet their viability as an instrument of spending restraint is questionable, since Congress has failed to pass concurrent budget resolutions in three budget years since 2002. When it has passed resolutions, Congress has amended the spending totals later in the budgetary process. Champions of budgetary restraint contend that a return to statutory caps, with a reliable enforcement mechanism, is the only way to bound discretionary spending.

America in the Global Economy

Americans are big spenders, not big savers. American consumers and their national government spend beyond their means, as discussed in the preceding chapter. Just as consumers go into debt to satisfy their appetite for the goods and services they want, the federal government borrows from a wide range of entities willing to loan it funds in exchange for interest-bearing securities. And just as Americans' appetite for foreign-made goods has risen sharply, so has the federal government's reliance on foreign loans to finance its deficit spending.

The search for value motivates both American consumers and foreign lenders. Consumers balance considerations of quality and price when making purchases. For the most part, the growing availability of foreign goods in the U.S. marketplace has held prices in check. Since 1990 import prices have risen only about one-fourth as fast as has the consumer price index (CPI) overall, benefiting buyers of electronic devices, clothing, shoes, and toys—the most frequently purchased consumer goods.[1] Foreign purchasers of U.S. bonds and notes also seek value, weighing market return and security of investment. Rising interest rates in mid-decade 2000, combined with the security afforded by the federal government's full faith and credit pledge behind its debt issues, have attracted no shortage of foreign investors willing to lend money to Washington. Despite high federal budget deficits and rising national debt, the performance of the U.S. economy, compared to that of the rest of the industrial world, underpins confidence in the ability of the U.S. government to make good on its promises. Between 1995 and 2005, which includes the 2001 recession, U.S. real GDP growth averaged 3.3 percent a year compared to 2.2 percent in the Euro area and 1.2 percent in Japan.

Central banks, like private investors, seek value in making foreign investments. Based on market considerations alone, it should not be surprising that foreign central banks would want to acquire U.S. securities. In fact, foreign central banks hold more than half of the outstanding stock of U.S. Treasury securities.[2] The return on their investment, paid in U.S. dollars, also builds their foreign reserves, adding to the ability of central banks to intervene in currency markets as desired. China's central bank, for example, accumulated foreign reserves approaching $1 trillion by the end of 2006.

In a nutshell, the United States is able to spend more than its national income and to invest more than it saves by drawing upon the savings of foreigners. Rates of national saving have risen sharply since 2000 in Japan, China, the emerging nations of East Asia, and most of continental Europe, exceeding domestic investment. Even in China, with the world's fastest growing investment rate, at 46 percent of GDP, savings grew faster than investment, generating a resource pool available to others.[3] Yet within national saving, the rate of household saving has declined since 2000 in Japan and several other Asian nations, with the marked exception of China.[4]

The United States' tapping of the so-called world saving glut—a term popularized by Ben Bernanke, current chairman of the Federal Reserve Board—has enabled Americans and their government to live well above their financial means.[5] The extent of that dependence is covered later, but first we need to discuss the ways in which the U.S. economy is interconnected with the rest of the world.

The U.S. Economy's Global Interconnections

Business enterprises in the United States sell goods and services to individuals, corporations, and governments all around the world, just as our foreign counterparts purchase goods and services from U.S. providers. For example, we buy BMWs from Germany, shoes from China, and wine from France, and we sell Cray computers to Japan, Boeing jet aircraft to Singapore, and wheat to Russia. Both U.S. corporations and individuals invest in the stocks and bonds of foreign companies, just as foreigners invest in U.S. companies. Some corporations may gain financial control of foreign enterprises or secure outright ownership of them (such as Sony's purchase of Columbia Pictures or Bridgestone's control of Firestone Tires). Foreign governments buy U.S. Treasury securities, and the U.S. Department of the Treasury buys foreign currencies on the open market. Foreign-headquartered banks make loans to American business enterprises, and U.S. banks lend funds to foreign enterprises.

International economic relationships are clearest when we look at U.S. companies selling products made in the United States to buyers in foreign lands or when U.S. consumers buy goods made overseas. They get far more complex when, for example, a U.S. company produces a product on foreign soil using materials imported from one or more other nations and then transports that product back to the United States for sale. Of course, these relationships can exist in reverse—that is, when foreign-owned companies produce products in the United States for sale here or in other countries. Illustrations are easy to find: Toyota automobiles assembled in

Table 6.1

**International Trade as a Component of National Economies:
Selected Countries, 2005**

Country	Trade as a Percentage of GDP	Exports as a Percentage of GDP	Imports as a Percentage of GDP
Taiwan	113.6	58.0	55.6
China	77.3	42.0	35.3
Korea	68.0	36.0	32.0
Canada	66.8	35.7	31.1
Germany	65.8	36.8	29.0
Mexico	62.6	30.6	32.0
Russia	49.9	33.0	16.9
United Kingdom	40.2	18.6	21.6
United States	26.2	10.2	16.0
Japan	20.7	11.4	9.3

Source: U.S. Central Intelligence Agency, *The World Factbook 2006*; Bureau of Economic Analysis, U.S. Department of Commerce.

Kentucky by American workers, using a combination of American- and Japanese-manufactured components; jet aircraft manufactured by Boeing but employing parts and technological devices made by Mitsubishi and Fuji; and McDonald's hamburgers and french fries prepared by foreign workers in countries on nearly every continent, using both domestic ingredients and those imported from the United States.

Just take a simple economic transaction and notice the complicated economic relationships inherent in it. Buy a new Subaru Legacy Outback automobile, assembled in Indiana, and create the following effects. Assuming that the purchase is made in the United States, the American-owned dealership profits from the sale; the salesperson earns a commission; the sale contributes to a sales volume sufficient to keep demand at a level that justifies the retention or addition of workers in the assembly plant, as it does for top Japanese management in the plant. Similar benefits accrue to component suppliers in both Japan and the United States. In addition, the money paid for the car ends up in a Japanese-owned bank account in the United States and becomes available to be lent to American borrowers. Stockholders, both foreign and domestic, also benefit to the extent that this sale parallels enough others to keep the company acceptably profitable. The sale value of the automobile adds to the U.S. GDP even though it is the product of a foreign-owned corporation.

Nations are caught in a web of international economic relations. In a real sense, a foreign economy may rely on both domestic and international investors

Table 6.2

**International Trade as a Component of the U.S. Economy:
Selected Years, 1961–2005**

	Exports (in $ billions)	Exports as a Percentage of GDP	Imports (in $ billions)	Imports as a Percentage of GDP
1961	26.0	4.8	22.7	4.1
1965	35.4	4.9	31.5	4.4
1969	49.3	5.0	50.5	5.1
1973	91.8	6.6	91.2	6.6
1977	158.8	7.8	182.4	9.0
1981	302.8	9.7	317.8	10.2
1985	303.0	7.2	417.2	10.0
1989	509.3	9.3	589.7	10.8
1993	658.6	10.0	719.3	11.0
1998	931.4	11.0	1,100.6	13.0
2000	1,064.2	10.8	1,442.9	14.7
2003	1,020.5	9.3	1,517.3	13.8
2005	1,272.2	10.2	1,995.8	16.0

Source: Bureau of Economic Analysis, U.S. Department of Commerce.

for its capital, on other nations for needed raw materials, and on the citizens of still other nations for consumer demand. Some national economies are more interdependent than others.

Table 6.1 compares the relative dependence of selected national economies on international trade. The U.S. economy is far less dependent on international trade than are the economies of most other nations. Consider the case of Taiwan, which is four times more dependent on international trade than is the United States. Japan's position at the bottom of the list probably surprises most readers. Although Japan enjoys a healthy favorable trade balance, led by a large surplus in manufacturing, its economy is far more self-sufficient than is generally appreciated. Other than importing needed raw materials and agricultural foodstuffs, Japanese firms tend not to import anything that they can make domestically.

The U.S. economy has steadily become more reliant on international trade over the past four decades. (See Table 6.2) Until 1969 U.S. exports and imports combined rarely amounted to more than one-tenth of the GDP. By 2005 the combined value of exports and imports constituted more than 26 percent of the GDP. That level is far from trivial. The volume of both exports and imports was larger than consumer spending for durable goods, nonresidential investment, or housing investment, to put its size in perspective. Within overall international trade, imports hold a decided edge over exports—the implications of which are discussed next.

Table 6.3

U.S. Current and Capital Account Balance Compared, 2005 (in $ billions)

			Current Balance		
				Net Unilateral	
	Goods	Services	Income Receipts	Transfers	Balance
Exports	892.6	379.6	465.6		
Imports	−1,674.2	−321.6	−458.2		
Balance	−781.6	58.0	7.4	−82.9	−799.1

Capital Balance			
U.S.-Owned Assets Abroad, Net		Foreign-Owned Assets in the United States, Net	
Direct Investment	−21.5	Direct Investment	128.6
Portfolio Investment	−155.2	Portfolio Investment	492.3
U.S. Claims on Foreigners	−340.2	U.S. Government Securities	365.0
U.S. Government Assets	21.7	Liabilities to Foreigners	281.6
Foreign Currencies	3.5	U.S. Currency	19.4
	−491.7	Statistical Discrepancy	3.9
			1,290.8

Foreign-Owned Assets in the United States, Net	1,290.8
U.S.-Owned Assets Abroad, Net	−491.7
Capital Balance	799.1

Source: U.S. Department of Commerce, Bureau of Economic Analysis.

The United States' International Economic Position

The United States' international economic position is popularly measured by its trade balance, or the difference between exports and imports of goods and services. Americans typically look to the trade balance as an indicator of how well the United States is doing vis-à-vis the rest of the world. They do so, however, in the sense of whether the United States is "winning" or "losing" in the international economic arena. For most Americans, a decidedly favorable trade balance indicates winning, whereas a negative balance points to losing. This simplistic view merits critical discussion, which follows later in this chapter.

Fewer Americans realize that international economic transactions include more than trade in goods and services. In reality, they also include flows of income on foreign investments and unilateral transfers abroad. Together, they constitute the current account of the U.S. balance of payments.

Foreign investment can take two forms: *direct* investment and *portfolio* investment. **Foreign direct investment** can be defined as the ownership or control by individuals or corporations in one country of 10 percent or more of the voting securities of a corporation in another country or the equivalent interest in an unincorporated enterprise. **Foreign portfolio investment** is the ownership or control of less than 10 percent of a company's voting securities plus foreign party holdings of company or government bonds. Thus investment income equates to the profits from direct investment, dividends on stocks, and interest.

Unilateral transfers include such transactions as government aid to other nations, private cross-national humanitarian aid, and personal income transfers from workers on foreign soils to family members back home. Net unilateral transfers involving the United States have been negative, reflecting the disproportionately heavy flow of U.S. foreign assistance, including military aid, from the United States to foreign nations.

Table 6.3 shows the U.S. current account balance for 2005. The account was $799.1 billion in deficit. The trade deficit alone totaled $723.6 billion, reflecting a deficit in goods that outstripped a surplus in services. The deficit in net unilateral transfers added to the overall deficit. The current account deficit continued a trend that began in the late 1970s. Before then, the current account was seldom far from balance. Since then, growing negative balances in goods have been the major factor contributing to the deficit condition.

But that trade deficit in goods needs to be put in perspective. Imports to the United States from its own multinational corporations constitute 37 percent of total U.S. imports.[6] Although the goods come from foreign operations or subsidiaries of U.S. companies, they are still treated as imports, because they enter the United States from foreign origins.

In addition to the current account component, the U.S. balance of payments keeps track of the *international flows of capital* that pay for the foreign trade, financial investments, and unilateral transfers. Both theoretically and from an accounting standpoint, the sum of foreign trade, income on foreign investments, and net unilateral transfers must equal the capital flows that finance these transactions. They fail to do so in practice because of statistical discrepancies in the data.

Table 6.3 shows the components and compares the value of U.S.-owned assets abroad to that of foreign-owned assets in the United States. The value of net foreign-owned assets in the United States exceeds that of U.S.-owned assets abroad by a 2.6 : 1 margin. Portfolio investment, U.S. Treasury securities, and financial liabilities to foreigners (largely held by financial institutions) constitute 88 percent of net foreign-owned assets in the United States. Direct investment adds another 10 percent, and foreign-held U.S. currency makes up the difference. U.S. claims on foreigners, together with portfolio investment, account for the lion's share of net U.S.-owned assets abroad. The United States remains an attractive destination for foreign savings.

Figure 6.1   **Net Capital Inflows to the United States, 1995–2005**

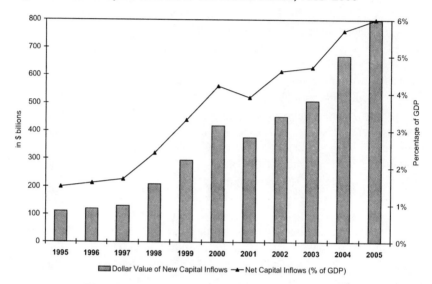

Source: *Economic Report of the President,* 2006, 126; Bureau of Economic Analysis, U.S. Department of Commerce.

Figure 6.1 illustrates the major growth of net capital inflows to the United States that have occurred since 1995. Not only has the dollar value greatly increased, from just above $100 billion in 1995 to almost $800 billion in 2005, but net capital inflows have increased their share of the GDP as well, rising from 1.5 percent in 1995 to 6 percent by 2005. During those years, the United States became much more reliant on foreign capital.

The U.S. trade deficit in goods is widespread geographically, as Figure 6.2 illustrates. By far, the United States' largest trade deficit in goods exists with China, at $202 billion, followed by a $123 billion deficit with the European Union. The United States runs sizable deficits with Japan, along with Canada and Mexico, the United States' regional trade partners in the North American Free Trade Agreement (NAFTA).

The trade gap with China has generated the most political controversy. Although China's economy has become reasonably open to foreign trade, critics point out that the Chinese government's control over the value of the yuan, whereby its value is largely pegged to the value of the dollar, has added to China's low labor-cost price advantage in international trade. Even though China relaxed its long-practiced peg in July 2005 and allowed the yuan to rise in value within government-set limits, critics argue that the yuan remains substantially overvalued (with estimates by investment banks ranging from 10

Figure 6.2 **U.S. Trade in Goods for Selected Areas and Countries, 2005**

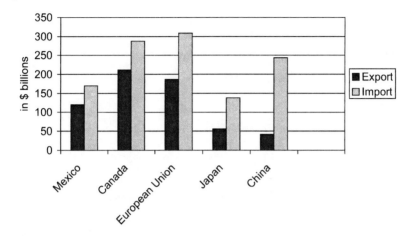

Source: U.S. Central Intelligence Agency, *The World Factbook*, 2006.

to 15 percent[7]), making Chinese goods sold to U.S. buyers artificially cheap and making U.S. goods sold to Chinese buyers more costly than they would be with a "fair" exchange rate.

Although China's admission into the World Trade Organization (WTO) in December 2001, and its associated obligation to conform to the WTO's many multilateral agreements, has opened up Chinese markets and afforded greater access to U.S. exports, the forces favoring Chinese imports into the United States have proved too strong to overcome. As Figure 6.3 illustrates, U.S. exports to China have grown sharply since China's admission into the WTO, while U.S. exports to the rest of the world have remained essentially flat.

Factors Affecting the U.S. Trade Balance

Several factors affect the U.S. trade balance with other nations. They are highlighted in Table 6.4. All exert some effect, but certain factors appear to be more consequential than others. Among them, the *condition of the U.S. economy and that of America's major trading partners* appears to be of greatest significance. When our trading partners' economies experience strong growth, the increased personal income generated by that growth provides the financial resources for individuals and businesses to buy more U.S. exports. Strong growth also fosters a consumer-minded psychology. As foreign consumers feel more inclined to spend and then act on that inclination, U.S. exports benefit along with other goods produced and sold in those lands. Of course, the

Figure 6.3   **U.S. Exports to China and the Rest of the World, 1990–2004**

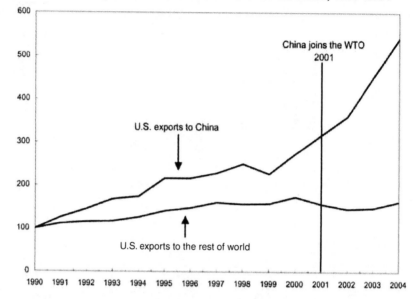

Source: Economic Report of the President, 2006, 167.
Note: Index of exports in 2000 U.S. dollars.

relative proportion of benefit is a product of the other factors listed in Table 6.4. Conversely, when foreign economies sag, the associated lower demand depresses U.S. export sales along with other sales.

When the U.S. economy grows healthily, American consumers and businesses are more inclined to increase their spending, benefiting both imports and domestically produced goods. Again, the other factors come into play in influencing the benefit distribution between imports and goods produced in the United States, as we shall soon see.

But before we get into that, this is probably a good time to complicate matters a bit, harkening back to an earlier discussion. Because we are considering forces that affect exports and imports, we should clarify how the U.S. government counts exports and imports. It is clear that a General Motors car produced in the United States and sold in Costa Rica is treated as a U.S. export and a Costa Rican import. But what about a General Motors car made in Mexico and sold there? It is counted neither as a U.S. export nor import. The sale, instead, becomes part of Mexico's GDP—not part of the United States', even though the car was produced by a U.S. corporation. Now, what if that General Motors car assembled in Mexico is brought across the border and sold in the United States? It then is treated as a U.S. import and a Mexi-

Table 6.4

Factors Affecting U.S. Exports and Imports

Factor	Export	Import
Economic growth of trading partners	Higher growth, higher U.S. exports	Not applicable
Economic growth of U.S. economy	Not applicable	Higher growth, higher imports
Value of the U.S. dollar	Higher dollar, lower exports	Higher dollar, higher imports
U.S. prices relative to foreign prices for similar goods	Higher U.S. prices, lower exports	Higher U.S. prices, higher imports
Quality and status of U.S. goods relative to foreign goods	Higher U.S. quality and status, higher exports	Higher foreign goods quality and status, higher imports
Trade policies, including barriers to trade	Higher foreign barriers, lower exports	Lower U.S. barriers, higher imports

can export. From an accounting perspective, it reduces U.S. GDP, because the GDP, in national income accounting terms, is the sum of consumption, investment, government spending, and exports *minus* imports. Does it make any difference if that Mexican-produced auto incorporates components and parts made in the United States? The auto itself counts as a U.S. import, but the components and parts manufactured in the United States are treated as U.S. exports.

The globalization of production obscures how economic growth can affect a country's trade balance. Take again the example of the General Motors car produced in Mexico but sold in the United States. To the extent that the production of General Motors cars sold in the United States increasingly moves to Mexico, a rapidly growing U.S. economy that heightens demand for General Motors cars would, in that case, contribute to rising U.S. imports, not exports. And indeed this is happening.

The *value of the U.S. dollar* can affect U.S. exports and imports. In theory, a higher dollar contributes to lower exports and higher imports. A rising dollar makes U.S. exports more expensive in foreign nations. Concomitantly, it makes U.S. imports cheaper. A falling dollar has the reverse effect, making exports cheaper and imports more expensive. The rise of the dollar on foreign exchange markets in the late 1990s reflected not only the sustained growth and fundamental strength of the U.S. economy but also the financial crisis taking place throughout much of Southeast Asia, with its economic ripples felt in the north of Asia, as well. The sinking value of Southeast Asian currencies against the dollar contributed to a quickened decline of the Japanese yen, a downturn that began almost two years before the onset of Southeast Asia's financial crisis and that has also been accelerated by falling Japanese interest rates. The U.S. dollar also rose against the Canadian dollar and the Mexican peso, the currencies of the United States' two biggest trading partners, but at a more moderate pace. In contrast, the Chinese yuan maintained its then-fixed value against the dollar.

The dollar's value reversed course following the 2001 recession, as the Federal Open Market Committee (FOMC) sharply reduced the federal funds rate (FFR) to spur economic recovery. Although the FOMC incrementally increased the FFR as the economy rebounded from its recessionary trough, the early bounce given the value of the dollar by higher interest rates failed to be sustained into the second half of the decade. One prominent school of thought suggests that the United States' high and rising twin deficits—its current account deficit and federal budget deficit—and uncertainties about the war in Iraq tarnished the dollar's allure despite the United States' comparatively strong economic growth.

A separate but related factor to the exchange rate is the *price of similar goods from one country to another*. If a drought in France, for example, greatly drives up the price of French wines relative to comparable premium California Napa Valley wines, American consumers will be more inclined to purchase the relatively cheaper California wines. Yet this tendency will be modified a bit if at the same time the value of the dollar rises against the euro. However, it would have to rise enough to sufficiently offset the basic price difference. If, as a twist to this example, France and most of the rest of Europe experienced general inflationary pressures (not shared by the United States) that significantly increased the price of their goods across the board, including the price of wine, then that inflation could contribute to a softening of the euro's value in relation to the dollar, thereby contravening somewhat the inflationary price increase. As this example suggests, prices and exchange rates can interact with each other in complex ways.

The relative perceived *quality of goods* and the *status* that they confer on their owners are other factors that can affect exports and imports. If Americans perceive Toyotas to be better built than Fords, they will gravitate toward Toyotas, all other considerations being equal. On price, they may even be willing to pay more for a comparably equipped Toyota if they believe that it provides greater value over its useful life. If "yuppie" tastes in the United States dictate that one be seen driving an Acura, an Audi, or a Honda, in contrast to a Lincoln, a Pontiac, or a Dodge, then peer status considerations will tend to prompt a person to purchase the more desirable foreign model, even if it is priced higher than a comparably equipped domestic model. Similarly, the desire of a Mexican youth to wear American-brand clothing in preference to domestic brands can exert the same kind of effect on consumer choice. The former predisposition operates in favor of U.S. imports, while the latter supports U.S. exports. One way to help improve the U.S. trade balance is to change tastes, so that both U.S. and foreign consumers prefer American products. Advertising can work toward that end, but advertising in the United States in support of American goods is counteracted by the advertising here of foreign-controlled multinational corporations which milk foreign-product status preferences for all they are worth. But, as has been discussed previously, lines get blurred when we consider American-brand Nike shoes made in Malaysia or Hondas assembled in Ohio. Still, the brand-name country association and the perceived quality and status of the product seem to exert the most compelling enticements.

Finally, national *trade policies* can affect a country's trade balance. A country can erect both legal and nonlegal barriers to trade that discourage the import of selected goods in order to protect domestic goods from foreign competition. Specific legal barriers include tariffs, quotas, and domestic content requirements. Each merits discussion. **Tariffs** are taxes on imported goods, which raise the effective price of those goods to consumers, making them less price competitive and thereby biasing the options of consumers away from imported goods. **Quotas** limit the amount of imported goods allowed into a country. **Domestic content requirements** mandate that a certain percentage of a final product be manufactured or assembled in the home country.

Short of these legal barriers, nations may negotiate *voluntary trade restrictions*, by which one country agrees to limit its exports of certain goods to another country. These agreements are not motivated by the unilateral magnanimity of the country doing the limiting. Rather, they are typically the product of intense negotiations between two nations, often prompted by threats of legal restrictions if exports are not curbed "voluntarily."

Long-standing relationships between suppliers and distributors can constitute still another significant nonlegal barrier to free trade, by rendering it difficult for outsiders to break into these entrenched networks. This can be the case even when outside enterprises are able to offer a comparable or better product at a cheaper price. Intranetwork loyalty weighs heavily in the business equation. Japan provides a case in point, as is discussed at greater length later in this chapter. Its interlocking structure of ownership reinforces this exclusivity. Yet Japan is not alone in this regard. Observers of the Southeast Asian economic crisis point to network cronyism as a central element of the overextended financial dealings that have led to bank closings, investor panic, and corporate failures.

Free Trade and U.S. Trade Relationships

The United States is one of the world's leading proponents of free trade, but that has not always been the case. For most of the nineteenth century, the

United States pursued a protectionist policy incorporating relatively high tariffs. Revenues from tariffs in the early 1900s generated about half of all federal revenues. Today they account for less than 2 percent.[8]

President Woodrow Wilson advanced an internationalist foreign policy, calling for the creation of a League of Nations, as well as promoting trade liberalization. At his behest, Congress enacted the Underwood Tariff Act of 1913, which reduced tariffs considerably. In the wake of the stock market crash of 1929 and the ensuing economic collapse, Republican President Herbert Hoover and the Republican-controlled Congress reverted back to the GOP's traditional preference for trade protection. The Tariff Act of 1930, popularly known as the Smoot-Hartley Tariff, raised tariff rates by about half, from an average of 40 percent to 60 percent. Other nations followed suit. International trade declined, in turn, by about two-thirds in just four years, contributing to the severity of the Great Depression.[9]

The elections of 1932 paved the way for a new direction in international trade policy. With Democrat Franklin Delano Roosevelt in the presidency and large Democratic majorities in both chambers of Congress, the stage was set for a reversal of federal trade policy. Following a historical Democratic preference for trade liberalization, Congress, under President Roosevelt's urging, passed the Reciprocal Trade Agreements Act of 1934. It adopted a new reciprocal bargaining framework for trade policy. The act suspended passage of product-specific trade laws and delegated the responsibility for tariff negotiation to the president.[10]

The shift toward increased trade liberalization continued during the Truman administration. In 1947 President Harry S. Truman signed the General Agreement on Tariffs and Trade (GATT), a formal multilateral forum for trade negotiations. National membership in GATT expanded significantly during the second half of the twentieth century, and multinational trade negotiations proceeded through a number of so-called trading rounds, typically named after the city or country hosting them. The early rounds focused mainly on tariff reduction, but later rounds expanded the agenda to include deliberations over governmental subsidies to industry, antidumping (selling goods at significantly lower prices in foreign markets than in a nation's domestic market), and protection of intellectual property. At the end of the Uruguay Round (1986–94), the members approved a major revision of the general agreement, which included creation of the World Trade Organization (WTO) as the administrative arm of the association of nearly 150 member nations.

The WTO, with its secretariat in Geneva, Switzerland, administers a process of dispute resolution, to which countries bring allegations that other nations have failed to abide by provisions under the general agreement. Panels of experts, commissioned by the WTO, rule on the claims' validity. Violators face WTO-endorsed sanctions, including retaliatory tariffs.[11]

One highly publicized case of WTO intervention occurred during President George W. Bush's first term and involved U.S. imposition of tariffs on imported steel to protect U.S. steel producers from lower-priced foreign competitors—an action sharply at odds with the president's free trade rhetoric. The WTO sided with the European Union in its objections, and the United States faced $2.2 billion in retaliatory tariffs. As the European Union's review process moved with its deliberate speed to impose them, the Bush administration lifted its tariffs, which were in place for twenty months, averting retaliatory actions and counterresponses that would have likely spread beyond steel.

Though the U.S. Constitution gives the legislative branch the ultimate authority to regulate international trade, Congress has delegated a great deal of operational authority to the executive branch, to which Congress looks for policy leadership. Typically, Congress allows the president to negotiate trade agreements, and the president has several advisers who assist him in leading international economic policy. The most important include the secretaries of the Departments of Treasury and Commerce, the Federal Reserve Board chair, and the U.S. trade representative, a special post created in 1963. It is the trade adviser and his top officials who, under the president's general direction, negotiate trade agreements and resolve trade disputes with foreign nations.[12] In addition to working within the framework of the WTO, U.S. trade representatives actively negotiate bilateral agreements with the United States' trading partners. And with congressional enactment of the Trade Act of 2002, Congress limited its authority to voting trade agreements up or down, taking away its power to amend agreements.

The United States' active participation in bilateral trade negotiations, as well as in multilateral deliberations, whether within the framework of the WTO or as part of NAFTA, discussed a little later, has resulted in substantially reduced U.S. tariffs on imported goods over the past seventy-plus years. The greatest came from bilaterally negotiated tariff reductions from the Great Depression through the end of World War II, but substantial reductions have continued to take place since that time, as Figure 6.4 illustrates.

America's normative attachment to free trade has its roots in America's cherished values of individual liberty, governmental restraint, and the market as the fairest allocator of resources in society, despite protracted episodes of protectionism in the United States' formative industrial years and selective politically motivated protection of specific industries. These classical liberal values[13] hold that the individual is best positioned to decide what is in his or her best interest and to act on it. Restraints on trade constrain economic free choice. They put the interests of a limited number of producers (those who benefit from trade restraint) above a vastly larger body of consumers.

Figure 6.4   **Average U.S. Tariff on Goods Subject to Duties, 1930–2005**

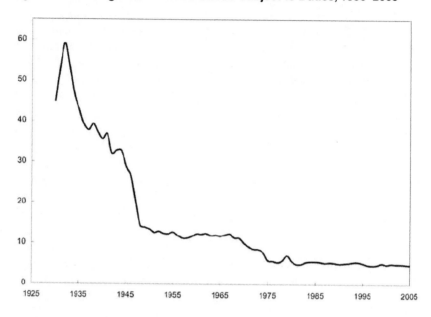

Source: Economic Report of the President, 2006, 154.

In doing so, barriers to free trade not only constrain economic choice, they also restrict the size of the economic pie. Free trade, conversely, expands economic output well beyond what a domestic economy could produce for its nation's citizens. Nations trading freely enjoy mutual benefit. Consumers benefit because they have a greater variety of goods from which to choose, and producers benefit because they can specialize in those areas in which they are favorably positioned to secure a profitable share of the international market, whether abundant natural resources, low costs of production, or a pool of skilled workers underlie that favorable positioning.

The benefits of specialization in international economic commerce were first recognized in the early nineteenth century by classical economist David Ricardo, who wrote about the virtues of what he labeled the law of comparative advantage.[14] Simply put, countries produce goods that people in other countries want and for which the exporting nation holds an advantage over other nations in producing those goods. Countries trade with nations enjoying a comparative advantage because they see it in their residents' best interest to do so. Assuming that a number of countries share a comparative advantage in exporting a natural resource or producing a given product, competition among them holds down prices and keeps other countries from being held captive by a single supplier or producer. A nation that turns to imports from countries that hold a comparative advantage in particular goods can marshal its resources to export to others goods for which it has a distinct advantage. In doing so, it can reap the advantages of economy of scale. World economic efficiency is enhanced, as nations are free from having to incur the investment and operating costs of producing all of what they need domestically and from suffering the many inefficiencies inherent in economic dependency.

The law of comparative advantage seems straightforward when we consider such goods as Colombian coffee, Saudi Arabian oil, Turkish hand-knotted rugs, and Swiss watches. None of these nations, however, has a corner on the market. But they still have elected to specialize in producing those goods in sizable numbers for sale in international markets. They have taken advantage of abundant natural resources or built on historical legacy. Yet other nations have elected to specialize in producing products for which they have no natural resource advantage or long-standing affinity. China's greatly expanded production of shoes and clothing and Japan's dominant position in electronic goods and automobiles serve as examples.

What accounts for this emphasis? In China's case it is differential costs in factors of production. The labor-intensive nature of production gives low-cost Chinese labor a comparative advantage in the manufacture of shoes and apparel. Worldwide demand justifies market entry; the Chinese have no intrinsic attachment to shoe or clothing production. Rather, Chinese entrepreneurs know that they can use their cost-of-labor advantage to compete effectively in those markets. In the case of Japan, its industries held no comparative advantage in electronic goods in the decades immediately following World War II. Moreover, its automobiles were highly suspect in international markets. They were hardly known for quality in the 1950s and 1960s. Yet Japanese industrialists saw a fertile market opportunity and, with government intervention to secure capital, invested heavily in modern plants and the technology necessary to produce quality automobiles that were price competitive. The same is true for electronic goods such as radios, stereos, and televisions. Both industrial entrepreneurs and government planners set out to acquire a sizable slice of the world market, and they did it.[15]

Regionalization and the North American Free Trade Agreement

The logic of increased economic efficiency and mutual benefit through free trade should prompt nations to reduce remaining barriers to trade, and that is just what has happened around the world since World War II. Still, nations have pursued different approaches toward that end. Most commonly, they have

Table 6.5

Major Provisions of NAFTA

Area	Provision (When Fully Implemented)
Tariffs	Eliminates all tariffs on roughly 9,000 categories of goods produced and sold in member nations.
Quotas and import licenses	Eliminates all quotas and import licenses applied at the border.
Investments	Prescribes the imposition of special requirements on investments made by businesses or individuals of one member nation in another member nation.
Rules of origin and domestic content requirements	Prevents goods produced either completely or in large part outside member nations from being exported duty-free among member nations. Requires that goods contain at least 50 percent North American content to move duty-free across the border.
Health and the environment	Guarantees that no member nation would be forced to reduce its health and environmental standards.

forged bilateral agreements with trading partners as well as pursued freer trade through the WTO, as discussed earlier. They have also participated within *regional* free-trade associations aimed at advancing the economic interests of affiliated members and the region as a whole. More than 170 regional agreements were in force in 2005. Prominent associations include the European Communities (EC), the Central European Free Trade Agreement (CEFTA), the Association of East Asian Free Trade Area (AFTA), the Common Market for Eastern and Southern Africa (COMESA), and NAFTA, of which the United States is a member along with its neighbors Canada and Mexico.

The North American regional agreement took effect on January 1, 1994, and is to be fully implemented by 2008. Table 6.5 summarizes its major provisions pertaining to tariffs, quotas and import licenses, investments, rules of origin and domestic content requirements, and health and the environment.[16] NAFTA's provisions, like all regional free trade agreements, advance free trade among member nations; yet they also give preferential treatment to members over nonmembers. Members share the benefits of multilateral reductions in tariffs and quota restrictions—benefits not shared by nonmembers. Moreover, rules of origin and domestic content requirements also advantage members over nonmembers. For example, under NAFTA, while motor vehicles and parts that contain at least 60 percent local content can move from one member nation to another without tariffs being imposed, those that do not are subject to existing tariff rates. The rationale behind this provision is to ensure that members benefit economically from foreign trade within North America, by limiting the extent to which they can incorporate into the final product components and parts made outside NAFTA countries. If this provision were not imposed, firms of member nations might succumb to the temptation to rely on cheaper foreign components and parts, thus reducing their costs and increasing their profits while escaping tariffs—a reward intended for member nations who share the economic pie. Still, there should be no doubt that domestic content provisions are anti–free trade. Although they fence in a certain amount of industrial production and its associated economic benefits, they depress worldwide economic efficiency and invite other nations to adopt similar barriers to free trade.

Congress approved U.S. participation in NAFTA partly in response to policies of the European Union (EU), an association of European nations formed in part to lower trade barriers among its members and to make them more competitive internationally. Just as the EU sought to realize the benefits of freer trade among its members, so did NAFTA. This was a rational economic strategy for the members of both associations because, after all, their leading trading partners could be found among their respective association's membership. Thus securing the benefits of intra-associational trade could be expected to pay immediate dividends to member nations.

Despite their protective elements, associational agreements can be seen as steps toward broadened free trade, as nations begin by liberalizing trade within their respective regions. Once successful, the lure of expanded cross-regional trade may well prompt participants to remove protective barriers. Too the extent that the international community, through instruments such as the WTO, can agree to further trade liberalization, the perceived need for either protection or retaliation should break down somewhat. However, if efforts toward broadened multilateral liberalization bog down, as they did during the WTO's recent Doha Round, we can likely expect further growth of regional trade agreements, creating what some see as stumbling blocks, rather than building blocks, to widened international trade.[17]

NAFTA has indeed accomplished its goal of greatly expanding trade among its three North American members. From 1993 to 2005, intermember trade increased by 173 percent, from $297 billion to $810 billion. Although Mexican and Canadian exports to the United States grew faster than U.S. exports to its two neighbors, U.S. exports to Mexico and Canada grew nearly twice as fast as U.S. exports to the rest of the world.[18] And even though Mexican and Canadian exports grew at faster rates, a U.S. Department of Commerce analysis concludes that the growth of U.S. exports to Mexico and Canada supported approximately 130,000 new jobs a year in the United States—jobs that paid 13 to 18 percent more than other U.S. employment. Mexican and Canadian workers in export-supported jobs benefited as well, earning 40 percent and 35 percent more, respectively, than workers in nonexport sectors.[19]

Foreign Direct Investment

When the United States runs a current account deficit, as it currently does, it must finance the deficit by either borrowing from foreigners or selling assets to them. And much like annual federal budget deficits add to accumulated national debt, foreign financing of annual current account deficits increases foreign ownership of U.S. assets. As the result of a long string of current account deficits, foreigners now hold over $2.5 trillion more in U.S. assets than Americans hold in foreign assets. Those assets may take the form of corporate stocks and bonds, government securities, financial institutions' liabilities, currency, and direct ownership of businesses and real estate. As noted previously, to be counted in this last category—foreign direct investment—foreign investors must control at least 10 percent of the voting securities of a corporation or of the equivalent interest in an unincorporated interest or property.

Of all the forms of foreign investment, foreign direct investment receives the greatest popular attention, even though foreign portfolio investment exceeds it by a nearly 4 : 1 margin. The U.S. Congress got in an uproar over the China National Overseas Oil Corporation's unsuccessful efforts to secure a controlling interest in Unocal, a U.S.-owned energy company. Nearly twenty years earlier, media accounts riled Americans over Mitsubishi's purchase of New York City's Rockefeller Center—an investment that lost money for its Japanese corporate owner, leading Mitsubishi to happily return the landmark to American ownership. Still, foreign corporations have acquired controlling interest in a number of prominent U.S. corporations, including Sony's takeover of Columbia Pictures, British Petroleum's acquisition of Shell Oil, and Deutsche Bank's control of Bankers Trust.

These acquisitions are more alarming to Americans than the knowledge that Japanese, Chinese, and other foreigners increasingly invest in Treasury bills or corporate bonds. Even their investment in U.S. stocks causes little alarm, as long as foreign investors stay far from management control. In a real sense, these so-called portfolio investments pay a compliment to the United States and its economy. And foreign purchase of U.S. Treasury securities keeps their interest rates lower than they would be without that foreign investment, thus reducing the federal government's interest costs; and foreign purchase of U.S. company stocks supports their price in equity markets. Outright foreign ownership or control of U.S. companies and landmarks is another matter.

Another form of foreign direct investment appears to be less troublesome to Americans, and that is the foreign ownership of production plants and branch offices in the United States. Just as large U.S. multinational corporations expanded production plants and branch offices around the world, building on their early foundations in Western Europe, so have foreign nations increasingly located them in the United States. Consider Mercedes Benz's automobile assembly plant in Alabama, Honda's in Ohio, or the many big-city locations for branches of Germany's Commerzbank or Japan's Sumimoto Bank.

The United States continues to lead all nations in both originating foreign direct investment and hosting it. The United Kingdom and Canada receive the greatest share of U.S. direct investment abroad, and the United Kingdom and Japan make the greatest direct investment in the United States.[20] About three-fourths of U.S. direct investment abroad remains in developed countries in spite of recent increases in U.S. direct investment in emerging markets. For instance, although China is the second largest host to worldwide foreign direct investment, China attracts less than 1 percent from the United States.[21]

Direct investment and trade are related. The Toyota Corporation, for example, could decide to expand its assembly plants in Japan in an effort to meet rising U.S. demand for Toyota automobiles, or it could elect to open assembly plants in the United States. Its choice represents both a business and a political decision. On the business side, Toyota could reduce both its transportation and labor costs by establishing new plants in the United States. As an economic offset, however, a U.S. location makes Toyota more dependent on American-made components and parts. But that increased dependence serves as a political asset, as do the American jobs created by the plants. An additional political consideration is that Toyotas made and sold in the United States do not count as Japanese exports, and they contribute to the U.S. GDP. If they were made in Japan and transported to the United States for sale, they would add to America's trade deficit with Japan—a touchy matter politically.

The benefits of foreign direct investment seem less clear than the benefits of trade that result from comparative advantage. Still, they can accrue to both the host and the investing country. The host country benefits not only from the jobs created in foreign-owned plants and offices but also from the demand that these new enterprises create for machinery, parts, supplies, and services—most of which are provided domestically. In fact, one study found that foreign companies operating in the United States purchased from U.S. suppliers 80 percent of the materials and services used in production.[22] Other benefits can come in the form of technology transfer and management improvement, both of which can increase productivity in the host country.

The investing country also stands to benefit. Direct investment in foreign nations increases their personal income, all other things being equal, enabling their residents to increase their consumption of imports, including those from the investing country. Direct investment can also create trade opportunities, improving a nation's trade balance. As is the case of the United States, its multinational corporations export more to their overseas affiliates than they import from them.[23]

What about the relationship between foreign direct investment and jobs? Don't U.S. corporations "export" jobs when they acquire productive facilities or expand their operations in other lands? Clearly they do. In 2004, U.S. multinational corporations employed 28 percent of their workforce in foreign affiliates. General Motors and Ford, for instance, operate assembly and parts plants around the globe. General Motors manufactures its cars and trucks in thirty-three countries and employs more than 20,000 employees in China alone. Ford operates 108 plants worldwide. Whirlpool, America's largest supplier of domestic appliances, has nearly fifty manufacturing and technology research centers around the world and makes most of its products in Mexico and Europe.

Does that mean, however, that those jobs would have otherwise been established in the United States? For reasons related to market proximity, supply, and labor cost differentials, it cannot be assumed that those jobs would have otherwise been created in the United States.

International Trade, Investment, and Employment

The debate over whether the United States should participate in NAFTA highlighted the relationship between trade policy and employment. In voicing his opposition to NAFTA, Ross Perot, a third-party candidate for the presidency in both 1992 and 1996, warned Americans of the "giant sucking sound" of jobs being pulled south of the border that would follow congressional approval of NAFTA. He predicted the loss of up to 6 million U.S. jobs to Mexico, compared to the legislation's supporters who forecast the creation of more than a million new jobs in the United States resulting from the added Mexican demand for U.S. goods that could be expected to flow from greater economic activity in Mexico. Organized labor in the United States echoed Perot's fears, creating the anomaly of a Democratic president championing NAFTA's approval and facing the strong opposition of a traditionally loyal political ally. President Clinton's position prevailed in Congress, but it took overwhelming Republican support in the House to bring about victory. Republicans voted 132–43 in favor of NAFTA approval, while Democrats opposed it by a 102–156 margin.

The rationale that trade liberalization between the United States and Mexico would benefit both economies won out. Supporters argued that NAFTA would open up Mexico's market for U.S. goods, repairing a relationship in which it had been more difficult for U.S. goods to get into Mexico than for Mexican goods to make it into the United States. Supporters also pointed to the potential rise in Mexican demand for U.S. exports that could be expected to accompany the personal income gains of Mexican workers.

Our earlier discussion of NAFTA as an agent of regional trade liberalization shows that it contributed to expanded intermember trade and corresponding export-oriented employment growth in all three nations. This is not to suggest that U.S. jobs have not been displaced to Mexico. Media accounts of plant closings in the United States and the movement of jobs to lower-cost operations in Mexico provide vivid illustration of selective job migration; however, there is no doubt that increased exports among NAFTA members have contributed to sizable net employment growth in all three nations.

Since Ross Perot's warnings about the "giant sucking sound," public focus on job loss has turned to China, India, and Southeast Asia, as U.S. multinational corporations increasingly look for low-cost labor and reduced costs of production and service delivery. Yet survey data from the Bureau of Labor Statistics show that for layoffs of fifty or more employees between 1996 and 2004, less than 3 percent were attributable to import competition or overseas job relocation. The surveys further show that trade-related job losses do not involve longer periods of unemployment or lower reemployment earnings than do job losses from other causes. Job turnover is a constant in the U.S. economy. Over the past ten years, the U.S. economy has created an average of 17 million jobs each year, while 15 million jobs have been eliminated in the same period. International investment and employment policies of multinational corporations still play a relatively minor role in job turnover.[24]

Global outsourcing has taken three forms over the past two decades. The first occurred in manufacturing. Multinational corporations expanded their overseas operations or acquired foreign subsidiaries to take advantage of low-cost labor and reduce their costs of production. The second transformed retailing, as large-volume discount stores, epitomized by Wal-Mart, went global in their search for the lowest cost suppliers of consumer goods. The third extended outsourcing to services, made possible by advances in information and communications technology.[25] These advances have enabled companies to segment activities and parcel them out to the lowest cost bidders. Activities such as software programming, accounting and financial analysis, tax preparation, and consumer relations have been the leading candidates for outsourcing.[26]

Although data on job loss associated with offshore outsourcing are limited, estimates by two prominent international business consulting companies—McKinsey and Company and Forrester Research—project them at less than 850,000 through 2005, a small fraction of the current 135 million U.S. workers.[27]

Department of Commerce data show that U.S. multinational corporations typically invest abroad for access to markets rather than for low-wage workers.[28]

Why Worry About the United States' Large Current Account Deficit?

Why worry about the United States' large current account deficit? After all, no consistent relationship exists between a nation's near-term economic performance and the size or rate of change in its trade deficit. Even a superficial glance at the contemporary short-run experience of the United States and Europe brings that point home. Between 2002 and 2005, the United States' current account *deficit* averaged $558 billion a year, or 5.3 percent of GDP. The Euro area nations,[29] on average, accumulated a current account *surplus* in each of those years, averaging about a half of 1 percent of GDP. However, the United States enjoyed much stronger economic performance over the four years. While U.S. real GDP growth averaged 3 percent, Europe's economy managed only a little more than 1 percent growth. Unemployment averaged 5.6 percent in the United States compared to nearly 9 percent in Europe. Adding Japan yields a similar relationship. Japan had a large current account *surplus* in each year, averaging 3.4 percent of GDP over the four years. And although Japan's average unemployment rate, at 5 percent, was somewhat lower than the United States' 5.6 percent average rate, Japan's economy grew by only 1.7 percent a year during that period, doing better than Europe's but growing at only about half the U.S. rate.[30]

With the U.S. economy performing comparatively strongly, foreign investors have been willing to finance the United States' balance of payments deficit by increasing their holdings of U.S. assets. Foreign central banks, particularly those of China and Japan, have been willing to increase their purchase of dollars to depress the value of their currency and hold down the price of their exports to the United States. The big question facing the United States is how much longer they will continue to do so, allowing Americans to consume more than they produce domestically and, on the flip side, to spend more than they earn.

The answer to that question is, as long as they believe it is in their interest to do so. Should foreign investors and central banks worry that growing U.S. indebtedness will erode the value of their U.S. assets, they will become less inclined to invest in the United States. If that were to happen, economic theory suggests that their growing disinclination to invest in the United States would help to drive up U.S. interest rates. Rising interest rates tend to depress economic demand, as economic theory also tells us. Reduced demand dampens economic growth and depresses personal income.

One sure way of safeguarding against that undesirable outcome is for the United States to increase its rate of national saving. If that were done, the current account deficit would decline. Saving would displace consumption, and increased domestic saving would narrow or eliminate the gap between domestic saving and investment. Thus it is not surprising that economists, such as Paul Krugman,[31] regard America's low saving rate as a key economic problem. Yet to reduce America's trade deficit in goods, it is not enough to decrease consumption in relation to personal income alone; consumption expenditures must be switched, as well. That involves changing U.S. consumers' appetite for foreign goods.

Government can act to increase national saving by cutting the federal budget deficit. That becomes easier, as recent U.S. experience suggests, when strong economic growth swells government revenues. When economies sag and government revenues fall short of estimates, deficit reduction requires tax increases or expenditure reductions. However, both tax increases and expenditure reductions act to dampen demand and make economic matters worse.

Should the economy go into recession, people and businesses would get hurt. Rising unemployment and falling personal income lead to reduced consumption. Consumption of both domestic and foreign goods falls, even though the rate of decline might be higher for one category than for the other. As consumption of foreign goods falls, so does the trade deficit. Thus, as Robert Eisner reminds us, recessions can cure trade deficits, but the "cure" inflicts far more economic pain than that created by the malady. Remember that strong economic growth at home fosters consumer confidence and demand that ripples through the economy as businesses increase production to meet that demand. To the extent that imports to meet some of that demand rise faster than do exports to the rest of the world, the trade deficit will rise. Would it make good policy sense to choke off prosperity in order to reduce the trade deficit? Of course not. So most American policy makers stand ready to tolerate a trade deficit in a sound economy.

Government Regulation and Deregulation

Although America's political culture highly values individual freedom, public policy makers and citizens alike recognize that the unbridled pursuit of private interest can harm the broader public interest and that government has an obligation to intervene selectively and limit individual freedom for the common good. Yet America's classical liberal inheritance puts the onus on government to justify its intervention in private spheres of activity. The issue of when and to what extent government should control individual or group activity is an inherently political question that lies at the heart of public policy making. Policy makers, both elected and appointed, make those choices on the public's behalf, and they typically justify their choices as being in the public interest. But what constitutes the public interest is itself a political question, one that gets resolved through authoritative governmental action, whether that takes the form of legislation, court decisions and rulings, or regulation.

This chapter focuses on regulation that has economic implications, broadly conceived, in which government requires individuals or organizations to behave in certain ways under the credible threat of sanctions for noncompliance. In the United States, federal government agencies exercise regulatory authority that is vested in them by acts of Congress or, under certain restrictions, by executive action of the president. Congressional acts provide the legal framework for regulation, empowering government agencies to issue the very regulations that command individuals or organizations to behave in certain ways, but those regulations must be consistent with the enabling legislation. That enabling legislation may be drawn quite narrowly, specifying not only the intent of the law but also the conditions, standards, and procedures pertaining to it; or it may attach only general statutory guidelines to its statement of legislative intent. In the latter case, Congress gives government agencies considerable discretion in implementing the law. In exercising delegated administrative discretion, government agencies engage in rule making, a process that results in their issuance of regulations that have the force of law. A similar process operates in the states.

The Normative Context of Regulation

Government regulation tends to evoke strong feelings—in the abstract and in application. Concerns in the abstract center on views of the appropriate role of government, particularly whether government is going too far in intervening in private affairs. Those who prefer self-interested action and limited government put the heaviest burden on government to justify its intervention. Others who see a constructive role for government to play in the economy and in society are more welcoming of government intervention as a check on the negative spillovers of self-interested behavior. The former view individuals as the best judges of their own interests, and they see the economy and society benefiting from this aggregate pursuit of self-interest. The latter worry that unrestrained pursuit of self-interest will come at the expense of collective goods.

In the contemporary rhetoric of politics, regulation has taken on a pejorative association with big government, bureaucratic red tape, and inefficiency. Those seeing it that way draw a reasonably rigid line between the private and public spheres; within the private sphere, they consider the market to be the best and most efficient allocator of value. The market makes goods available that individuals and organizations want, as firms—motivated by profit—compete to satisfy those wants, using price as the information medium of voluntary exchange. For Milton Friedman, the wonder of the market is that an efficient economic order can emerge as the *unintended* consequence of the actions of many individuals or organizations, each acting in the pursuit of self-interest.[1] Friedman's presumption is to let the market work—that is, unless the conditions that allow markets to function effectively are threatened or fail to be met. Government, then, has an obligation to step in and correct the defect. Preservation of the market becomes the justification for intervention.

Certain conditions must be met for the market to work effectively. First, exchange must be voluntary. Second, prospective buyers must be able to choose from among available equivalent goods; and, other than price differences, the choice of doing business with one seller rather than another must be relatively costless. For instance, this dictum would be violated if transportation costs of doing business with a competitor were so high as to render it uneconomical, even after consideration of price competitiveness. Third, there must be freedom of entry and exit. Would-be competitors must be free to enter into competition in search of a share of the market, and enterprises must be free to pull up stakes when market conditions dictate. Fourth, all costs must be borne by the parties involved in a market transaction; uncompensated costs must not spill over to third parties. Finally, government must not define the substance of the economic product, the specific array of goods and services available, or their distribution.

Confronting Threats to the Market: Monopoly Practices and Negative Externalities

The greatest threats to the free market come from **monopoly practices** and **negative externalities**. The effective working of the market is premised on free choice. Consumers must be free to take their business elsewhere if they find prices too high or quality lacking. However, consumers cannot exercise that freedom of choice if businesses are not free to enter the market and provide them with viable alternatives. Businesses will enter the market only when they see an opportunity to compete successfully and make a satisfactory profit. Unrestrained market economies offer incentives for firms to increase their market share. Firms can do that by raising the perceived value of their products, by improving product quality and offering competitively low prices, and through the effective use of advertising that stimulates consumer desire. Their success at expanding market share may prompt some of their less successful competitors to decide that it is in their self-interest to exit the market altogether rather than to pursue unsuccessful competition. Other firms may find it in their interest to be taken over by successful competitors who are seeking opportunities to expand their market presence.

As another means to expand market share, successful firms may elect to join forces and merge their enterprises. Mergers not only can broaden market penetration and increase the operating efficiency of the resulting enterprises, they also can improve their competitive position, squeezing out less well-positioned competitors. Extending this scenario, it is possible to end up with only one or a few firms dominating a market. When a single firm reaches a dominant position over ineffective competition and is able to influence prices through independent action, economic theory suggests that consumers will be the losers, facing reduced choice and higher prices than would occur with competition. When only a couple of viable firms remain in a market, the danger exists that they may be tempted to collude rather than to compete, dividing the market between them and sharing the profits garnered from prices set higher than would exist if they were in competition.

Not only do consumers face the potential of restricted supply and high prices under these conditions, but the economy suffers as well, as firms no longer face the competitive pressures that prompt them to operate as efficiently as possible. Thus government has an incentive to intervene and restrict monopolistic practices. It does this by applying antitrust policy.

Externalities arise when the actions of private participants in the economy impose costs on others who fail to be compensated for them (negative externalities) or when the actions of private participants confer benefits on others who fail to pay for the benefits derived (**positive externalities**). Government regulators tend not to concern themselves with positive externalities, because no party is directly harmed or disadvantaged in the relationship, even though it becomes possible for some individuals to reap benefits while avoiding costs, raising the problem of inequity. A prominent example is the open union shop, in which workers need not be union members. Union members pay dues that, in part, pay the salaries of union officials who bargain with management for higher wages for workers. If their bargaining proves successful, union members benefit through higher earnings, but so do nonmembers, who bear none of the costs of union endeavors. Other than considerations of cross-worker inequity, no uncompensated costs are *imposed* by one party on another, although the very possibility of "free rider" benefits probably depresses would-be union membership. That is why many states have laws requiring all workers to join the required union, an option permitted by federal law.

The case of negative externalities is different. One party benefits by offloading costs, and another is harmed by absorbing the consequences of the first party's actions. Industrial point-source pollution (pollution that can be traced to a fixed point of discharge) provides a salient example. Polluters impose costs on others. Those who pollute a river or stream can impose costs on downstream users. The costs may be direct—for example, when downstream communities must pay to treat the water to standards of drinkable quality—or they can be indirect, such as when pollution levels prevent people from swimming or fishing in those waters, depriving them of valued recreation. Air pollution also imposes costs—the personal costs of respiratory illness on the most medically vulnerable and the larger burden on society of paying for the health-care costs of those requiring treatment for conditions exacerbated by air pollution. Although government can employ fines to exact payment from industrial plants that exceed allowable emission levels, those directly affected go uncompensated, unless they successfully sue polluters as compensation for the effects they have suffered. Fines serve as surrogate compensation for the costs borne by society, and they also serve as a policy tool to bias the options of industry, which must weigh the costs of fines against the costs necessary to reduce pollutants to acceptable levels.

An industry operating purely in its corporate self-interest, focusing on the financial bottom line, has an incentive to pass costs outside the corporation. Reducing pollution emissions entails increased expenditures. Therefore, industries have to balance the costs of investing in devices that reduce emissions with the consequences of not doing so, including fines and negative public opinion that might cost them sales in the marketplace. If there were no government-imposed counterbalance, firms might be more willing to push the limits of negative public opinion in order to maximize profits.

What about pollution that cannot be readily attributed to specific sources?

It is one thing to be able to trace chemical pollution in a waterway to an industrial source and allocate costs back to it, and it is quite another thing to be able to trace auto emission air pollution back to the respective vehicle operators. It is much easier for government to place requirements on automobile manufacturers to design their products in ways that reduce emissions. Beyond that, the external costs that automobile users impose on society through air pollution essentially go uncompensated. Sure, gasoline taxes impose costs on users, but the revenues from those user charges go toward highway and road improvement—improvements that often facilitate more automobile use, which produces even greater pollution. Although government can enact pollution taxes of various sorts, such as a tax imposed on the annual mileage use of registered motor vehicles, with the revenues directed toward environmental cleanup, such an initiative would likely fail the test of political feasibility. As an alternative, government could increase existing motor fuel taxes in an effort to raise revenue while discouraging use, perhaps allocating some of the newly found revenue to subsidize mass transit as part of an effort to entice motorists to abandon their automobiles in favor of public transportation. To the extent that motorists make the shift in large numbers, vehicle emissions could be significantly reduced. However, policy makers in the United States have been far less inclined than their European counterparts, for example, to bias individual options to that extent. On behalf of individual freedom, U.S. policy makers, for the most part, have left to individuals the largely unhindered vehicle-use choices that collectively impose environmental costs on the rest of us—a policy stance that contrasts with the regulation of point-source pollution.

Protecting the Public: Reducing Risk and Ensuring Equity

In addition to protecting against market failure and addressing externalities, government regulation also seeks to *control or reduce the risk* faced by individuals in the marketplace.[2] Government does this by developing standards for products, production processes, and the information that manufacturers are required to disclose to consumers. Common illustrations include the control of financial institutions, insurance, prescription drugs, food safety, television and radio broadcast standards, and workplace safety, as well as ingredient and nutritional labeling on consumable products. In addition, government licenses providers of certain services, such as physicians, nurses, attorneys, stockbrokers, and even cosmetologists.

Government also intervenes in the marketplace to *ensure equity of service provision and fair price* in those markets in which self-interest might lead monopolies or near monopolies to allocate service and price in ways that maximize user revenues and corporate profits. The areas of public utility and transportation regulation serve as prominent examples. The former covers such services as telephone, natural gas, electricity, and water. The latter applies to rail, airline, and trucking transportation. With public utilities, government regulation might mandate universal service and control the prices charged to residential users, which, based on cost allocation, would be higher in the absence of governmental control. Government regulators fill the revenue gap by allowing utilities to charge business users more than cost allocation justifies, creating, in effect, a cross-subsidy. A similar relationship pertains to urban residential and rural residential users, in which urban users subsidize rural users.

With the regulation of transportation, government has acted to require providers to serve unprofitable geographic areas in exchange for the right to serve highly profitable ones. In both public utilities and transportation, government has granted providers a reasonable operating profit and, in return for their cooperation, has restricted competition. Yet as is discussed later in greater detail, legislative action at both the federal and state levels has selectively removed government from the business of directing service provision, setting rates, and controlling the entry of competitors in commercial transportation.

States play a significant regulatory role in the U.S. federal system. For instance, they license practitioners in certain professions and occupations serving the public; they have the primary responsibility for regulating public building safety, insurance, and electrical power; and they have secondary responsibility in regulating banking and environmental pollution. At the same time, federal law has greatly limited or reshaped the states' regulatory power in such areas as trucking, natural gas, and telephone service.

Government regulatory policy has taken different turns over time, and those turns have largely been a response to changing perceptions of what constitute public problems. The following section traces the currents of regulatory policy in the United States and the tools that regulatory policy makers have chosen to use over time in several important sectors of the American economy.

Problem Perception and Regulatory Policy

The roots of modern government regulation lie in the late nineteenth century, a time of rapid industrialization and transition from competing regional economies to a truly national economy.[3] Railroad expansion, added to established steam-powered waterway transportation, provided a national transportation infrastructure that fostered the growth of a national economy and greatly expanded interstate commerce. Nationally chartered banks and growing stock exchanges provided the capital in support of the industrial consolidations that led to a swiftly expanding corporate-based national economy. A growing number of state-chartered banks capitalized more limited regional economic operations.

The late nineteenth century was a period of steep economic growth punctuated by wide swings of the business cycle. It was also a period of increasing tension between the emerging corporate-based economy and family-owned businesses, on the one hand, and between industrially led urbanization and increasingly radicalized agrarian interests, on the other. This tension was exacerbated by foreign immigration, the swelling of central cities, changes in the organization of production, and rising labor militancy—changes that foreshadowed even more intensified social pressures in the early twentieth century. Corporations engaged in takeovers and mergers and formed trusts (in which the trust held stock in a number of related industries and exercised management authority over them). The largest and most prominent trust was the Standard Oil Trust, which in 1879 controlled 40 different oil companies. Mergers combined 4,227 businesses into 257 corporations in the years between 1897 and 1904 alone, giving birth to industrial giants such as U.S. Steel and International Harvester.[4]

The rise of third-party political movements in the 1890s reflected growing social dislocations and discontent with change. Feeling squeezed by urban industrial interests, radical agrarians threw their support behind the newly formed People's Party, commonly referred to as the Populists. The Populists called for the institution of an income tax and government-induced economic stimulation through unlimited coinage of silver. They also advanced a platform of nationalization of railroads and telegraph companies.

As rails came to crisscross the nation, the railroad became the predominant commercial transportation mode in America. It provided shippers with the most flexible, efficient, and timely mode of transportation available. Yet despite the railroad's national geographic reach, made possible by both federal and state land grants, the states, not the federal government, played the major role in regulating railroads for most of the nineteenth century. Shippers soon came to argue that the different and often conflicting regulations undermined the very efficiency that the railroad offered. Moreover, shippers in the Midwest and the West raised their voices against the growing monopolistic practices of the few railroads serving their regions, some of which were sanctioned by state regulation. Agricultural interests were successful in forcing new state railroad regulations and antitrust laws in seventeen states.[5]

The Rise of Economic Regulation

Faced with rising complaints from both agricultural and other commercial interests over rates and reacting to an important 1886 U.S. Supreme Court

decision that struck down state regulation on the basis that the "right of continuous transportation" was necessary for commerce, both the House and
Senate quickly took up legislation that would substitute national regulation
for state regulation.[6] Their efforts resulted in passage of the Interstate Commerce Act of 1887, which created the Interstate Commerce Commission
(ICC). Congress granted the ICC power to set "just and reasonable" rates in
the public interest and delegated to the regulators the authority to implement
that criterion. These actions marked the federal government's entry into national economic regulation.

For the remainder of the nineteenth century and through the first five
decades of the twentieth, the federal government pretty much confined its
regulatory intervention to economic matters. A shift to social regulation, also
referred to as protective regulation, would largely wait until the 1960s.

The Sherman Antitrust Act of 1890, following closely on the heels of the
Interstate Commerce Act, was the first in a series of congressional initiatives designed to constrain the ability of companies to merge, form trusts, or
conspire to fix fares, rates, and prices. However, it created no enforcement
mechanism. It was not until 1903, during Theodore Roosevelt's first term as
president, that Congress created the Antitrust Division of the Justice Department to lead antitrust enforcement. Yet the legislation's ambiguous intent
and questions about the extent of the division's authority rendered it less
than an aggressive enforcer, leading its administrators to demur to the courts
for guidance.

Reacting to the courts' ready willingness to intervene, Congress, with
President Woodrow Wilson's blessing, created the independent Federal Trade
Commission (FTC) in 1914 and gave it the powers to promulgate rules, initi-
ate complaints based on its investigatory analysis, and take enforcement actions against violators. In that same year, Congress strengthened the federal
government's regulatory hand by enacting the Clayton Act, which extended
antitrust controls, principally by prohibiting price discrimination if its effects
were to lessen competition significantly or to create a monopoly. It was not
long, however, before the courts jealously reined in the FTC's enforcement
power. With the exception of Congress's creation in 1920 of the Federal Power
Commission to regulate the *interstate* sale of electric energy and natural gas
on the *wholesale* market, the next wave of national economic regulation would
come in the 1930s from a Democrat-controlled Congress sympathetic with
Franklin Delano Roosevelt's New Deal.

Under the pressure of economic dislocations caused by the Great Depression, New Deal regulations were aimed at reducing risks to participants in the
market economy, as well as restoring their confidence in America's financial
institutions. Toward that end, new regulatory initiatives included the Federal

Deposit Insurance Corporation (FDIC) in 1933 and the Securities and Exchange Commission (SEC) a year later. The former was instituted to insure bank deposits against loss resulting from bank failure, a growing occurrence during the Great Depression's early years. The latter was established to regulate the selling and buying of stocks and securities, to provide consumers with information about transactions, and to prohibit transactions based on insider information—that is, information about corporations' business intentions not available to the public.[7]

Congress, in 1935, acted again to protect investors and consumers by passing the Public Utility Holding Company Act (PUHCA). **Holding companies** are corporations that own companies outright or hold a controlling interest in their stock. Utility holding companies are corporations that own or control utility companies. Because states regulate the retail sale of electric power, including approving the rates charged to both commercial and residential customers, utility companies are guaranteed a secure stream of revenue. With holding companies controlling the utilities, the parent corporation could use secure utility revenues to finance or guarantee riskier business ventures of its affiliated companies, thus potentially jeopardizing the financial security of the utilities themselves. And that is what happened following the stock market crash and the Great Depression that followed. Between 1929 and 1936, fifty-three utility holding companies went bankrupt in the United States.[8]

Congress's passage of PUHCA subjected multistate utility holding companies to regulation by the SEC and required them to incorporate in the same state as the utility they owned, effectively restricting their geographic reach and thereby greatly limiting their economic incentive to acquire utility companies. Under PUHCA, holding companies desiring to own utilities in more than one state would have to divest themselves of the other, nonutility companies they owned or controlled—a price typically far too great for holding companies to pay. As a result, investors in utility companies received protection against financially ruinous risk taking by parent corporations, and utility customers enjoyed the confidence of secure service. Parenthetically, Congress repealed PUHCA as part of the 2005 energy bill, signed into law by President Bush. More will be said about this turn of events as the discussion later turns to deregulation.

New Deal legislation also authorized the federal government to regulate telephone and radio communications, in addition to interstate trucking and interstate commercial airline transportation. Congress created the Federal Communications Commission (FCC) in 1934. Not only would the FCC regulate what could be transmitted by telephone line or radio signal (later by broadcast or cable television), it also controlled service entry through its authority to grant licenses. Congress, the following year, extended the government's regulatory authority by charging the ICC to regulate interstate trucking. Prior to Congress's passage of the Federal Motor Carrier Act of 1935, motor carrier regulation fell to the states, creating a national patchwork of inconsistent intrastate regulatory practices. No regulation of interstate trucking existed at all. Under the 1935 legislation, federal regulation of interstate trucking extended to entry, routes, rates, service abandonment, and mergers. The federal act became a model for subsequent amendments of state regulation of intrastate trucking, fostering greater uniformity of state regulation than existed prior to federal regulation.[9] Three years later, in 1938, Congress created the Civil Aeronautics Authority (renamed the Civil Aeronautics Board in 1940) to regulate the commercial airline industry and gave it the authority to control entry and approve routes, flight schedules, and service abandonment.

All of these regulatory initiatives functioned to restrain competition, instead of promoting it, as was the goal of much nineteenth- and early twentieth-century regulation. They had as their goal to ensure reliable service provision without destabilizing competition. To do so, competition would have to be controlled, with regulated providers guaranteed a "just and reasonable" return on their investment. In all three instances already noted, the regulated industries actively supported federal regulation. In turning to protection over competition, the federal government set itself up for what would be increasing criticism that the regulated industries had come to capture the government's regulatory authority and advance their own economic interests rather than the public interest.

The United States' entry into World War II turned national policy makers' attention toward mobilizing the economy for war. New Deal regulations remained in place, but America's industrial output significantly shifted to the manufacture of military goods, although early in the war corporations moved with less than alacrity in leaving their domestic markets. The War Production Board, created by President Roosevelt under the authority granted to him by the War Powers Act of 1941, hastened the process of conversion by restricting industry's ability to use raw materials for the production of consumer goods. The board came to exercise central control over the allocation of raw materials and production.

With war's end, central planning and control gave way to a transition back to a consumer-oriented domestic economy, initially involving canceling defense contracts and compensating firms for foregone income. In addition, the federal government faced the daunting task of disposing of the large surplus of raw materials and equipment that had accumulated toward the end of the U.S. military campaign. With these challenges met, and with the regulatory inheritance of the Progressive Era and the New Deal firmly in place, policy makers and organized interests turned their attention to providing the infrastructure and services necessary to accommodate the population explosion that took place following the war. Waves of baby boomers filled schools, triggered a construction boom, and increasingly placed demands on America's transportation systems. Regulation took a respite as Americans focused on education, jobs, and family life—that is, until rising social activism in the 1960s reenergized and redirected regulatory fervor.

The New Social Regulation

While the so-called old regulation tends to focus on economic relationships, particularly those pertaining to markets, rates, and the obligation to serve, the new social regulation shifts the focus to the *conditions* under which goods and services are produced and the physical characteristics of the products and the by-products produced.[10] Whereas economic regulation typically affects one industry (such as communications or commercial transportation) at a time, social regulation spreads its effects broadly across the economy and society. Social regulation, like economic regulation, responds to changes taking place in society and the extent to which policy makers see them as problematic and meriting public action.

The environmental movement, which gained strength in the 1960s, is a case in point. It raised the specter of growing environmental risks and mobilized citizen activism that found expression through the rise of environmental interest groups. The publication in 1962 of Rachel Carson's *Silent Spring* provided dramatic testimony of how agricultural pesticides find their way into the air, water, crops, animals, and humans. Beyond their effects, she argued that government and the scientific community did not seem to care much about the consequences of environmental pollution for public health. The resulting highly publicized counterattack from the chemical industry sparked the beginnings of a national debate.

Other notable events focused the public's attention. The Cuyahoga River, running through Cleveland, Ohio, became so polluted with combustible wastes that it caught on fire in 1969, creating a spectacular image on prime-time national television and on the front pages of newspapers throughout the country. Accounts of polluted lakes and other waterways, hazardous dump sites, and worsening air pollution in metropolitan areas increasingly captured the attention of the media and the public at large. Americans apparently came to realize that the environment could not be taken for granted; benign neglect would not solve what had popularly come to be recognized as real and growing problems. The throngs who turned out across the country for the first Earth Day, in April 1970, gave vivid testimony to the fact that environmental quality had taken its place on America's policy agenda.

Growing public attention to the risks of environmental pollution both sensitized and motivated fledgling consumer interests to explore and raise the risks of unsafe consumer products. Books such as *Unsafe at Any Speed* became popular best sellers, and Ralph Nader became the recognized leader of the consumer protection movement in America. Its activism followed a wide array of consumer interests, including automobile and consumer product safety, food and drug safety, deceptive advertising, and financial dealings.

About the same time, organized labor took an increasing interest in workplace safety, concentrating on measures to prevent job-related injury and illness. It used a 1968 mine disaster in West Virginia, which killed seventy-eight miners and received prime-time media attention, to symbolize the workers' plight. Public interest groups played a negligible role in the ensuing debate. In reality, fortuitous political events paved the way for legislative attention. President Richard Nixon took interest in identifying himself with a governmental response, seeing it as a way of wooing blue-collar workers and thereby broadening his political appeal.[11]

Of the three areas, the national public debate became most intense over environmental protection and consumer product safety. Workplace safety never received the same amount of media attention as that devoted to the other two areas. Its debate was largely confined within Washington circles—among the executive branch, Congress, and organized labor and business associations. Each, however, percolated during the late 1960s, leading to legislation enacted in the early 1970s during the Nixon administration. That legislation together created three new regulatory authorities: the Environmental Protection Agency (EPA) in 1970; the Occupational Safety and Health Administration (OSHA), also in 1970; and the Consumer Product Safety Commission (CPSC) in 1972. Congress established the EPA within the executive branch, giving the president the power to appoint its administrator, subject to Senate confirmation, and it created OSHA as an agency within the Department of Labor. In contrast, Congress established the CPSC as an independent regulatory agency, one of the few independent commissions created after the New Deal. Of the three, the EPA has engendered the greatest controversy and has had the widest impact, yet has been able to expand its regulatory reach while enjoying sustained public support, even as policy makers advanced deregulation in other policy areas. It merits closer scrutiny.

The Environmental Protection Agency and Environmental Protection: The Embodiment of Social Regulation[12]

Prior to Congress's 1970 passage of the Environmental Protection Act, which created the EPA, and subsequent enabling legislation directed at air and water pollution control, the federal government played only a limited role in environmental protection. The scant authority that existed was spread among several executive branch agencies, including the Departments of Health, Education, and Welfare (HEW), of the Interior, and of Agriculture. What little environmental regulation that existed fell to the states, selectively assisted by local governments. But that fact should not be interpreted to mean that the United States has been free of environmental problems.

In its formative years, the vast expanse of the western frontier held the promise of unbounded resources that settlers could put to their use. The sheer quantity of land and unspoiled natural resources accommodated the needs of the early pioneers, seemingly without adverse effects on those resources. At the same time, the industrial revolution of the late nineteenth and early twentieth centuries and rising urban populations in the Midwest and Northeast offered early evidence of a tension between economic growth and environmental quality. Extensive coal burning blackened the skies of many an industrial city by the early twentieth century. Outbreaks of contaminated drinking water prompted cities to regulate water systems. In rural areas, loggers cleared large tracks of virgin lands, spurring Congress to create national forests and a national park system for protection. State legislatures, urged on by Progressive or Populist governors, enacted parallel legislation that created state forests and wildlife preserves. Despite these actions, government's role, at all levels, remained limited.

Before Congress greatly strengthened the federal government's environmental regulatory hand in the early 1970s, its early role in water pollution control was restricted to providing grants and technical assistance to local governments for the construction of sewage treatment plants. And although Congress in the mid-1960s required states to establish their own water quality standards and draft plans to implement them, the states were slow in responding. Without minimum national standards, many states were hesitant to take any action that might give nonresponsive states a competitive advantage in keeping and attracting industrial development.

The federal government was somewhat more active in addressing air pollution. Following California's lead, Congress focused its attention on the automobile as a major source of air pollution in urban areas. It authorized HEW to set emission standards for all automobiles sold in the United States, and HEW, in turn, applied California's already-existing standards nationally. Beyond the control of emissions, President Johnson in 1967 urged the adoption of national air quality standards, a tougher position than he had taken on water quality. Congress approved only a study of the matter and passed the legislative ball to the states, requiring them to adopt their own air quality standards, paralleling national legislative action on water quality. Not surprisingly, the vast majority of states once again put off compliance.[13]

The year 1970 marked a significant point of departure in federal environmental policy making. Three reasons can be offered for the policy breakthrough. The first centers on the growing media attention given to environmental pollution and such happenings as the Cuyahoga River fire and the national Earth Day demonstrations mentioned earlier. The second points to the heightened activity of environmental interest groups and their influence on the public debate. Two reports from Ralph Nader's group, entitled *Vanishing Air* and *Water Wasteland*, presented highly critical assessments of what he viewed as federal neglect of serious air and water pollution problems, adding fuel to the proverbial fire. The former publication pointed the finger of blame at Maine Senator Edmund Muskie, a prominent Democratic leader in the Senate, who refused to throw his support behind national air quality standards. The third reason touches on pure political advantage. President Nixon's 1970 State of the Union address devoted considerable attention to the environment, prompting observers to view his emphasis as a direct challenge to Muskie, who was then the front-runner for the Democratic presidential nomination in 1972. Nixon's stance levered Muskie to reverse his position on national standards.[14]

Congress's passage of the 1970 Environmental Protection Act created the regulatory infrastructure to place the federal government firmly in the lead on environmental protection nationally. Yet the newly created EPA still lacked the policy tools it needed to protect the quality of America's air and water. Without additional enabling legislation, the federal government's role would continue to be one of monitoring pollution; assisting the states in defining their own policies, priorities, and standards; and providing limited financial assistance to support state efforts.

Subsequent companion legislation gave the EPA the authority it needed to oversee the cleanup of the nation's air and water. Congress first addressed air pollution. The Clean Air Act of 1970 served as the legal foundation for the national government's partial preemption of what had been a role essentially left to the states. It contained four major provisions. First, Congress charged the EPA with setting air quality standards that would apply nationwide. No longer would the states be allowed to determine what constitutes acceptable levels of air pollution within their borders. After all, polluted air can be blown across state lines, theoretically from states possessing lax standards to adjoining states having much tougher ones. In addition, given interstate competition over economic development, some states might elect to gain a competitive advantage over others by limiting their environmental regulations. Under the legislation, states could only elect to establish tougher standards for major pollutants and could not loosen the minimum federal standards. Second, the act required the states to prepare implementation plans for the EPA's approval, showing what efforts would be made to bring a state's air quality into compliance. Third, it required automobile manufacturers to reduce emissions by 90 percent for all 1975 models, even though the technology to do so was not available at the time, or face a fine of $10,000 per vehicle. Fourth, it charged the EPA with establishing emission standards for electric power plants. Procedurally, the act also importantly gave citizens the right to sue polluters (for not complying with the standards) and the EPA (for not enforcing them).

Under the federal government's oversight, this landmark legislation delegated to the states the responsibility to monitor compliance and enforce it. The states, in turn, could carry out those functions directly or delegate the day-to-day tasks to local government agencies. In the latter case, that responsibility frequently resides at the county level or with metropolitan air quality districts that cut across county lines. But if states or local governments failed to carry out their delegated responsibilities properly, EPA personnel could step in and take over the job of monitoring and enforcing compliance.

In 1977 Congress amended the Clean Air Act, ironically both to expand the EPA's authority and to extend compliance deadlines. Under the 1977 amendments, states were required to submit plans for controlling industrial pollution, including illustrations of how emissions from new industrial sources in noncomplying areas would be offset by corresponding reductions from existing sources. The legislation also required states to use permits to control the addition of new fixed-pollution sources, and it mandated that smokestack scrubbers be installed on all coal-burning power plants. The amendments also required states to establish vehicle emission testing programs in counties whose air failed to meet federal air quality standards. For states not in compliance, the federal law authorized the EPA to withhold federal grants-in-aid for highways and sewage treatment (an example of the use of sanctions that cross over to other policy areas), as well as to prohibit states from issuing permits that would increase aggregate air pollution from industrial sources. At the same time, the amendments extended the heretofore unmet deadline for automakers to comply with the strict federally prescribed auto emission standards, in recognition that significant progress had been made, although the mandated 90 percent reduction had not been fully attained on schedule.

Government's strengthened regulatory role over air pollution during the 1970s made a difference in improving America's air quality. Despite economic growth and an expanding population, the President's Council on Environmental Quality found that the five major air pollution emissions (particulates, sulfur oxides, nitrogen oxides, hydrocarbons, and carbon monoxide) declined by 21 percent between 1970 and 1980.[15] Days in which the air was determined to be unhealthy declined by about one-third in forty metropolitan areas between 1974 and 1980. Nonetheless, air pollution remained a serious national problem: seven major cites still averaged more than 100 unhealthy days a year from 1978 to 1980.[16]

Water pollution regulation followed a similar path. Again following President Nixon's lead, Congress passed enabling legislation that greatly increased the EPA's regulatory authority over water quality. The Water Pollution Control Act of 1972, commonly referred to as the Clean Water Act, set minimum national standards, industry by industry, for the release of point-source pollution. It also addressed the problem of non-point-source pollution, such as that caused by fertilizer or agricultural waste runoff into groundwater, rivers, lakes, and other waterways, although Congress stopped short of setting national standards. Instead, it authorized funds for state and local planning bodies to analyze the extent of non-point-source pollution and develop plans to address the identified problems. Without any accompanying federal mandate, little came of the effort.

Subsequent national water quality legislation extended the federal government's reach. The Safe Drinking Water Act of 1974 directed the EPA to promulgate maximum allowable levels of different chemicals and bacteriological pollutants in local water systems. Subsequently, the 1977 amendments to the Clean Water Act authorized additional federal aid for sewage treatment plant construction and, as we have seen with air quality policy, extended deadlines for industries to comply with the point-source standards set in 1972.

Compared with the documented improvement found in air quality, the picture appears to be less clear for water quality. The more than $30 billion in federal sewage grants helped to give communities the resources necessary to treat raw sewage before it is discharged into public waterways, but most U.S. cities still did not have adequate secondary sewage treatment facilities by 1980.[17]

Adequate data do not exist to allow any definitive conclusion about whether America's rivers, streams, and lakes were cleaner in 1980 than in 1970, although Lakes Erie and Ontario showed well-publicized signs of rejuvenation. Conventional wisdom is that water quality at least did not deteriorate during the 1970s, despite population and industrial growth, and that it probably improved somewhat.[18]

President Jimmy Carter, toward the end of his administration and prior to his defeat in November 1980, vowed to continue to move forward in protecting the environment and extending the progress that had already been made—progress, he noted, "for which we are being repaid many times over."[19] His successor, Ronald Reagan, failed to share these sentiments. Instead, he questioned whether America's investment in environmental regulation and pollution control could meet the scrutiny of cost-benefit analysis. He also challenged the EPA's record on ideological grounds, seeing it as an example of overextended big government. Holding up the ideals of private enterprise and the free market, Reagan focused on the costs to the private sector of complying with what he viewed as the burgeoning environmental regulation of the 1970s. He promised to reverse what he saw as overregulation.[20]

Symbolizing the administration's altered policy course, President Reagan appointed Anne Gorsuch (later Burford) as administrator of the EPA. Gorsuch, a corporate attorney whose clients included many industries hostile to the EPA's expanded environmental role, came into office clearly sympathetic to industry's perspective on regulation. Several other top appointees came from the very industries that the EPA regulates. Kathleen Bennett, a lobbyist for the American Paper Institute, became assistant administrator for air, noise, and radiation; Robert Perry, a ranking attorney with the Exxon Corporation, became general counsel; and Rita Lavelle, a public relations officer for Aerojet-General, became assistant administrator for hazardous and toxic wastes.[21]

Gorsuch kept many agency positions vacant and used Reagan-initiated budget cuts to eliminate still others. Total employment at the EPA dropped from 14,269 at the beginning of 1981 to 11,474 by November 1982. The headquarters staff in Washington dropped from 4,700 to 2,500.[22] These reductions took a significant bite out of the agency's ability to monitor and enforce compliance with environmental protection legislation. In Gorsuch's first year in office, the number of lawsuits filed by the EPA against the biggest polluters fell from 250 to 78.[23]

Mounting congressional opposition, particularly among Democrats, spurred on by highly mobilized environmental interest groups, forced Gorsuch to resign in 1984, but not until Congress took the extraordinary step of citing her for contempt. The resignations of other initial Reagan appointees soon followed. Gorsuch's replacement, the highly regarded William Ruckelshaus, who had previously served as EPA administrator and who enjoyed bipartisan support in Congress, ushered in a period of restored stability to the EPA, along with renewed enforcement activity.

In the aftermath of rocky relations with Congress during his first term and faced with rising popular support for environmental protection, Reagan and his Office of Management and Budget (OMB) eased their hostile forays against environmental regulation. Yet that softened stance did not keep President Reagan in 1986 from vetoing a congressionally approved revision of the Clean Water Act. In response, Congress overrode his veto, drawing on the sizable support of Republicans in both chambers. Importantly, the 1987 amendments added the requirement that the states develop EPA-approved plans for controlling pollution from non-point sources. Toward that end, Congress required municipalities to regulate storm water runoff in the same way they regulate the discharge of polluted water from industrial plants.

George H.W. Bush, Reagan's presidential successor, campaigned in support of the environment. Once elected, he proclaimed himself to be the "environmental president," separating himself and his administration from the policy stance of his predecessor. As a gesture of his commitment, Bush appointed William Reilly, a former president of a major environmental interest group, the Conservation Foundation, to head the EPA. The real test of Bush's commitment to the environment would come from deliberations with Congress over amending the Clean Air Act, which had last been modified in 1977—a task put off during the Reagan years.

The product of presidential-congressional negotiations, the Clean Air Act of 1990 attempted to create a balanced approach aimed at making continued progress in cleaning up the air. Nonattainment areas and mobile-source pollution were singled out for attention. The amendments gave states time limits within which to bring the areas into compliance with federal standards, ranging from three to twenty years for ozone and from five to ten years for carbon monoxide. They also placed controls on a wider range of emission sources than ever before, including gasoline stations, body shops, paint manufacturers, industrial-sized bakeries, and many other enterprises. Enhanced controls on mobile sources of pollution required conversion to oxygenated fuels in areas not complying with carbon monoxide standards, affecting areas in which one-third of the nation's population resides.

The 1990 amendments also toughened the automobile inspection and maintenance requirements included in the 1977 amendments, requiring more sophisticated testing methods for those metropolitan areas most out of compliance with federal standards for ozone emissions. The enhanced test measures auto emissions during both acceleration and deceleration and tests the effectiveness of the governing electronic sensors and controls found in newer cars.

Reflecting the Bush administration's initiative and its influence at the apex of Bush's popularity, the 1990 legislation is notable for departing, in part, from the traditional approach to environmental regulation. Previous legislation relied on a "command and control" approach, built on the concepts of standards and enforcement. Congress established the goals, the EPA developed standards, and the states developed plans to apply and enforce them. Threatened sanctions or legal action by the EPA often won compliance, but they also kicked off what was commonly a protracted series of negotiations and moves and countermoves that resulted in compromise, frequently culminating in the EPA's conditional approval of state plans. Attention then moved to the steps that state and local governments, as their agents, might take to remove the conditions, commonly precipitating another wave of negotiations.[24]

The traditional regulatory approach relied on technology-forcing standards tied to permit granting, which led industries to install smokestack scrubbers, filters, and other equipment to reduce emissions. A new approach introduced *market-based incentives* into air pollution regulation, aimed at reducing components of urban smog and sulfur dioxide emissions that create acid rain. Although the EPA continued to set overall emission caps, it permitted states to develop plans that allowed regulated industries to buy and sell **emission credits**. The system works like this: as long as the aggregate emission ceiling for an area is not penetrated, a firm could increase its emissions beyond what it would be allowed if other industries in a nonattainment area reduced their emissions below target levels, in effect leaving room for the first firm to pollute more than it would otherwise be allowed. But what incentives exist for firms to reduce their emissions even more than required by the EPA?

Based on the market principle of self-interested behavior, the 1990 act provided an incentive for firms to do more than required, and that incentive is economic return. By adopting technology that reduces pollutants more than required, firms produce "excess pollution credits" that can be sold to other industries faced with reducing their own emissions. Rather than incurring the capital expense required to come into compliance, these other industries can elect to buy some or all of the excess credits—a proposition that might appear to be a good short-run business deal for the company doing the buying. Thus, as the rationale goes, the overall ceiling on emissions is not broken, and the individual firms doing the trading are acting in what they believe to be their corporate self-interest. Experience already suggests that electric utilities, which emit about 70 percent of the sulfur dioxide pollution in the United States, will be the major players in emission credit trading. Across the nation, trading in emission credits has been most active in California and in the Northeast.

As President Clinton began his second term in office, the EPA further toughened its air quality standards. The 1990 Clean Air Act requires the EPA to review air quality standards every five years to ensure that they adequately protect the public health. In November 1996 the EPA proposed new, more restrictive standards for ozone and particulate matter. After a series of hearings, the EPA announced the final version of the new standards on July 16, 1997, amid opponents' efforts to get Congress to pass a bill blocking their implementation. Industry officials, aligned with the National League of Cities and the National Association of Counties, led the opposition. Facing a certain presidential veto, Congress demurred.

Under the new regulations, the ozone standard changed from 0.12 parts per million measured over one hour to 0.08 parts per million measured over eight hours. For particulate matter, particles as small as 2.5 microns in diameter would be regulated, compared to the previous standard of 10 microns.

The regulations gave states until 2010 to bring noncomplying metropolitan areas into compliance. Opponents questioned whether the incremental health benefits justify enterprises' costs of compliance, and both opponents and supporters of the toughened standards have debated not only the assumptions underlying projections of costs and benefits but the quality of the supporting science as well.[25]

In a second wave of initiatives to reduce air pollution, President Clinton announced new regulations on May 1, 1999, subjecting medium-duty passenger vehicles (those weighing between 8,500 and 10,000 pounds) to the same tailpipe emission standards that apply to light-duty passenger vehicles (those weighing up to 8,500 pounds). This change picked up the rapidly growing number of large sport utility vehicles (SUVs), vans, and trucks. These standards, commonly referred to as Tier 2, took effect beginning in 2004, and states are expected to be fully in compliance by 2010. In a companion action, the Clinton administration also announced regulations to reduce the sulfur content of gasoline by an average of 90 percent upon full implementation by 2010.[26]

On May 17, 2000, President Clinton announced his administration's third major regulatory initiative to reduce air pollution even further, this time striking at the sulfur content of diesel fuel, reducing it by 97 percent. The EPA projects that when fully implemented in 2010, the new regulations will reduce smog-causing nitrogen oxides from buses and heavy trucks by 95 percent. It also reduces bus- and truck-emitted particulate matter by 90 percent. Such a dramatic reduction also produces a tandem benefit, allowing buses and heavy trucks to use pollution-control devices for the first time—devices that would not have worked without a major reduction in the sulfur content of diesel fuel.[27]

The George W. Bush administration proposed new legislation in July 2002 that would greatly expand the system of market-based pollution credits introduced in 1990 during his father's administration. The legislative initiative, called Clear Skies, would place higher caps on nitrogen oxides, starting in 2008, and on sulfur dioxide, starting in 2010. It would also place a new cap for the first time on mercury emissions, also starting in 2010. Under the proposal, industries could buy or trade credits across the three pollutants. For example, an industry able to reduce its emissions below the cap for sulfur dioxide could sell its excess emissions credits to another firm that fails to bring its nitrogen oxides emissions under the allowable level. The EPA projects that the legislation would cut sulfur dioxide emissions by 73 percent, from 11 million tons in 2002 to 4.5 million tons in 2010. The EPA also projects reductions of 67 percent for nitrogen oxides and 69 percent for mercury over the same period.[28]

The Bush proposal faced considerable opposition in Congress, and its prospects for passage were dealt a near-death blow by the Senate in 2005. Opponents were able to bottle up the Clear Skies bill in the Senate Environment and Public Works Committee. Critics argued for tighter caps and complained that the Bush administration's initiative drew out deadlines for compliance too far. They also objected to a related provision in the legislation that would have rolled back a Clean Air Act mandate that older plants that upgrade or add equipment to increase output must also modernize their pollution controls. The Bush administration countered that its recommended caps and credit trading would still reduce aggregate emissions.[29]

Critics of the Bush administration's environmental record were quick to portray the legislation as part of a pattern of efforts to weaken environmental protection and favoring the interests of industry. Using EPA data, the National Resources Defense Council pointed out that during the first three years of Bush's presidency, the EPA's citations for pollution violations were down by 57 percent compared to the last three years of the Clinton administration, and lawsuits filed by the EPA against companies violating federal environmental laws declined by three-fourths over the same years compared.[30]

Yet, in a move that elicited the support of environmentalists, the EPA in December 2005 promulgated regulations to strengthen the existing 2.5-micron standard for particulate matter, by cutting almost in half the allowable concentration in the air, averaged over twenty-four-hour periods. The EPA estimates that the tougher standard, when phased in through 2009, will increase the number of nonattaining counties from 208 to at least 283.[31]

Environmental protection has proved to be an area of enduring popular public support. Public support has been the counterbalance against efforts to reverse the expansionary course of environmental regulation. It mitigated attempts by the Reagan administration to weaken the EPA's rule-making and enforcement roles, and it served as a trump card in Bill Clinton's struggles with Congress over national policy and budgetary priorities. The expansion of environmental regulation, despite a slowdown of enforcement during the George W. Bush administration, stands in contrast to the wave of deregulation that swept through some areas of government regulation in the late 1970s and continued to the turn of the century.

Deregulation

Deregulation is the reduction or elimination of government-imposed restrictions. When applied to business, deregulation seeks to enhance competition and increase market efficiency. It may also be aimed at reducing the prospect of agency capture, in which the regulated interests greatly influence regulatory policy and its application toward benefiting themselves economically. In doing so, they may attempt to use government regulation to "fence themselves in" and keep prospective competitors out.

Early Economic Deregulation

Well before presidential candidate Ronald Reagan campaigned successfully on an agenda that called for lower taxes, reduced domestic spending, and a retrenchment in government regulation, progress had already been made in reducing economic regulation. Deregulation of commercial transportation that occurred during the late years of the Carter administration set the stage for a host of deregulatory initiatives that followed in the 1980s and 1990s.[32]

Airline deregulation started the ball rolling. Prior to deregulation, the Civil Aeronautics Board (CAB) regulated five central aspects of interstate commercial airline operations: entry; routes; exit, or route abandonment; fares; and airline mergers. The CAB's guiding principle seemed to be ensuring the stability of the airline industry and the service it provides. Regulation insulated airlines from competition with each other, as well as from would-be new entrants. It also protected the jobs of airline employees and set up a structure that permitted wage demands from organized labor to be readily built into the approved rates. It should not be surprising, therefore, that both the established airline industry and its employee unions opposed deregulation.

The impetus for deregulation came from within the regulatory agency itself, although increasing pressure from consumer groups for expanded and cheaper airline service encouraged the CAB's inclinations. Both the CAB regulators and consumer advocates were influenced by entrepreneurial experiments taking place in Texas and California in *intrastate* commercial air transportation. CAB's authority was limited to interstate operations; it did not apply to intrastate air transportation. Thus absent state regulation, new entrants could enter and compete for service between a state's major metropolitan areas. And that is what the new maverick airline, Southwest Airlines, did in Texas. Operating smaller, more economical aircraft and offering no-frills service, Southwest charged lower fares than could the regulated carriers. It also frequently flew into smaller, secondary airports located closer to city centers, making its flights highly accessible to intrastate commuters. Another carrier, Pacific Southwest Airlines, followed suit in California. Although the state of California regulated fares for intrastate flights, they were based on the lowest-cost carrier, not the average cost followed by the CAB, so Pacific Southwest enjoyed a price advantage over the interstate carriers. Both airlines quickly proved popular with the public and expanded their passenger loads. They became exemplars for consumer groups of what greater competition could mean for the airline passenger.

In 1975, after John Robson became chairman, the CAB allowed limited experimentation with discount fares and commissioned a thorough study of regulation and its effects. Although the study recognized the element of service equity that regulation ensured, in balance its tone was critical, reflecting the resulting operational inefficiencies and high costs to consumers. The new chairman, Alfred Kahn, became a champion of deregulation within the Carter administration, and he had little difficulty winning the support of the efficiency-oriented, engineering-educated president. With the administration's active support, Congress passed the Airline Deregulation Act of 1978 (the same year Congress also partly deregulated interstate wholesale sales of natural gas). The act allowed the CAB to give up all control of routes and fares, leaving fare setting to competition in the marketplace, and to grant entry to any "fit, willing, and able" applicant. Concerning route abandonment, the legislation established a subsidy program to make it financially worthwhile during a transition period for a certified carrier to continue to provide service to those smaller communities previously served under regulation. Thereafter, the market would determine whether airlines would choose to continue service. Left with nothing significant to regulate, the CAB ceased to exist after 1984.

Following airline deregulation, the Carter administration and Congress turned their attention to interstate commercial rail and trucking transportation. American industry and agriculture relies heavily on railroads and trucks to carry their goods and products across the nation. Railroads offer shippers less flexibility than do trucks, but they also charge much lower rates for service. They carry approximately three-fourths of intercity freight ton miles but account for only about one-fourth of the costs of domestic freight transportation.[33] Railroads are best suited to shipments over long hauls and to points that have convenient access to the fixed rails. Heavy and bulky goods, such as agricultural machinery and construction materials, are most efficiently transported by rail. So are agricultural commodities and natural resources, such as coal and iron ore, that must travel long distances to market. Trucks tend to carry shipments over shorter distances than do the railroads, and their inherent flexibility and timeliness make them the mode of choice for most shippers—that is, unless shipping destinations, the types of goods carried, and delivery timelines are satisfactory enough to prompt shippers to take advantage of sizable cost savings that rail transportation affords.

As discussed earlier, rail transportation has been subject to government regulation far longer than has trucking. The ICC regulated rates, the abandonment of service, freight car utilization, and mergers. Compared to trucking, the entry of new competitors has not been a prominent focus of railroad regulation. The high fixed costs of operation and the railroad industry's declining share of interstate freight miles have combined to discourage prospective new entrants into the industry. In approving rates, the ICC used value-of-service pricing, pricing based on the value of goods being shipped rather than the costs of providing the service. High-value shipments of manufactured goods subsidized shipments of low-value goods, such as grain and other agricultural produce. In response, shippers of manufactured products turned to trucking as a better value. As railroads lost revenues to trucking, they petitioned the ICC to permit them to abandon service on unprofitable route segments—a practice to which the ICC was typically unsympathetic. Yet, at the same time, the pricing system continued to give the railroads a decided government-approved advantage over trucking for the transport of low-value goods.

The ICC also regulated freight car utilization. The nation's network of fixed track created interrailroad dependence, as freight often moves from an origin served by one railroad, through areas served by another, and out to a destination served by a third. Because it would be highly inefficient to transfer goods from one railroad's cars to another's, railroads rent the other's cars and hitch them to their own locomotives for their portion of the haul. The ICC regulated the interline rental rates that railroads can charge one another and set the rates low, creating another cross-subsidy of sorts. In effect, the larger railroads with the greatest geographic coverage and number of cars subsidized the smaller railroads having fewer cars. As would be expected, the subsidizers argued for a fairer, market rate of return on their loaned capital.

Drawing on the experience of airline deregulation, President Carter threw his support behind railroad deregulation. In October 1980 Congress passed the Staggers Rail Act, which opened the way for greater market pricing of service and allowed for the abandonment of unprofitable routes. In passing the legislation, Congress also addressed the market disadvantage that regulation had placed the railroads in vis-à-vis trucking. The act provided that where sufficient intermodal competition exists, the ICC could exempt a number of commodities from rate regulation altogether, allowing the market to set prices. Under the partial deregulation that occurred, the ICC allowed double-stack containers, which increased the railroads' operating efficiency and rendered them even more price competitive with trucking for the transport of manufactured goods.

Trucking deregulation followed a similar timeline as that of railroad deregulation. Compared to rail deregulation, the movement to trucking deregulation turned even more to rooting out the inefficiencies of the regulated system and reducing costs to shippers. In fact, the debate over trucking deregulation more closely resembled the debate over commercial airline deregulation than that over railroad deregulation. As noted earlier, the ICC exercised many of the same regulatory functions as did the CAB, including entry, routes, exit, rates, and mergers. Its regulation of entry included controls not only on the ability of existing licensed carriers to compete in the industry itself but on their ability to transport goods other than those they were expressly authorized to carry. Once a motor carrier obtained the authority to transport a particular type of commodity—agricultural products, for example—it then had to secure the authority for specific routes. This combination of commodity and route authorization created a highly segmented system, often causing truckers to make empty backhauls because either they lacked the route authority to carry goods of whatever type back to their point of origin or they possessed the route authority but lacked the authority to carry a type of commodity that was otherwise available for transport. Thus entry and routes became central foci of the case to improve efficiency.

Based on the experience of airline deregulation, which included increased flight availability and price reduction for most consumers,[34] advocates of trucking deregulation assumed that freer entry and greater trucker flexibility in serving routes would improve the entire system's efficiency and result in lower costs to shippers. ICC regulators came to share this perspective toward the end of the decade. Unlike rail, with its high fixed costs and rigid route structure, which mitigated competition from within the industry (with the railroads worried much more about their ability to compete with another transportation mode, namely trucking), trucking offered few intrinsic obstacles to competition from within. In the absence of regulation, an enterprising entrepreneur need only acquire a truck and licensed drivers to begin competing on the basis of price and service quality. Compare that to the start-up costs in the railroad business of purchasing locomotives, rail cars, and track rights. It was this relative ease of entry that, in the first place, prompted the trucking industry in the early twentieth century to seek ICC regulation in an effort to restrain competition and ensure profitability.

Unlike the path to railroad deregulation, trucking deregulation got a boost from the courts. Under a 1977 decision that supported the complaint of an applicant denied entry by the ICC, the court ruled that the ICC could no longer consider whether existing carriers could provide the service sought by a new entrant. It could base its decision only on whether entry would serve a useful purpose and whether existing carriers would be harmed. Congress's enactment of the Motor Carrier Act of 1980 followed the judiciary's lead and opened up entry widely. Under the act, new entrants only had to show that the proposed service was useful and that they were fit, willing, and able service providers. The statutory basis of presumption shifted in favor of ICC approving the application. Competition ballooned as a result, and the rates charged shippers fell accordingly. The increased competition brought with it improved service. Where carriers used their newly found freedom to readily abandon unprofitable routes, greater freedom of entry brought in new carriers in many instances to serve abandoned routes.[35]

With deregulation, the ICC did not go out of business, as had the CAB. Yet its workforce declined by more than two-thirds in the ten years following enactment of the Motor Carrier Act of 1980.[36] Congress replaced it with the Surface Transportation Board in 1995.

The deregulation of commercial transportation embodied an idea whose time had come. The ingredients for policy change were present and reinforcing. Martha Derthick and Paul Quirk offer five reasons why deregulation of commercial airline and trucking became such a compelling force in commercial transportation policy making. They argue that (1) elite opinion converged in support of reform, cutting across political parties, ideological predispositions, and academic disciplines, (2) officeholders in positions of leadership advocated reform and took supportive initiatives, (3) the early pro-competitive initiatives of the regulatory commissions set the deregulatory agenda and precipitated the opposition of the regulated industries, which turned to Congress for protection—inviting Congress to take an institutional stand on the issue, (4) the combined weight of factors one to three influenced Congress to pass legislation in support of deregulation, and (5) the affected industries found themselves at a disadvantage in their efforts to poke holes in the widely supported idea of deregulation and to mobilize the support of opinion leaders and policy makers.[37]

The cases of commercial airline, railroad, and trucking deregulation also appear to fit John Kingdon's theoretical framework created to help us understand agenda setting and policy change.[38] These cases seem to be instances in which the independent streams of problem recognition, policy development, and political support came together to set the deregulatory agenda and coalesce political support for a preferred policy option that appeared to solve the problem as defined. Policy makers and policy entrepreneurs came together in defining the problem in airline and trucking regulation as one of economic inefficiency, whereas they viewed the problem in railroad regulation as primarily one of rate and service inequity, even though deregulation did allow the railroads to operate more efficiently through more flexible freight car utilization and expanded cooperative ventures with the trucking industry. The regulators themselves pursued a policy course that had been shaped by expert policy entrepreneurs who drew on the findings of empirical studies of the effects of regulation. That policy course found the support of presidents and congressional leaders who used the same standards of judgment as had the regulators and policy entrepreneurs in defining the problem and evaluating alternative courses of action to solve it as defined.

The deregulation of commercial transportation also illustrates the phenom-enon of policy learning at work. The debate over trucking and railroad deregu-lation was greatly influenced by the earlier debate over airline deregulation. It established the "givens"[39] of problem definition and the choice of policy instruments, facilitating their transfer from one related policy area to another. It also influenced the terms of future debates over deregulation, although an important new ingredient—technological change—came to affect problem definition and alternative possibilities in contemporary debates. Its effects were felt most in telecommunications deregulation and, to a lesser but still significant degree, in electric energy deregulation.

Telecommunications Deregulation

Congress's passage of the Telecommunications Act of 1996 represented the first major overhaul of federal telecommunications policy since the Communi-cations Act of 1934, which created the Federal Communications Commission and gave it the power to regulate long-distance telephone services and prices. The original act also waived federal antitrust laws, essentially sanctioning AT&T's hegemony in a highly noncompetitive market. The telecommuni-cations giant enjoyed an unchallenged monopoly position in long-distance service, was the exclusive provider of telephone equipment nationally, and provided more than two-thirds of local telephone service.[40] The burden fell on would-be competitors to demonstrate that their entry was both "necessary and desirable in the public interest," a criterion similar to that applied earlier to commercial transportation.[41] The company promised in return to run a widely accessible, technically advanced and reliable interconnected system. Non-AT&T local providers connected for a price to the Bell network for ac-cess to AT&T long-distance lines. This pattern held into the 1970s.

While AT&T controlled the line-based national telephone network, changes in technology enabled entrepreneurs to position themselves as prospective competitors. The development of microwave technology in the 1950s offered the potential to send high-quality voice transmission along microwave relay points. A new company, Microwave Communications, Inc. (MCI), petitioned the FCC in 1963 for the right to establish a microwave link between Chicago and St. Louis to service business users, arguing that the experiment would not harm the existing telephone network or users' ability to connect to it. The FCC granted its approval by a narrow four to three vote. The majority recognized that the relatively new technology held promise for expanded future use, and they saw the immediate limited application as a minuscule threat to AT&T's revenues.

After a successful but highly limited beginning, MCI wanted to expand its operations and connect its private-line business users to AT&T's local telephone switches. The FCC denied its 1978 request. MCI then successfully appealed the FCC's ruling to a federal appellate court, which ruled that the FCC had no compelling reason to deny connection.[42] The concept of competition was gaining a foothold in telecommunications decision making, which should not be surprising, given the times. Recall that 1978 was also the year in which Congress deregulated both commercial air service and interstate wholesale sales of natural gas.

Four years earlier, the increasingly competition-oriented Antitrust Division of the Justice Department filed suit in federal district court alleging that AT&T used its monopoly power to prevent manufacturers other than its wholly owned subsidiary, Western Electric, from competing to connect customer equipment to the AT&T-controlled network and that AT&T's entrenched position in long-distance service thwarted competition. But before the court could decide the case, the FCC decided to begin certifying competitors' equipment for use on the AT&T network. That decision, coupled with MCI's victory, prefaced the greater deregulation that was to come.[43] Neither case, however, derailed the suit, which picked up steam after the 1980 general election.

In 1980 AT&T asked to have the suit dismissed. The presiding judge, Harold Greene, refused the petition in a strongly worded statement that signaled his pro-competitive sympathies. With the handwriting on the wall, AT&T and the Justice Department settled the suit in January 1982. AT&T agreed to divest itself of its seven regional operating companies that provided networked local telephone service, but it would retain its long-distance services, Western Electric, and its Yellow Pages directory services. The divestiture decree also required that competing long-distance companies get the same connections to local networks as those afforded to AT&T.[44] Despite the agreement, telecommunications regulation changed little at the state level. States continued to regulate local telephone companies, including entry and rate setting.

At the federal level, the deregulation bandwagon continued to roll. In 1984 Congress deregulated the cable television industry, an action that would later be reversed in 1992, following steep increases in subscription fees charged to consumers. The Cable Communications Policy Act of 1984 expressly proscribed local telephone companies from offering cable television services, a market they were eager to enter. Local companies also chafed to get into the long-distance business, and cable companies wanted to offer local telephone service. The long-distance companies also wanted to provide local telephone service but worried that their entry into the local-service market would enable local companies to justify their desire to offer long distance. The growing appetite for interservice competition and the business prospects it offered loomed large in the public debate into the 1990s, but not much changed legislatively or on the regulatory front. It was not until 1995 that the FCC removed AT&T's dominant provider status and allowed it to compete freely in pricing its long-distance services.[45]

Technology continued to change, however. By the early to mid-1990s, advances in digital technologies, along with a greatly expanded fiber-optic communications highway that crisscrossed the nation, removed the remaining technical barriers to interservice competition. They permitted competitors to bypass local companies' connections, and they opened up the possibility of bundling services, including regular and cellular telephones, Internet access, and cable television.[46] The new digital-compression technology, developed in 1990 by researchers at General Instrument Corporation, provided the capability to transmit high-quality television pictures in digital form. In doing so, it also created the ability for the binary information flowing over cable television, telephones, and computers to be interchangeable. As Dick Oluffs puts it:

> Once a transmission is digitized, there is no principal difference, aside from volume of information, between a telephone call and a televised baseball game. If the conduit for the information is big enough, and the machines at both ends are capable of sending and receiving the information, the distinctions between cable, broadcast, and telephone companies disappear.[47]

Both regulators and the regulated interests appreciated full well that these technological developments brought down the technical walls that had divided telecommunications service providers and, with them, a justification for separate regulation of the different telecommunications services. Technically, cable operators could offer local telephone service, and local telephone companies could offer video programming and long-distance telephone services. Local telephone companies could provide communications and information services through Internet connections, and long-distance telephone companies could provide local telephone service. Broadcast television could sell its signals and programs over land-based cable and fiber-optic lines, in addition to over the airwaves. Without regulatory impediments, a single provider, such as a local phone company, could provide local and long-distance telephone service, cable television programming, and Internet connection.

Because these possibilities exist technically, the key issue then becomes the extent to which government will permit unbridled competition in a giant communications market. That question was answered preliminarily through the Telecommunications Act of 1996, which passed both chambers of Congress by lopsided margins (414–16 in the House and 91–5 in the Senate).

Congress set in motion a process that, when followed, would lead to significant deregulation of telecommunications. The act granted the regional Bells the right to offer long-distance services once the FCC determined that they had opened their markets to viable competition over local telephone service. It required local telephone companies to allow competitors to connect with their networks at any technically feasible point in order to complete calls, and it required that the connection be equal in quality to that which the local company provides itself. The act also set a course toward deregulation of cable television, eliminating price controls in April 1999 for more than basic service packages or earlier if local telephone companies entered the market and provided video programming to a comparable number of households. Price controls on basic service packages would remain in place until the competition requirement is met, even if that were to occur after March 31, 1999. To allow cable television competition by local phone companies, the law eliminated a ban on telephone companies' offering video services.[48]

The act gave the FCC power to preempt state or local regulatory efforts to inhibit competition. Yet it also charged the states with taking steps to ensure universal service at a reasonable cost. Congress's juxtaposition of market-based competition and universal access to service at a reasonable cost represents a compromise between those wanting full deregulation (the Republican leadership in Congress) and those committed to the principle of universal service (President Clinton and Democratic congressional leaders). The resulting partial preemption put a premium on interservice provider competition within a more integrated telecommunications system while guarding the public's right to local telephone service at a fair price.

In signing the Telecommunications Act of 1996, President Clinton praised it as a tool for advancing a telecommunications revolution led by technological innovation that chafed under "outdated laws, designed for a time when there was one phone company, three TV networks, and no such thing as a personal computer." Continuing, he remarked that "today, with the stroke of a pen, our laws will catch up with our future. We will help to create an open marketplace where competition and innovation can move as quick as light."[49]

The experience of the first four years following deregulation has shown that, contrary to President Clinton's optimism, competition in the telecommunications industry has not moved as fast as light. In fact, the record is at best mixed. The regional Bell companies were slow to provide new competitors with interconnections for local telephone service, prompting critics to conclude that the regional Bells prize holding on to their monopoly position more than they do the opportunity to compete in the already highly competitive long-distance market.[50] In fact, by the spring of 1999, other carriers had gained only 2.7 percent of the local telephone service market.[51]

In passing telecommunications regulatory reform, Congress not only hoped that requiring telephone companies to make their communications facilities available to competitors, in whole or in so-called unbundled elements, would broaden competition in the marketplace; it also saw facility sharing as an intermediate step toward facility expansion. Competitors would use facility sharing as a means of getting their feet wet in the business, later making capital investments to build their own capacity.

However, the way in which Congress structured the sharing obligation created a strong financial incentive for competitors to lease former monopoly providers' facilities. New entrants could interconnect with existing facilities at a wholesale price, and FCC regulations required that the interconnected service provided to their customers be equal in quality to that provided by the lessor to its own customers. The Telecommunications Act and the FCC regulations that followed from it biased providers' options against facility investment. The incumbent, former monopoly companies proved hesitant to expand facilities that would-be competitors could use at rates favorable to them, and new entrants had little incentive to invest in telecommunications facilities when they could tap into those of others on favorable terms.

Data show that investment by wire-line carriers declined from approximately $105 billion in 2000 to $43 billion just two years later—a 60 percent decline. As a percentage of revenues, the decline was steepest for the so-called competitive local-exchange carriers (those competing with incumbent, former monopoly carriers), falling from 54 percent of revenues in 2000 to about 10 percent in 2002, continuing an almost continuous decline since 1997.[52]

The expanding market demand for broadband service and the substantial costs entailed to meet it reinforced existing incentives. Telephone companies faced a dilemma. Because telecommunications deregulation did not require cable television companies to provide access to competitors, they enjoyed a distinct competitive advantage in meeting rising market demands for faster Internet connections, sharper video, and high-speed data transmission. The free-rider problem inhibiting investment, discussed earlier, dampened the enthusiasm of incumbent telephone companies to pour large resources into expanding digital subscriber lines (DSL); yet not to do so would all but surrender the market to cable operators.

The environment changed markedly in 2004, as the result of a January U.S. Supreme Court decision, followed by a March federal appeals court ruling. In the first case, *Verizon v. Trinko*,[53] the Supreme Court ruled that broadband providers cannot be forced to share new investments with competitors and that failing to do so is not a violation under the Sherman Antitrust Act. The D.C. Court of Appeals' ruling in the second case, *United States Telephone Association v. FCC*,[54] dealt a deathblow to the entire system of network sharing created by the 1996 act. In its decision, which the U.S. Department of Justice refused to appeal, the court ruled that the network-sharing requirements failed to achieve the legislation's objectives of expanding capacity and improving quality. As a result of the appeals court's ruling, the FCC rescinded its rules requiring facility sharing for competitors.[55] With the disincentives removed, the traditional monopoly telephone companies significantly increased investment in upgrading and expanding their DSL service.

The real competition in telecommunications, however, was to come from outside rather than from within the wire-line industry. Cable television remained a strong competitor for Internet access and high-speed data transmission. But cable also made inroads into voice communication, using voice-over Internet protocols (VoIP), and its prospects for increasing market share look promising. Wireless telecommunications offer another formidable competitor to wire-line providers, allowing customers to substitute cell phones for telephones, instead of adding them as a mobile option.

To preserve market share and hopefully capture an increasing share, telecommunications companies are positioning themselves for interservice competition. AT&T purchased Tele-Communications, Inc. (TCI), the United States' second largest cable provider, along with Media One, another large cable company. In another move, Quest acquired Continental Cablevision. Other recent combinations include Sprint and Nextel, Cingular and AT&T Wireless, SBC and AT&T, and Verizon and MCI.

Electricity Deregulation

Just as technological advances provided the means for expanded competition in telecommunications, they also opened the door to competition in the electric power industry. Advances in the generation and distribution of electric power have led the way. They enabled policy makers to question tenets underlying the traditional belief that electric power provision best took the form of a natural monopoly—given the need for large, high-cost plants, particularly coal-fired plants—that could produce power on an efficient and cost-effective economy of scale and maintain large reserves of emergency capacity. However, the introduction of advanced natural gas-turbine technology has allowed power producers to reach the same economies of scale in much smaller, lower-cost plants. In fact, a new innovation allows gas-turbine technology to reach even higher levels of efficiency than made possible by the traditional coal-fired plants. It involves combining two turbines so that the waste heat from the primary turbine is used in a second turbine.[56] Gas-turbine technologies have also been able to generate and store competitively priced energy in small quantities that can be used to complement other energy sources during peak demands. Yet it should be recognized that the efficiencies realized by these new technological innovations are dependent on the price of natural gas remaining roughly in its present position relative to other energy-generating sources.

Another restraint on competition that changing technology has diminished deals with optimum loading of the electricity grid. Service reliability is enhanced when the grid contains only as much power as will be used. Because of the technical nature of loading the grid, supporters of monopoly have argued that a single enterprise is best suited to manage grid loading and that additional players would only increase the chances of grid failure, leading to power outages. Technological advances have allowed for greater control of the electrons on the grid and have thereby reduced failure rates. That technology, called Flexible AC Transmission System (FACTS), allows for electronic rather than mechanical switching on the electricity grid, greatly increasing control of electrons and making single-enterprise management of demand placed on the grid far less significant in ensuring grid reliability.[57]

Although technological barriers to competition have been coming down, government regulation still limits competition over electric power provision. Change, however, is in the air. The proponents of deregulation have won significant victories at the state level, and the debate over federal deregulation is building nationally. In the current environment, the states, through public service commissions, are responsible for regulating investor-owned utilities, including universal-service requirements, retail rates, safety standards, and relations with customers. For municipal-owned utilities, local government councils establish service parameters and set retail rates. At the national level, the Federal Energy Regulatory Commission regulates the wholesale sale of electric power and its interstate transmission. Its powers extend to rate setting, as well as to service and safety standards.

Federal regulation dates back to 1935, when Congress passed two major pieces of legislation: the Federal Power Act, which created the Federal Power Commission (later renamed the Federal Energy Regulatory Commission) to regulate interstate electricity transmissions, and the Public Utility Holding Company Act (subsequently repealed as part of the Energy Policy Act of 2005, discussed shortly, which split up the handful of large holding companies operating across state lines that controlled most of America's electric-power generation.) The act also restricted the activities of the resulting enterprises to defined geographic areas. It was the latter action that solidified the vertical integration of the industry, by which those companies came to own the generating facilities, transmission lines, and distribution systems within their own exclusive service areas. State regulation, which preceded federal regulation and had its roots in the Progressive Era, regulated providers' virtual monopoly status and guaranteed them a cost-plus rate of return on their investment.

In addition to its regulatory role, the federal government became a direct provider of electricity in the 1930s. In 1933 Congress created the Tennessee Valley Authority (TVA) to provide electricity to much of Appalachia. Three years later Congress took another step to electrify rural America by establishing the Rural Electrification Administration (now known as the Rural Utilities Service) and charging it with providing subsidized loans and grants to rural electric cooperatives. Congress took both initiatives to help develop rural areas economically and widen access to electric power where investor-owned utilities were least likely to provide it. Those programs continue today, even though the rationale for their creation no longer seems to apply, given rural America's transformation since the New Deal.[58]

The patterns of regulation established in the 1930s remained largely intact until the 1990s, when two federal initiatives, influenced by technological change and the growing debate over telecommunications deregulation, spurred competition in the interstate wholesale electricity business. The first saw Congress take action when it passed the Energy Policy Act of 1992, which permitted electricity-generating facilities not sharing cost accounts with a parent utility to compete with one another and sell electricity in the wholesale market. The act also required utilities owning transmission lines to carry that power to electricity wholesalers and end-use retail customers (the latter as part of a state-mandated direct-access program) at nondiscriminatory, cost-based rates. The second action came four years later from the Federal Energy Regulatory Commission itself, when it mandated that transmission-owning utilities charge themselves for transmission service at the same rates they charge other parties under the 1992 act's terms.[59]

Following those inroads, the contemporary debate, both in the nation's capital and in the states, focused on whether competition among electricity providers should be broadened so that deregulated "freewheeling" of electricity over transmission lines could be extended to all utility customers. That could happen as a result of either state-by-state deregulation or federal statutory preemption. Regardless of the route, such deregulation would allow retail customers to choose their energy provider in much the same way they choose who provides their long-distance telephone service. Most observers expect that the resulting competition should lower the market price of electric power. Yet deregulation of retail utility service raises a number of thorny issues, including those of universal access to service at a fair price; potential cost and rate shifts from large industrial customers to small businesses and residential customers; reliability of service; and the recovery of "stranded costs"—that is, those costs tied to previous investments in power generation that do not contribute to competitive pricing.[60] Examples of stranded costs include investments in old-technology power plants, long-term fuel and power contracts, and the costs associated with decommissioning nuclear power plants. Whereas regulation allows utilities to build cost recovery into the rates they charge customers, competition puts utilities with high stranded costs at a decided disadvantage.

Since the Federal Energy Regulatory Commission's 1996 order, subsequent deregulatory initiatives have come from the states, not the federal government. Deregulation has been variously accomplished through legislation, public service commission rule making, or a combination of the two. As of February 2006, legislatures in twenty-two states, typically responding to gubernatorial initiatives, had approved legislation to deregulate or restructure the electric utility industry and pave the way for competition in retail sales.[61] Several states that approved deregulation instituted so-called transitional rate caps or freezes to control retail rates while the expected competition grew.

California's brand of restructuring deregulated energy generation and *wholesale* electricity pricing, allowing retail customers to choose their electricity provider, but continued to permit state regulators to set the rates that utilities could charge their retail customers. Faced with rising consumer demand and spot shortages (some of which were the result of wholesalers such as the Enron Corporation withholding supplies from the market) that pushed up unregulated wholesale prices, along with the utilities' operating losses resulting from their inability to increase regulated retail prices high enough to cover the costs of wholesale energy in the deregulated market, California suspended its restructuring. California's experience prompted five states—Arkansas, Montana, New Mexico, Nevada, and Oklahoma—to delay implementation of deregulation.

The early flurry of state activity divided congressional leaders over the desirability of federal deregulation of electric power. For those supporting federal legislative action, giving states the option to deregulate is not sufficient. Supporters argue that the federal government has an obligation to require all states to let their residents decide who will provide them with electricity and enjoy the savings that they expect competition to bring. Opponents worry that national deregulation would redistribute costs by drawing power away from states with low-cost electricity to more financially attractive markets in other states, thus raising the price of electricity for those who had previously benefited from lower prices. Opponents also worry that national deregulation would primarily benefit the largest electricity users, whose business competitors would covet most, and leave residential users with little rate relief or even with rate increases. They see residential users in rural areas to be most in jeopardy. Yet supporters counter that competitors have doggedly gone after households' business after deregulation of long-distance telephone service. They also argue that competition should benefit all users, even though the extent of that benefit may vary. In any event, supporters point to the expected aggregate cost savings nationally.

Before advancing preemptive federal deregulation, Congress appears to be willing to wait to see how many states elect to deregulate electric power on their own. States that have initiated deregulation by the time of this writing have been those with relatively high energy costs. Legislators in states where consumers are already enjoying low costs tend to be less than enthusiastic about deregulation. Although deregulation could lower costs further, it also is likely to draw power away from low-cost areas to higher-cost areas. The task of putting together a coalition in Congress large enough to pass preemptive federal deregulation will not be as easy as finding majority support for deregulation in a high-cost state.

The politics of electricity deregulation are also complicated by government's involvement in power production. Greater competition poses a threat to the small and less-efficient municipal power providers. If municipal power users switch to competitor-supplied power, the affected municipalities will suffer revenue losses. Those high-cost municipal providers that use comparatively high electric rates as a form of taxation will be most vulnerable. Congressional representatives whose districts include a high number of municipally owned power plants will feel the cross-pressures of their constituents' interests in the potentially lower electricity rates that competition can bring and the likely loss of business and tax revenues that competition can pose for their political colleagues who lead municipalities in their districts.

Rising Process Constraints on Regulation

This chapter has looked at regulation and deregulation along distinct substantive policy lines, exploring the rationale for government action; the political forces arrayed in support of, and in opposition to, government action; and the economic implications of government's authoritative choices. As has been apparent, government regulatory and deregulatory policy has taken different turns over time, and those turns have largely been a response to changing perceptions of what constitutes pressing public problems. But in addition to using regulation or deregulation to address problems along sectoral lines, policy makers have altered their perceptions over time about the desirability of regulation and deregulation as desirable tools of statecraft. Regulation won out for most of the twentieth century; both presidents and members of Congress viewed it, in balance, as promoting the public interest. Yet, as Jeffrey Cohen argues, until the 1970s policy makers rendered that judgment more on what they believed to be perceived problems and economic and political forces at work in the substantive policy areas under scrutiny than on normative grounds or any real sense of the macroeconomic implications of regulation.[62] That came to change in the 1970s, as regulations grew and extended further into areas of social policy and as the economy went into recession in mid-decade and suffered from stagflation (both high unemployment and high inflation) toward the decade's end.

Both Presidents Ford and Carter connected expanded regulation to America's economic ills and lent their support to deregulation as an appropriate policy response. President Reagan gave regulatory restraint an ideological wrapping, consistent with his call for reduced government penetration in society and the economy, striking a chord that resonated with America's liberal normative inheritance. For candidate and then president Reagan, the federal government needed to tax and regulate less—leaving more income in the hands of individuals to decide how to spend it and more room for the market to determine economic outcomes. That sentiment and the public's response to it made a strong impression on Reagan's presidential successors and the Congresses with which they dealt. Not only did it release a second wave of deregulation; it also engendered a string of presidential controls on new regulation. The presumption had shifted. Presidential controls placed the onus on government to justify its regulatory interventions and forced regulators to maneuver their proposals through executive screens and tests.

President Reagan set up the most formidable controls. In addition to creating the Task Force on Regulatory Relief and appointing Vice President George Bush as its chairman, Reagan issued two important executive orders that erected regulatory hurdles. The first, issued in 1981, required that a cost-benefit analysis accompany all proposed major regulations. It also charged the Office of Information and Regulatory Affairs (OIRA), which had been created in the OMB as a provision of the 1980 Paperwork Reduction Act, to review agency analysis, perform independent cost-benefit analysis when deemed needed, and screen out proposed regulations that failed to meet the standard of efficiency.

Early in his second term, Reagan raised the bar again, requiring that regulatory agencies disclose regulations being planned, not just those in the process of being advanced. The new order forced regulatory agencies to evaluate how consistent the planned regulations were with the president's policy agenda. On the basis of that review, the OIRA could prevent executive-branch agencies from promulgating regulations inconsistent with the president's program. President George H.W. Bush continued these practices.[63]

When President Clinton took office in 1993, he rescinded the order requiring cost-benefit analysis and replaced it with one of his own, Executive Order 12866. In doing so, Clinton took away the OMB's authority to detain proposed regulations that fail to meet the cost-benefit test. In its place, the new order required agencies to identify and evaluate alternative regulatory options, including comparing their costs and benefits, before advancing a regulatory proposal. However, a study of the OIRA's review of proposed regulations found that agencies widely ignored the requirement, either focusing only on the preferred alternative or failing to compare benefits to costs.[64] In response, the Clinton administration chose not to enforce the requirements stringently, giving agencies greater freedom to shape their case in support of regulation when it was consistent with the president's agenda. Republican congressional leaders threatened to make every effort to pass legislation that imposed a rigid cost-benefit test on the OMB, reining in the administration's freedom to apply that standard as it saw fit.[65]

President George W. Bush, early in his first term, affirmed his administration's intention to aggressively review proposed federal regulations. Along with the traditional foci on regulations' costs and benefits and their effect on state and local governments, the Bush administration added another: the effect on small business. Still another new requirement, however, generated the greatest controversy, and that involved the mandate that federal agencies commission external peer reviews of proposed regulations that are based on scientific research. Advanced as a means to ascertain the scientific soundness underlying regulation in areas such as public health and the environment, the new requirement has been branded by critics as a means to delay and sidetrack regulations following from legislation at odds with the administration's policy priorities. They worry that the White House will use the conflict-inducing procedural hurdle against prospective regulations that are closely spelled out by Congress in the legislation itself. They worry especially that it will be used as a tool to thwart congressional intent in such policy areas as climate change and environmental protection.[66]

Government and Social Provisioning

Writing in the late nineteenth century, at a time when waves of European immigrants swept across the United States seeking better lives, Horatio Alger extolled the opportunity offered by America. For Alger, the United States presented few barriers to upward mobility, in contrast to Europe's much more rigid social divisions. His popular accounts of boys from poor families who rose to social and financial heights widely captivated American readers. For Alger and his millions of readers, the United States offered unbridled opportunity, if only individuals worked hard to succeed and had a little luck along the way. Escaping feudalism, Americans grew up cherishing the ethos of individualism and equality. They embraced what Louis Hartz labeled America's liberal tradition[1]—a tradition whose roots were deeply planted in the philosophical soil of classical liberalism, as discussed in chapter 1.

That liberal tradition continues to shape Americans' attitudes and behavior. Individualism is deeply imprinted in America's political culture. Americans continue to prize personal responsibility and share optimism about their ability to succeed. This optimism, however, is based on personal initiative, not on active government intervention. Public opinion polls have consistently provided evidence in support of this conclusion, as was illustrated in chapter 1.

Comparative public opinion research shows Americans to be an outlier among nations in the emphasis they place on personal responsibility. When asked who should be responsible to provide food, clothes, and housing, 82 percent of American respondents put that responsibility entirely on the individual, compared to 57 percent of Europeans, who are more willing to assign a significant role to government.[2] In response to the question of whether government should provide jobs to all who need them, three-quarters of the Europeans queried responded affirmatively, compared to 39 percent of the Americans.[3]

What, specifically, are Americans' views of poverty and the poor? Public opinion surveys indicate that a majority consistently sees poverty as a significant problem in American society.[4] Yet Americans are divided on the issue of what causes poverty. As part of an ongoing study of poverty in America, poll data suggest that about half of the public believes that the poor are not doing enough to keep themselves out of poverty, while the other half sees circumstances beyond the control of the poor as the culprit. More than two-thirds of Americans (69 percent) say there are jobs available for anyone willing to work, reflecting an underlying belief in the opportunity that the U.S. economy offers.[5] Nonetheless, a majority of Americans agree that government should do more to help the poor, and the percentage of respondents favoring increased government involvement has risen slightly since 1994, reaching 57 percent in 2004.[6] Both citizens and their policy makers, however, hold differing views over *how* government should best help the poor. At the center of that difference lies the tension between a perceived need to alleviate the effects of poverty, which degrade human dignity, and the values of opportunity, personal responsibility, and just deserts.

So, how then does this widely shared public sentiment influence how government uses public policy to respond to the needs of those who fall through the cracks of American capitalism: those who find themselves part of the long-term unemployed and have children to support; those who had good jobs but lost them when their jobs were outsourced overseas; those who are employed but whose earnings are insufficient to raise them out of poverty; those who lack the financial ability to secure housing in the marketplace; those who lack health insurance because their employer does not provide it or because they earn too much to qualify for Medicaid even though they fall under the poverty line? The generalized response is that Americans' faith in personal responsibility and earned deserts does indeed influence social policy in the United States.

Public policy makers in the United States rely far more on the private marketplace to provide employment, housing, and health care than do their European counterparts. While America's economy—which has grown considerably faster than the Euro area's over the past fifteen years—has made it easier for job seekers in the United States to find employment than has been the case in Europe, American public policy has made it harder for those unable to find work in the private sector to obtain adequate public financial assistance, publicly provided or subsidized housing, publicly financed health care, or government-created public service jobs. That generalization also holds for immigrants to the United States, who are afforded greater opportunity to obtain steady employment than are Europe's immigrants but who face greater obstacles to receive public assistance in the United States compared to immigrants in European nations.

Essential differences can also be seen in how the United States and European nations provide financial resources for retirees. While the United States has turned to private employers to carry a large share of the burden, European nations have looked more toward government. Government-provided retirement benefits are far more generous in the Euro area than in the United States. Government pensions in Europe pay on average 74 percent of *preretirement* earnings, whereas the U.S. Social Security program replaces 57 percent of low-income workers' *average* annual earnings and only 38 percent of high-income workers' *average* yearly earnings.[7]

Before we examine specific government programs to help the needy and later look at how the elderly are provided for in retirement, we should understand who is poor in America.

The Poor in America

Approximately one in eight Americans lives in poverty, as measured by the U.S. Census Bureau. Looking at children alone, the proportion rises to about one in six. Children are almost twice as likely as adults sixty-five years of age or older to be poor. In addition to age, race and ethnicity correlate with poverty. Although more whites than either African Americans or Hispanics are poor, African Americans and Hispanics are about three times more likely than whites to be poor. Regardless of race or ethnicity, female-headed households with children are over five times more likely than married-couple families to be poor, illustrating what has become the feminization of poverty. Still, families headed by African American and Hispanic women are almost twice again more likely than those headed by white women to be poor. Recent immigrants are nearly twice as likely as native-born Americans to be poor, yet that difference erodes over time.[8] In fact, after immigrants have been in the United States for twenty-five years or more, their average income parallels that of the native born.[9]

In 2005 there were 37 million poor people in the United States, about the same number as in 1959. During that forty-six-year period, however, the poverty rate (the percentage of persons in poverty) fell by 44 percent.[10] (See Figure 8.1.) As Figure 8.2 illustrates, the elderly realized the biggest gains among age groups. Considering race, while 18 percent of whites were poor in 1959, only 8 percent were in 2005.[11] The poverty rate declined even more steeply for African Americans. In 1959, 55 percent of African Americans were poor compared to 25 percent in 2005. Unfortunately, the Census Bureau did not begin recording poverty rates for Hispanics until 1972, making it impossible to extend the forty-six-year comparison to include them. Nevertheless, the data since 1972 show that the poverty rate for Hispanics has not declined as sharply as it has for African Americans. Although African Americans were more likely to be poor than were Hispanics in 1972 (33 percent to 23 percent), as they continued to be in 2005 (25 percent to 22 percent), the gap between them closed.[12]

Figure 8.1   **Number in Poverty and Poverty Rate, 1959–2005**

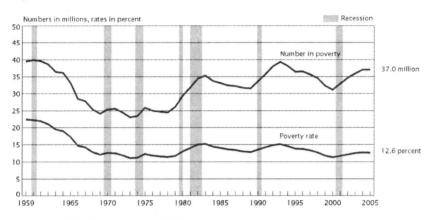

Source: U.S. Census Bureau, U.S. Department of Commerce, Current
Population Survey, 1960 to 2006 Annual Social and Economic Supplements.
Note: The data points are placed at the midpoints of the respective years.

Figure 8.2   **Poverty Rates by Age, 1959–2005**

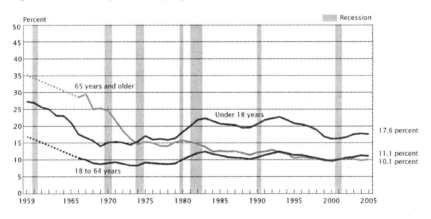

Source: U.S. Census Bureau, U.S. Department of Commerce, Current Population
Survey. 1960 to 2006 Annual Social and Economic Supplements.
Note: The data points are placed at the midpoints of the respective years. Data for
people 18 to 64 and 65 and older are not available from 1960 to 1965.

Irrespective of race, members of two-parent families fared best of all
in pulling themselves out of poverty. In 2005 only 5 percent of two-parent
families fell below the federal poverty standard compared to one in five in
1959.[13] The poverty rate for individuals living in female-headed households
also dropped, by 38 percent, over those years yet still stood at 29 percent in

2005—ten times that of two-parent families. The poverty rate was even higher for African American female-headed households in 2005, at 39 percent, but still represented a marked decline from a rate of 71 percent in 1959.[14]

It is one thing to get a sense of who is poor and how poverty rates have changed over time and quite another to put poverty in a personal perspective. Perhaps the most immediate way to do that is to equate poverty with money. We all know how much income we earn annually, and we know how far it goes in meeting our needs. Using guidelines developed by the Department of Health and Human Services to establish a base for determining the financial eligibility of needy individuals for federal assistance, a single person was considered poor in 2006 if his or her income fell at or below $9,800—that's a little more than $816 a month. A family of four with an income of $20,000, or about $1,666 a month, before taxes, would also be considered poor.[15] Given the cost of housing, food, and transportation, that income does not stretch very far. And as we shall see, the benefits provided by public assistance programs, both cash and in-kind support, fail to raise recipients out of poverty. Typically, such benefits fall considerably short.

Government Assistance

A distinction must be made in discussing government assistance. We typically associate government assistance with the redistribution of taxpayer revenues. Welfare payments come most readily to mind. General tax revenues support payments that go only to those individuals who meet a legally established means test. Almost everyone pays taxes to provide income assistance to a subset of the population that government officially determines to be needy. Welfare, therefore, constitutes public assistance. Yet not all programs that provide financial assistance to Americans take the form of public assistance, for which taxpayers foot the bill. Others are organized as social insurance programs, in which the recipients of financial support and/or their employers pay into a fund from which monies are drawn to cover the cost of benefits. General taxpayer support is not involved. Only individuals who have paid into the fund or on whose behalf employers have paid are eligible for benefits. Contributions support benefits.

Social insurance benefits go to workers (or to dependents in some cases after the worker's death) who have retired or become injured, disabled, or temporarily unemployed—*regardless of financial need.* Major social insurance programs include Social Security and its companion health-care program, Medicare; Unemployment Compensation; and Workers' Compensation. Social Security and Medicare are exclusively federal programs that rely on taxes paid by both workers and their employers to cover the cost of benefits on retirement. Unemployment Compensation is a joint federal-state program funded by taxes paid by employers, which provides cash benefits to workers during periods of temporary unemployment. Workers' Compensation is an exclusively state program providing income support and medical care to workers who have been injured or disabled on the job.

The distinctions between public assistance and social insurance programs are deeper than just the differences in their sources of funding and accounting. They affect how the public regards them. Whereas people equate public assistance with welfare, with a handout, they view social insurance programs as draws on prepaid accounts—accounts that were established and paid for through work. The popular perception is that benefits rightly belong to their recipients. These differences in public perception carry with them important social connotations that influence program content, conditions, and levels of financial and political support.

Public Assistance[16]

Public assistance programs, generally labeled as welfare, are aimed at society's needy, who must meet a means test to receive benefits. They consist of cash and in-kind assistance. Cash-assistance programs take two forms in the United States: assistance directed to families with dependent children, through the Temporary Assistance to Needy Families (TANF) program, and to the so-called categorically dependent—the needy elderly, blind, or disabled through the Supplemental Security Income (SSI) program. Unlike Social Security, categorical aid to the elderly is funded by general taxpayer revenue and is intended for those who have not worked enough to be eligible for Social Security or who are eligible but whose benefits fall below SSI standards. In that case, SSI supplements Social Security to bring monthly payments up to the SSI-guaranteed level. Major in-kind programs include health care, food stamps and other nutrition programs, and housing assistance. These will be covered after we discuss cash assistance.

Cash Assistance for Needy Families

Cash assistance for needy families has been synonymous with public welfare in the United States. Before the 1996 reform, the program bore the title Aid to Families with Dependent Children. Yet people most commonly referred to it by its acronym, AFDC. Its roots trace back to the New Deal, although Congress expanded the program in response to President Johnson's Great Society initiatives. With the 1996 reform, Congress changed its name to Temporary Assistance for Needy Families (TANF), symbolic of the program's reorientation from long-term dependency to temporary assistance leading to work.

The TANF program is the most recent and the most comprehensive of a series of efforts to reform public welfare in the United States. The new law gives states almost complete discretion to determine eligibility requirements and benefit levels. It places welfare-to-work performance requirements on the states and allows states to impose more restrictive work requirements on recipients than the federal government minimally requires. The federal legislation lets states decide how best to design programs that meet the federally imposed performance standards.

Most states had a head start in experimenting with welfare reform well before the new law took effect. The Family Support Act of 1988 allowed states to experiment with welfare reform but required them first to get approval of the federal Department of Health and Human Services. By the act's demise in August 1996, forty-three states had secured waivers from regulatory requirements.[17] Widespread state experimentation shifted substantial policy-making discretion from the federal government to the states, and advocates of even greater state administrative and programmatic discretion pointed to the large reduction of welfare caseloads that seemed to accompany state experimentation in support of their position. Caseloads indeed fell; that is not in question. Between 1993 and 1997, the number of persons receiving welfare fell by 28 percent, totaling almost 4 million recipients nationally. (See Figure 8.3.) What was disputed in this period of state experimentation was the extent to which welfare experimentation resulted in caseload decline. A report by the president's Council of Economic Advisers attributed about one-third of the decrease to state-initiated policy changes. The council attributed another 40 percent to national economic growth, which created 12 million new jobs over the period.[18] Nevertheless, buoyed by what they saw as the fruits of state experimentation, reformers pressed for giving states broad flexibility in using welfare funds, without the necessity of seeking waivers.

Republican congressional leaders led the campaign for devolution. Having gained control of both chambers of Congress in the 1994 election and drawing on the support of Republican governors whose states led the way in experimenting with welfare reform, Republican leaders successfully ushered a series of reform bills through Congress. President Clinton vetoed the first two, objecting to the first because it would have eliminated Medicaid as an entitlement program and to the second because it would have forced states to deny cash assistance to additional children born to welfare recipients and would have reduced benefits to some disabled children who receive SSI. But with those provisions removed in the GOP's third attempt and with the 1996 election shortly approaching, President Clinton, who promised as early as the 1992 presidential campaign to end welfare as we know it, finally signed the

Figure 8.3 **Welfare Caseloads, 1936–2005**

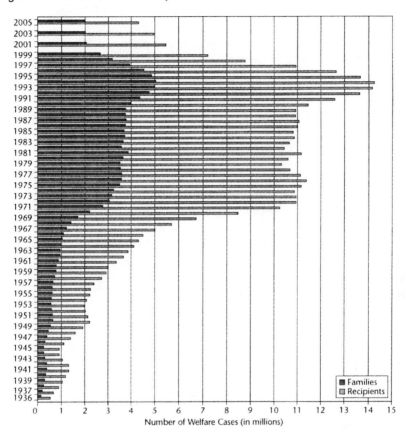

Number of Welfare Cases (in millions)

Source: Administration for Children and Families, U.S. Department of Health and Human Services.

reform legislation. Clinton called the occasion a historic opportunity to make welfare what it is meant to be: a second chance, not a way of life.[19]

In abolishing the AFDC program, Congress eliminated public assistance as a federal entitlement, ending its sixty-one-year-old guarantee of providing whatever amount of funding is necessary to pay benefits to all who meet eligibility requirements. In its place, Congress created a fixed-appropriation **block grant** to the states. The federal government's financial contribution became effectively capped. The states could elect to spend more if they wished, but the legislation allowed them to spend less than they had in the past. This is the case because, unlike the former AFDC program, TANF requires no state match of federal funding, requiring only that states spend at least 75 percent of what they spent on AFDC and related programs. In return, they still receive from the federal government about what they got under the AFDC program.

Welfare reform not only limited the federal government's financial exposure, it allowed state officials to reallocate state funds once spent on public assistance to other needs. The legislation also gave states the flexibility to transfer up to 30 percent of the new federal block grant funds to the already existing child care block grant and up to 10 percent to the social services block grant, depending upon how state policy makers weigh their priorities.

Overall, the conversion of the AFDC entitlement program to the new block grant program represented a fiscal wash of sorts, as Congress set the block grant at a level that approximated spending in the base years used for conversion. However, removing welfare's entitlement status assures that spending will no longer grow automatically as welfare caseloads rise. Spending can grow only to the extent that Congress appropriates the additional funds to pay for it. Yet this looks to have been a moot point. Strong economic growth during the late 1990s and in 2000 sent caseloads plummeting at the very time that states had been allocated grant amounts based on past spending that served the needs of higher caseloads. And that decline continued through 2005, even though the U.S. economy fell into recession in 2001. Reduced caseloads have meant that states found themselves with more aid per recipient than they had prior to the program's conversion.

The Requirements of the Temporary Assistance for Needy Families Program Placed on the States and on Recipients

Federal welfare reform follows from a central premise: states should be in the driver's seat to design the specifics of programs that meet the objectives of the reform legislation. The new legislation puts the focus on results, not on means. States must meet requirements in order to receive federal grants without penalty, but state policy makers have a great deal of freedom to determine how the requirements can best be met. Key requirements center on the states' ability to move welfare recipients into jobs. The act requires states to have at least half their welfare caseload working. For states to be in compliance, single parents must work a minimum of thirty hours per week. The primary wage earner in a two-parent family must work at least thirty-five hours per week, and both parents must work at least that amount if the family receives federally funded child care. Adults receiving welfare benefits must begin working within two years of receiving aid. States can exempt parents who have a child under one year of age from this requirement, but the act limits this exemption to a total of twelve months cumulatively.

Although the reform legislation places work requirements on the states, the use of the term *work*, in its traditional sense, is a bit of a misnomer. States can satisfy the work requirements of the law by placing recipients in educational, training, and work experience programs. Actual work can include both subsidized and unsubsidized private-sector and public-sector employment, on-the-job training, and community service. States face having their block grant reduced by 5 percent in the first year they fail to meet the law's work requirements. Escalating penalties can increase the amount reduced to 21 percent of the block grant's value by the fourth year of noncompliance.

Along with the states, recipients themselves face penalties for not meeting the law's work requirements. Individual recipients who fail to meet the work requirements placed on them face grant reductions commensurate with the amount of work or equivalent activity missed. For example, a recipient who is absent 50 percent of the time in a given period receives a 50 percent reduction in aid for that period. The law ultimately gives states the right to terminate the benefits of adults who refuse to work at all, although states cannot rescind Medicaid coverage for their children. It also requires states to reduce recipients' benefits by at least 25 percent if they fail to cooperate with authorities in establishing the paternity of dependent children covered under the act. States can choose to withdraw their benefits altogether. Finally, the law requires unmarried parents under the age of eighteen to attend school or a training program and live with a parent or legal guardian in order to qualify for federal block grant funding.

Restrictions on the Duration of Benefits

The law also limits the time that recipients can receive benefits financed by federal funds. States are prohibited from using block grant funds to assist recipients who have received welfare for more than five years. Previously, no such limit existed in federal law; however, nearly half the states had already imposed time limits through the waiver route.[20] The new legislation provides some flexibility in applying time limits to individual recipients, giving state administrators the prerogative to exempt up to 20 percent of their caseload from the time limit. It also allows states to impose a shorter time limit.

For the congressional architects of the law, the time limit feature lies at the heart of welfare reform. As the new program's title suggests, they view welfare as temporary assistance, available to see people through periods of need on their way to employment. They see the work requirements, discussed earlier, as the tools necessary to speed up that transition.

The Debate over Reauthorization

The original authorizations included in the Personal Responsibility and Work Opportunity Reconciliation Act expired on September 30, 2002, but Congress has extended them. President Bush supported reauthorization legislation that would continue the program through 2007, but at the 2002 funding level. He also proposed strengthening the act's work requirements, by mandating that 70 percent of families receiving welfare must work forty hours a week. Training could count toward the requirement, up to twenty-four hours a week, for no more than three months in a two-year period.

President Bush's recommendations drew strong reactions from welfare advocates, who argued that the administration's proposal called for a return to Reagan's "workfare." Many state officials saw the proposal as tying their hands, giving them less latitude to offer recipients programs that upgrade their job skills and ultimately improve their employability.

After approving a series of continuing resolutions to fund the program, the Republican majority was able to secure sufficient support to include reauthorization within the Deficit Reduction Act of 2005, which President Bush signed into law on February 6, 2006. The legislation reauthorized the TANF program through 2010 but capped the basic block grant at $16 billion, a ceiling demanded by Republican negotiators. The reauthorization also increased the work participation rate required of states, progressively increasing it from 50 percent in 2006 to 70 percent in 2010, meaning that 70 percent of TANF recipients would have to be working or participating in work-preparation programs by 2010, ultimately giving the Bush administration what it wanted.

Questions About the Future

The most central question about the future is how families with dependent children will fare without their entitlement to benefits. Funding can run out with discretionary spending programs. Eligible recipients can go without benefits if funds are lacking to meet their collective needs. This will not be a problem as long as recipients consistently move from welfare to work in numbers that allow available welfare funds to cover the benefit costs of those still reliant on public assistance. A strongly growing economy can provide the jobs to make that happen. Yet there will always be some individuals who will have great difficulty finding employment even in the best of economic times. What will happen to them? Perhaps the only realistic option they will have if they wish to receive public aid is to satisfy the new law's work requirement by performing various forms of community service. Others will get discouraged and no longer seek public support. Still others, faced with the requirement to work, will elect not to apply in the first place. Despite this dilemma, supporters of reform hope that a combination of incentives to work and a favorable economy will move a growing number of Americans from economic dependence to independence.

The problem is that it is difficult to assess validly what is happening to those who leave the welfare rolls. One thing is clear: caseloads have fallen dramatically from a peak of 5,046,263 families on welfare in 1994 to 1,870,039 in 2005—a reduction of 63 percent. What is less clear is the extent to which welfare recipients have found their way into the jobs created by economic growth. They have come off caseloads in surprising numbers; beyond that fact, we systematically know little more.[21]

Dependency and the Value of Work

Getting recipients off welfare and into jobs is not a new emphasis of federal welfare policy. The former AFDC program required recipients to register with state employment service offices and to actively seek employment as a condition for receiving aid. AFDC's now-defunct Work Incentive Program (WIN), established by Congress in 1967, added support services, such as remedial education, job training, and child care, to improve the employability of young welfare mothers. Yet most reviews of the WIN program questioned its success in getting recipients off the rolls and into jobs.[22]

This facilitative approach gave way in the 1980s to a more coercive orientation. Shortly after assuming office in 1981, President Ronald Reagan called on Congress to adopt a national *workfare* program requiring all able-bodied AFDC recipients to work for their benefits. Under his proposal, those recipients who failed to find jobs would be required to work a specified number of hours a week in public-sector employment, performing such tasks as snow shoveling, trash cleanup, and routine clerical duties. In comparison to the WIN program, the emphasis shifted from improving employability to actual work itself. Critics labeled the proposed program as "slavefare."

Although Congress rejected the notion of a national mandatory workfare program, it passed legislation in 1981 that provided incentives for states to enact their own workfare programs. In response, more than half the states created programs, but many elected to impose forced public service work only after employability and job search efforts proved unsuccessful.

State experimentation under the Family Support Act of 1988, alluded to earlier, contained a mix of traditional and new approaches. Although states continued to require recipients to participate in training aimed at enhancing their employability, they also secured federal waivers limiting the time recipients could receive assistance without actually working, and they instituted a number of provisions designed to modify recipients' behavior. States selectively refused to increase the benefits of welfare mothers who gave birth to additional children while on public assistance, cut the benefits of teen mothers or recipients whose children failed to attend school regularly, and required teen mothers and their children to live at home with a parent or legal guardian in order to receive benefits.

The Personal Responsibility and Work Opportunity Reconciliation Act of 1996, which abolished the AFDC program and replaced it with TANF, gave states the opportunity to continue their use of incentives and disincentives to bias recipients' behavior, but it also went further than any prior act of Congress in establishing work requirements and cutting off financial assistance to those who do not work after a period of time. As noted earlier, both states and recipients face financial penalties if they fail to meet work requirements—states in failing to move a sufficient percentage of recipients from welfare to work and the recipients themselves for failing to work enough hours per week. Those unable to find employment face time limits on the welfare payments they receive in lieu of work.

America's normative inheritance, shaped by classical liberalism and the Protestant work ethic, has long valued work. European immigrants, most of whom came to the United States with few material resources, improved their economic and social lot through work. They may have started out poor, but they were poor *despite* work. The U.S. Census Bureau reports that about 60 percent of the poor's income in 2004 came from employment earnings, a percentage consistent with that reported in 1996, the year of federal welfare reform.[23] This contrast has led political scientist Lawrence Mead to conclude that "the working poor left poverty, and the poor became almost by definition nonworking."[24] Although poverty for most persons is transient, Mead focuses his concern on the long-term poor—the 6 percent to 7 percent who are poor for more than two years. These tend to be the nonworking poor, most commonly living in female-headed families receiving public assistance.[25] Mead recognizes that the expanded public assistance born of the Great Society's war on poverty did indeed reduce poverty statistically, but he, like Charles Murray,[26] argued that it failed to achieve the hoped-for self-sufficiency that was expected to follow government's helping hand. Mead sees grave social implications in this shift from the working poor to the dependent nonworking poor. Not only does it weaken the valued link between personal effort and reward, it also offers dysfunctional lessons to the children of dependent adults. For Mead, the answer lies in substituting work for dependence. Government's efforts must be put into getting the long-term dependent poor into jobs and off public assistance, whatever the nature of the work involved and even if that work is coerced.

Mead's 1992 book, *The New Politics of Poverty*, which highlighted the shift, discussed its implications, and offered policy advice, caught the attention of welfare reformers. Its analysis and policy recommendations particularly struck a resonant chord with Republican congressional leaders, who found academic support for their predisposed preference for work-centered welfare reform. Its findings and normative arguments found a central spot in the congressional debate leading to the landmark 1996 reform legislation. The value placed on work and the antipathy felt toward dependency led policy makers to the position of denying benefits to those who fail to find sustained work and exhaust their eligibility for *temporary* assistance.

Taking Issue with the Direction of Welfare Reform

Critics of welfare reform, while recognizing the value of work, see the 1996 reform as potentially hurting the poor. One prominent critic has been Mary Jo Bane, former assistant secretary for children and families in the federal Department of Health and Human Services during the Clinton administration, who resigned in protest from her position shortly after President Clinton signed the welfare reform legislation. Her objections centered on four key features of the legislation: the elimination of welfare's entitlement status and the associated loss of guaranteed assistance to dependent children; the states' prerogative to reduce their spending commitments to public assistance, leading to what she refers to as a "race to the bottom"; the dangers of the legislation's work and time provisions, which offer the prospect that unemployable recipients will be left without the means to support even a meager existence; and the social consequences of "child abandonment" arising from mothers with young children being forced to take jobs outside the home.[27]

Bane worries about the assumed feasibility of long-term welfare recipients transitioning to self-sufficiency, even in a good economy. Clearly, a good economy increases the job prospects of the more employable recipients—those who have the basic skills and aptitude to find employment, if only demand in the economy is strong enough to create the jobs necessary to employ them. If the economy stagnates or declines, their employment prospects dim, as do those of competing job seekers. But what about the fortunes of the long-term unemployed, who typically face major impediments to employment? Although states can exempt some of them from benefit termination after they reach the five-year lifetime limit on financial assistance, critics question what will happen to those still unemployed recipients and their dependent children who are not exempted. Will they join the ranks of the homeless, increasingly turning to community-based, nonprofit social service agencies for assistance?

Another visible critic of welfare reform, Harvard professor Christopher Jencks, shares Bane's concerns. He, too, questions the feasibility of moving welfare recipients into jobs. Yet, at the same time, he ponders the fortunes of those able to find minimum-wage jobs in a good economy. Jencks notes that Congress, at President Clinton's behest, acted to improve the lot of those welfare recipients able to find even minimum-wage employment, by expanding the Earned Income Tax Credit (EITC) available to the working poor. The liberalized EITC effectively adds about two dollars an hour to the pay of a minimum-wage job for a single mother of two children who works thirty-five hours a week—just barely raising that family out of poverty. So, those recipients at least able to find a steady, minimum-wage job improve their income, on the average, over what they received from public assistance, although minimum-wage employment can be anything but steady, being highly responsive to economic conditions. Yet for those able to find steady minimum-wage employment, their food stamp allotment is typically cut, as is any housing assistance they may have received. With these offsets, Jencks questions the extent to which their material situation is really improved, and he calls upon government to do more to support the material well-being of working mothers and their children. Like the supporters of welfare reform, Jencks sees social value in work; however, he wants the rewards of work to yield more than the market alone is prepared to provide.[28]

Although most social analysts acknowledge the intrinsic value of work, even though they take issue with the feasibility of employing welfare recipients or with the adequacy of rewards that low-level employment brings, some challenge that very value base. Social critics such as Frances Fox Piven and Richard Cloward place a higher value on government-provided income protection for the poor than they do on the poor competing in the marketplace for subsistence employment. In their view, "social provisioning" provides security for the poor, protecting them from the effects of the market. It also benefits those more regularly attached to the labor force who do not have to compete for jobs with those to whom government provides income protection. Fox Piven and Cloward see social provisioning as strengthening the bargaining position of working people, as competition for jobs is reduced. For them, then, functional social policy must include an adequate social parachute for the structurally unemployed or those who, at best, occasionally drift into jobs but who largely remain jobless—a policy they see benefiting workers, as well.[29] Their voices fall far from the mainstream in the era of work-oriented welfare reform.

Cash Assistance for the Categorically Dependent: The Blind, Disabled, and Elderly

In addition to public financial assistance to needy families with dependent children, government provides aid through the Supplemental Security Income (SSI) program to the so-called categorically dependent: the blind, disabled, and the elderly poor who either have not qualified for Social Security or have Social Security benefits below SSI standards.

Congress created the SSI program in 1974, using it to replace a web of federal and state programs that individually provided cash assistance to the needy blind, disabled, and noncovered elderly. Under consolidation within the federal government, the Social Security Administration administers the program, and Congress appropriates general revenues to finance basic grants, which apply nationwide. Many states, however, choose to supplement them. For 2006 federal basic grants amounted to $603 per month for an individual living independently and $904 a month for an eligible couple. State supplements vary considerably and depend upon recipients' living arrangements (living independently or in the household of someone else) and the amount of outside income, if any, they receive. For example, Vermont adds $52 a month for a single recipient and $98 a month for a couple living independently. California is far more generous, adding $230 and $568, respectively.[30]

In-Kind Assistance

In addition to cash payments, the needy also receive in-kind assistance, that is, assistance that has cash value but is not in the form of cash. In-kind assistance primarily includes medical care, food aid, and subsidized housing. Each is discussed in turn.

Medical Care

Sixty percent of Americans rely on employers for their health insurance coverage.[31] However, that percentage drops to just 20 percent for those members of families with incomes that put them in the bottom fifth of income earners.[32] Most of the other 80 percent in the lowest income quintile rely on the federal-state Medicaid program to pay the costs of their medical care. Overall, Medicaid covers 13 percent of all Americans.

More than 45 million people received Medicaid benefits in 2004.[33] The federal government pays the majority of the costs of benefits and administration, about 57 percent. Medicaid consumes approximately 7 percent of federal spending. The states pay the other 43 percent of program costs. The states' contribution to Medicaid constitutes 20 percent of state general-fund spending, up from only 4 percent in 1970, illustrating the stress that Medicaid has placed on state budgets. Based on their per capita income, states receive federal aid that ranges between 50 percent and 83 percent of their actual program expenditures.

Congress enacted Medicaid, along with Medicare, in 1965.[34] Unlike Medicare, Medicaid is limited to the financially needy. Medicaid is jointly administered and financed by the federal government and the states. Although state participation is optional, all states participate. Yet only TANF and SSI recipients are eligible for Medicaid in twenty-one states. The remaining states open the program to other medically needy persons as well. To participate in the latter category, individuals, by federal law, cannot have income in excess of one-third above the TANF cash payment for a similar size family, with only marginal exceptions made for those with low income and extraordinarily high medical bills.

The Medicaid program complements the Medicare program, which will be discussed later in this chapter. Medicaid can be used to pay the premiums for Supplementary Medical Insurance (covering health-care providers' services) and the deductible and coinsurance costs for poor Social Security recipients who lack the means to pay the required patient contribution or deductible.

To receive federal funds, states must provide the following basic medical services to patients: physicians' and nurses' services; inpatient and outpatient hospital services; laboratory and x-ray services; skilled-nursing care; home health services; and screening, diagnostic, and treatment services for children.

In addition to these mandatory services, the states, at their option, may provide other services or devices and still receive federal reimbursement for the costs. Such services or devices might include chiropractic care, dental care, eyeglasses, hearing aids, and prescription medicines.

Some states provide almost all thirty-two services or devices permitted by federal law, whereas others provide only a few beyond the required core. Given this state discretion, Medicaid recipients are comparatively advantaged or disadvantaged depending on where they live.

Although TANF families constitute two-thirds of Medicaid beneficiaries, their medical bills account for only about a fifth of all Medicaid benefits paid. SSI recipients make up about one-third of Medicaid recipients but represent nearly two-thirds of Medicaid costs, and their share of costs has been growing the fastest of all, with the rising costs of long-term care (such as that provided in nursing homes) leading the way. The remaining claims come from the non-TANF medically needy in those states that have elected to extend Medicaid benefits to them.

Many states have also requested waivers from federal regulations governing the Medicaid program. Waiver requests approved by the federal Department of Health and Human Services have taken different forms. One approach has been to expand eligibility to include more families considered to be part of the working poor while, at the same time, reducing the services available to recipients under the traditional program or requiring them to pay more out of their own pockets for care. To make ends meet fiscally, a number of states have offered slimmed-down programs to the new pool of eligible recipients—an initiative that would not be possible without the states securing so-called Section 1115 waivers.

In contrast to America's categorical approach to providing medical care to the needy, European countries have incorporated medical care for low-income and poor individuals within a national system of universal health care, commonly employing one of two approaches: a **national health service** or a single-payer insurance system. With the national health service approach, adopted in the United Kingdom, Ireland, Italy, Spain, Portugal, and Scandinavia, public employees provide medical care in publicly owned offices and hospitals. Single-payer systems, employed in the other continental European nations, variously incorporate a mix of public and private service providers, but as a common element government pays the cost of ensuring universal access to health care, either by financing the cost of insurance or paying the salaries of public employees.[35]

Food Assistance

While most European nations employ comparatively generous cash payments to enable members of low-income and poor households to meet the cost of putting food on the table, the United States relies upon an in-kind cash proxy to help ensure that its assistance goes to food and not to other uses. The federal food stamp program is the major U.S. government vehicle for providing food assistance to the needy. Administered by the U.S. Department of Agriculture (DOA) and costing more than $31 billion annually, food stamps benefited more than 11 million households and approximately 26 million individuals in 2006, providing food benefits averaging about $93 a month. The actual benefit, however, depends upon family size and the amount of the TANF grant provided in a given state. Food stamp benefits tend to be relatively lower in states with high TANF benefits, and vice versa.[36]

The label *food stamp* is somewhat a misnomer today, because most recipients receive debit cards that can be read electronically. The DOA made the switch in an effort to reduce counterfeiting and the illegal sale of food stamps.

Eligibility for food stamps is cast more inclusively than for the TANF and SSI programs. For a household to be eligible for food stamps, its gross monthly income must be no more than 130 percent of federal poverty guidelines. Thus TANF and SSI recipients are clearly included, but so are some low-income workers and their dependents. Slightly more than half of the participants are children, and 65 percent of children benefiting from food stamps live in single-parent households.

To ensure that food stamps are spent on food, they cannot be used to purchase alcoholic beverages or tobacco products, nor can they be used to buy nonfood items or pet food. In that respect, they are not the same as money, because federal regulations restrict their use.

Other significant forms of food assistance include in-school breakfast and lunch programs, as well as a special supplemental nutrition program for low-income pregnant women, infants, and children up to age five. This latter program, commonly referred to as WIC, opens eligibility to households with incomes up to 185 percent of federal poverty guidelines. It served an average of 8 million participants in 2006.[37]

Housing

Housing is another area in which U.S. and European policy differ significantly.[38] In most European countries, government policy recognizes housing as a basic human right, and government supports extensive programs of government-owned housing and rental assistance, although recent steps toward greater privatization have reduced the supply of "social housing" somewhat. Nonetheless, housing allowances tied to income are more readily available and more generous than in the United States. For example, more than half the renters in the United Kingdom receive housing aid, as do almost half in Denmark, more than a third in France, and about a quarter in the Netherlands.[39]

Instead of emphasizing rental subsidy, policy makers in the United States have elected to subsidize home ownership across the income spectrum, by permitting homeowners to deduct mortgage interest and local real property taxes from their income tax liability. Regarding housing for the needy, U.S. policy has shifted from providing them with public housing to subsidizing their rents in privately owned units. From 1960 to 1980, the number of public housing units tripled, from 400,000 to 1.2 million, only to decline sharply during the Reagan years.[40] The Reagan administration viewed public housing as dysfunctional, contributing to cycles of dependence and crime. During the Reagan administration, federal housing assistance fell to its lowest per capita post–World War II level. It has continued to fall below the level of need. About three-fourths of low-income households eligible for vouchers do not receive any form of federal housing assistance,[41] and only about one-third of welfare recipients receive it.[42]

Housing for the needy has not held a privileged position on the U.S. public policy agenda. American policy makers have largely relied upon the market to meet demands for housing. They have come to hold large-scale public housing projects in disrepute, and federal housing assistance has not fared well in competition over domestic discretionary spending. Housing is far from being considered a right in American policy.

Social Insurance

Social insurance carries the distinct connotation of personal responsibility and just deserts. In return for contributing earned income into government-administered funds, people get something back: either a stream of income or medical care during their retirement years. In the popular conception, a bargain between payer and the government is struck, and the public holds the clear expectation that government will hold up its end of the bargain, given that individuals have held up theirs by making benefit contributions during their working years.

This sense of obligation has strengthened in recent years, as retirees have become more dependent on Social Security. That growing dependence is the product of two forces: a marked shrinkage of traditional pensions provided by private-sector employers and a precipitous decline in the rate of personal savings. As business increasingly eliminates or reduces pension benefits, government programs of social insurance become more critical.

Social Security

Both policy makers and the general public look at Social Security differently than they do welfare. The value of work and the principles of social insurance and just deserts undergird their view of Social Security. Because Social Security has no means test, as does public welfare, all eligible recipients with sufficient covered employment receive benefits, regardless of need. Benefit levels reflect both the duration of work and the amounts of income subject to the Social Security tax.

Both employers and their employees pay Social Security taxes that finance benefits paid to covered retirees. No general purpose taxes support benefits. The popular view is that retirees drawing benefits are only getting back what they deserve, based on their employers' and their contributions. Nevertheless, there is no question that Social Security redistributes income in society. Recipients who earned less during their working years receive a higher proportional return on taxes paid than do those who earned more and worked about the same amount of time.

Created by Congress in 1935 as part the New Deal, Social Security, or Old Age Survivors Disability Insurance (OASDI), is administered exclusively by the federal government and covers 96 percent of the working population. Most federal workers and some state employees covered by their own retirement systems constitute the 4 percent not participating. Like public welfare, Social Security reduces poverty. Monthly Social Security checks keep about 40 percent of beneficiaries age sixty-five or older out of poverty. Benefits constitute the major source of income for almost two-thirds of Social Security recipients age sixty-five or older, and they contribute 90 percent or more of the income for about one-third. Nevertheless, about 40 percent of Social Security benefits go to recipients with incomes above the U.S. median. Social Security benefits provide only about 20 percent of the income for the top 20 percent of elderly income earners.[43] In 2006 retired workers received an average monthly benefit of $1,007.

In addition to providing retirement benefits, the Social Security program also provides cash assistance to dependent survivors of covered workers and to workers themselves who become disabled and can no longer work. For the typical worker, the survivor's benefit is worth about $403,000 over the survivors' lifetimes, and the disability benefit has a dollar value of approximately $353,000, according to actuarial estimates.[44]

The Trust Fund: Reality or Fiction?

Social Security taxes pay for Social Security benefits. Under current law, employers and employees each pay a tax equal to 5.3 percent of the employee's gross salary, up to a salary limit established by law, to finance the program's retirement and survivor's (OASI) benefits. That limit was $94,200 a year in 2006. Employers and employees each pay another 0.9 percent to finance the disability insurance (DI) part of the program. Self-employed individuals have to pick up both the employee and employer portions, contributing 12.4 percent on the same taxable base toward both OASI and DI benefits. And, as will be discussed later, employers and employees each contribute another 1.45 percent of gross salary to pay for Medicare hospitalization (HI) benefits. However, no taxable salary cap exists for Medicare, as it does for OASI and DI.

The federal government credits Social Security taxes to two separate trust funds, the Old Age and Survivors Insurance (OASI) and the Disability Insurance (DI) trust funds. Tax revenues supporting Medicare's hospitalization benefits are credited to the Federal Hospitalization Insurance (HI) trust fund. The tax revenues themselves are deposited in accounts of Federal Reserve banks and affiliated financial institutions across the country, from which the Treasury can borrow to pay for other federal spending when the rest of the federal budget is in deficit. The trust funds receive an IOU in exchange for the borrowed money, which promises to credit to the fund the going rate of interest on Treasury bonds as well as ultimately to pay back the loaned principal.

The U.S. Treasury accounts for each of the trust funds separately, paying benefits from available tax revenues and investing any surplus revenues not needed to pay benefits in U.S. government securities, which pay the prevailing market rate of interest. Interest is credited to the respective trust fund account.

From an accounting standpoint, any principal and interest available beyond what is needed to pay benefits constitute fund reserves. The Social Security trustees estimate that Social Security taxes for OASI and DI will exceed benefit payments by about $177 billion in 2006, contributing to a combined OASI and DI fund balance of $2.04 trillion—the value of U.S. bonds held by the funds, along with the interest credited to them.[45] For now, the trust funds are solid fiscally; yet, as will soon be evident, that positive fiscal balance will evaporate and turn sizably negative if no policy changes are made.

Employing the unified-budget concept, which includes all fund accounts in the federal budget, not just the general fund, the large federal budget deficits accumulated over the past three decades would have been larger still had offsetting positive year-end balances not been available in many trust fund accounts, including those for Social Security. For example, the unified-budget deficit amounted to $248 billion at the end of FY 2006. If the budget surplus in the Social Security trust fund were not available, the federal budget deficit would have been $425 billion.

It should be clear by now that Social Security is financed on a pay-as-you-go basis. Current revenues cover current costs, which means that current taxpayers pay the cost of retirees' benefits. Today about 3.3 workers covered by Social Security contribute to pay the benefits of every retiree, sufficient not only to meet outlays but to build up a U.S. securities–based reserve. As the wave of baby boomers starts to retire in large numbers in about 2011, the cost of retirement benefits will increase significantly. Retirements will increase faster than the number of workers paying Social Security taxes. By 2020 the number of covered workers per retiree will drop to about 2.6 to 1. By 2030 forecasts point to only 2.2 covered workers per retiree.[46] These changing demographics spell trouble for the solvency of the combined OASI and DI trust funds.

Trust Fund Financial Integrity and Retirement Security

National policy makers tend to put off tough political decisions on problems that have distant consequences. The financial problems facing Social Security fall into this category: the alternatives are tough politically, and the policy consequences are reasonably distant. Analysts argue about the extent of the problem and when the day of reckoning will come; the *OASDI Trustees Report* on the status of the Social Security trust funds serves as the focal point in that debate. In its 2006 report, the trustees[47] forecast that annual tax revenues coming into the combined OASI and DI trust funds will exceed annual expenditures from those funds through 2016. Tax revenues begin to fall short of expenditures in the following year, and the trust fund will need to tap into its credited interest. In 2027 total annual income, including interest income on accumulated assets, begins to fall short of annual expenditures, requiring that Treasury securities credited to the fund be redeemed to cover the shortfall.[48]

The Department of the Treasury faces a burden: it must turn to Congress to come up with the cash necessary to actually pay the interest and redeem the securities. Congress, in turn, will have only a few options: raise taxes, cut benefits, cut other federal programs and reallocate the resources, or borrow the money. The last option entails selling other federal securities to willing buyers in the marketplace. And because general obligation securities have the "full faith and credit" of the federal government behind them, they will be marketable, although large sales could drive up the interest costs—costs that future operating budgets will bear. Still, even if Congress comes up with the money to pay back its debt to the trust funds, unless it changes the law, the trustees estimate that OASDI tax revenues will be sufficient to cover only about three-fourths of program costs beginning in 2040.

The trustees based their projections on what they believe is the best estimate for the future. That estimate follows assumptions about each of the factors that affect the trust funds' tax revenues and expenditures. They include economic performance, wage growth, inflation, employment, birth rates, immigration, and mortality rates. For instance, if the economy performs better than assumed and all other assumptions prove reasonably sound, the key dates just discussed will be moved back in time somewhat. Similarly, if mortality rates drop faster than expected and all other assumptions square with reality, OASDI will have greater financial difficulty than the best estimate projects.

Options abound for fixing the problem. They include extending Social Security coverage to those currently exempted; increasing the retirement age; increasing payroll taxes; reducing benefits; allowing trust fund administrators to invest a portion of trust fund reserves in private capital markets (rendering that portion unavailable for use in paying for other government expenditures); and permitting participants to invest a portion of their Social Security tax in individual retirement accounts, from which they could make their own investment choices drawn from a set of defined options. The most radical option would do away with the present Social Security system altogether, replacing it with a system of forced saving, similar to those found in Singapore and Chile. With this option, individuals would have broad flexibility in directing savings into investment instruments, but their ability to tap those savings, short of retirement or for a defined emergency, would be greatly restricted. These last two options would fundamentally change the nature of the existing Social Security program. They would move it, in part or in whole, from a pay-as-you-go (PAYGO) system to one that is prefunded, in which individual and employer contributions grow in line with market yields to provide income in retirement.

Public opinion polls have traditionally shown that Americans overwhelmingly support Social Security. Demographics play a significant role here. With a highly favorable ratio of taxpaying covered workers to retirees, retirees enjoyed returns well in excess of contributions. For instance, a man with average lifetime earnings who retired at age sixty-five in 1980 received benefits nearly four times higher than he and his employer contributed during his working years. Women, with their greater longevity, did even better.[49] But young workers today can expect considerably less favorable returns when they retire, because there will be far fewer workers to support their benefits, likely necessitating tax increases or benefit cuts.

The options of raising taxes and reducing benefits most affect the needy. Given that Social Security taxes are forms of **proportional**, not **progressive, taxation**, they weigh most heavily on low-income taxpayers. The fact that the law caps income subject to taxation magnifies the taxes' regressivity. Any increase in the tax rate would raise the relative financial burden put on low-income taxpayers. Across-the-board benefit cuts would disproportionately hurt those most dependent on Social Security for their retirement income. Thus it is not surprising that advocates for the needy look to benefit cuts targeted at high-income recipients as the answer. They reason that Social Security benefits merely augment the income of high-income retirees, whereas low-income retirees rely on Social Security benefits just to make ends meet.

These issues lead to a debate about the nature of the Social Security program. Was it really meant to be a social welfare program under the guise of social *insurance*? Although there is no doubt that it redistributes income, policy makers may have to grapple anew with the extent to which they make Social Security an instrument of even greater redistribution. That could be accomplished by such options as removing the income limit on the payroll tax or phasing out benefits for participants having retirement incomes above a certain level, say $50,000 annually. These indeed are tough options politically. They affect the economic interests of the best-educated and most successful elderly—a political force with which to reckon.

Transition to some form of privatization would also have implications for the low-income needy. As discussed earlier, retirees who earned low incomes during their working years receive a higher rate of return on contributions than do high-income workers. Redistribution makes that possible. A pure system of privatization would remove that redistributional feature. To retain it, Congress either would have to set aside a portion of Social Security tax revenue to augment the contributions made on behalf of low-income workers or would have to use general purpose tax revenues for that purpose.

Distributing the Benefits of Economic Growth: Rising Income Inequality and the Middle-Class Squeeze

Willing buyers and sellers enter into economic transactions to advance their self-interest. Buyers turn to the marketplace to satisfy their wants. Sellers strive to produce goods and services that are wanted and attempt to influence those very wants themselves. Sellers do not offer their wares out of a sense of altruism but out of a desire to earn profit. As Adam Smith famously put it in the eighteenth century, "It is not from the benevolence of the butcher, the brewer, or the baker that we expect our dinner, but from their regard for their own self-interest. We address ourselves not to their humanity but to their self-love, and never talk to them of our own necessities but of their advantages."[1] For Smith, an economic order emerges as the unintended consequence of multiple autonomous and uncoordinated voluntary transactions, as if "an invisible hand" were at work.

Not only does market demand drive the array of goods and services produced, it also greatly influences the jobs that employers seek to fill. Demand for labor bids up its costs. In a labor market, workers compete for jobs, and employers compete for workers. That competition in good part determines the wages that workers can command.

These market-based transactions come together to constitute market outcomes. The sale of goods and services generates income that, in turn, can be spent or saved. Most of the income finds its way into workers' pockets in the form of salaries, wages, and the cash value of fringe benefits. The remainder largely goes to corporations and small businesses. Workers make choices about how much of their after-tax income to spend and to save; corporate officers decide how much income should be passed down to equity shareholders in the form of dividends; and both corporate officers and small business owners decide how much income should go to employee compensation and how much should be plowed into investment. The aggregation of these choices tells us about the distribution of benefits from market outcomes. The market allocates economic value but is unable to adjust its distribution. That responsibility falls to government. Government can indeed redistribute income and benefits using its taxing and spending powers. The extent to which policy makers elect to alter market outcomes rests on collective political choice.

Economic growth increases the size of the overall economic pie. Assuming adequate demand, production can be expanded in two ways: through the addition of new workers or the increased productivity of existing workers. In either case, as output grows, so does income. Yet what needs to be explored further is who gets that income growth and in what proportion. That is the subject of our next discussion.

Income Distribution Between Labor and Capital

Economists view increased worker productivity as the key source of real (inflation-adjusted) income growth and an improved standard of living. As workers produce more per hour, the tenet goes that employers will be willing to pay them more for their more productive labor. And that happened for the most part in the last half of the twentieth century, with the greatest gains in wage and salary income as a share of GDP following high productivity growth in the twenty-five years between 1950 and 1975 and again during the last five years of the past century. From 1950 through the early 1970s, growth in labor compensation pretty much paralleled growth in worker productivity. From the early 1970s on, growth in labor compensation lagged behind productivity growth, with the gap widening to the time of this writing.[2] By the mid-1970s, productivity growth had slowed, averaging an annual rate of growth of 1.5 percent between 1975 and 1995, compared to annual growth rates of 2.4 percent between 1950 and 1975 and 2.6 percent from 1996 and through 2000.

During those periods of higher productivity growth, worker compensation increased its share of the GDP, as Figure 9.1 illustrates. Compensation's share declined moderately from the early 1970s through the mid-1990s, with the wages and salary component of compensation losing the most ground, offset somewhat by the rising claim of fringe benefits, especially the share devoted to health insurance.

That positive relationship between productivity growth and compensation growth reversed itself during the first half of the first decade in the new century. Between 2000 and 2005, annual growth in worker productivity averaged 3.1 percent—the highest five-year spurt of productivity since the first half of the 1960s. What happened to worker compensation? Its share of the GDP *fell*, and wages and salaries bore the largest brunt of the fall, dropping nearly five percentage points from 2000 to 2005—the biggest five-year shift since the end of World War II in the share of GDP going to wages and salary. As

Figure 9.1   **Employee Compensation and Corporate Profits as a Share of GDP, 1960–2006**

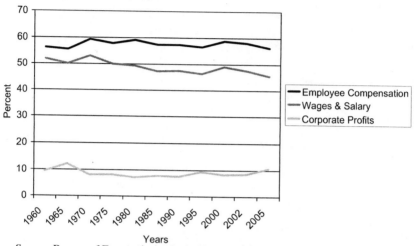

Years

Source: Bureau of Economic Analysis, U.S. Department of Commerce.

labor's share of the GDP fell, corporations' share rose sharply, hitting a level not attained since the mid-1960s.

The United States, however, was not an outlier here. Corporate profits as a percentage of GDP rose sharply in the Euro area, Canada, and Japan as well, approaching or reaching all-time highs. In fact, corporate profits as a percentage of GDP climbed by about four percentage points for the G-7 nations[3] between 2000 and 2005, nearly reaching the percentage gain enjoyed by U.S. corporations.[4]

The Economist suggests that economic globalization accounts in good part for the shifting fortunes of capital and labor, especially the rapid economic advancement of China, India, and other emerging Asian economies. Firms headquartered in developed industrial economies have been able to reduce wage and salary costs by shifting production to low-wage emerging economies, taking advantage of rising skill levels, and by relying more heavily on immigrant labor in their own countries. Moreover, as emerging economies increase their share of high-tech goods production, contributing to price reduction in world markets, the wages of skilled workers in developed countries can be expected to fall as a percentage of GDP.[5]

Growing Income Inequality

Turning the focus again to income gains in the United States, Figure 9.2 shows that real median household income declined from 2000 to 2005, falling

Figure 9.2   **Real Median Household Income, 1967–2005**

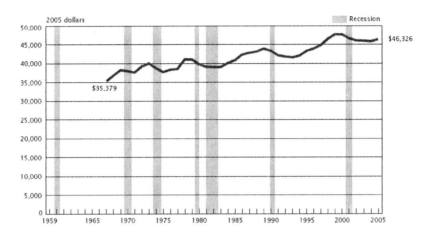

Note: The data points are at the midpoints of the respective years.
Source: Census Bureau, U.S. Department of Commerce Current Population Survey,
1968 to 2006 Annual Social Economic Supplements.

back to the 1997 level and wiping out the significant gains of the late 1990s.
Focusing just on economic recovery following recession, median household
income actually declined by one-half of 1 percent during the four-year period
of recovery from the trough of the 2001 recession. For households headed by
working-age adults under sixty-five, real median income declined even more,
by 3.7 percent from 2001 to 2005, down by $2,000 over the four years. That
decline can be compared to the 8.7 percent growth realized over a comparable
period from the 1974 recession and to the 8.3 percent growth from 1982. And
although the four-year growth rate in real median household income from
the 1990 recessionary year reached only 2.9 percent, it still was positive and
was followed by a sharp increase in real median income over the remainder
of the decade.[6]

While looking at median income gives a picture of how the typical household in America has fared, it can hide disparities in real income gains (or,
conceivably, losses) realized at different points on the income spectrum. To
discern how well different income groups have done, we need to turn to an
examination of income distribution.

The U.S. Census Bureau employs the Gini coefficient to measure income
inequality based on household income data drawn from the bureau's monthly
sample survey of U.S. households. The resulting Gini coefficient, which can
be used to measure inequality of any distribution, is a number between zero
and one, with zero representing perfect equality and one representing perfect

Figure 9.3   **Change in Household Income Inequality, 1967–2005**

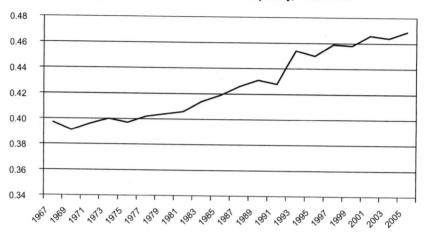

Source: Census Bureau, U.S. Department of Commerce, *Income, Poverty, and Health Insurance Coverage in the United States: 2005*, August 2006, Table A-3.

inequality. Its use allows government officials, economists, the media, and other interested parties to track changes in income inequality over time. Figure 9.3 shows changes in income dispersion since the Census Bureau began reporting it in 1967. Using Census Bureau data from its Current Population Survey (CPS), the conclusion is inescapable that income inequality has steadily increased since the late 1960s, and the steepest increases occurred during the 1980s and 1990s. However, the CPS data understate the true degree of inequality of earned income because the bureau has "top-coded" income reported above a certain level, and the threshold for top-coding has changed over the years. Today it stands at $150,000; thus reported annual income of $250,000 or $2.5 million, for instance, are currently classified as falling above $150,000.

The Census Bureau also reports the share of total household income received by each quintile (each 20 percent grouping) of earners, but the practice of top-coding again understates the true top ranges of the top 20 percent of income earners. Nevertheless, Table 9.1 shows that since 1975 all quintiles but the top lost share of household income. The top 20 percent improved their share of household income by nearly seven percentage points.

The Census Bureau data has another limitation that goes beyond top-coding but is related to it. The bureau does not break down income shares within the top quintile, so it is impossible to know how well those at the very top of income earners have done over time. We are therefore unable to compare the

Table 9.1

Shares of Household Income by Quintiles: Selected Years, 1967–2005

	1967	1970	1975	1980	1985	1990	1995	2000	2005
Bottom 20%	4.0	4.1	4.3	4.2	3.9	3.8	3.7	3.6	3.4
Second 20%	10.8	10.8	10.4	10.2	9.8	9.6	9.1	8.9	8.6
Middle 20%	17.3	17.4	17.0	16.8	16.2	15.9	15.2	14.8	14.6
Fourth 20%	24.2	24.5	24.7	24.7	24.4	24.0	23.3	23.0	23.0
Top 20%	43.6	43.3	43.6	44.1	45.6	46.6	48.7	49.8	50.4

Source: Census Bureau, U.S. Department of Commerce, *Income, Poverty, and Health Insurance Coverage in the United States: 2005*, August 2006, Table 4-3.

income gains received by the top 10 percent of income earners with, say, the top 1 percent or even the top one-tenth of 1 percent. To examine disaggregated income gains, we must turn to income data included on individual income tax returns and released by the Internal Revenue Service (IRS). Fortunately, economists Thomas Piketty and Emmanuel Saez have calculated the respective income shares received by subdivided groups within the top 10 percent of income earners and have made them available for public use.[7] Table 9.2, which uses their computations, shows the respective income shares received by the top 10 percent of income earners, the top 1 percent, and the top one-tenth of 1 percent.

In 2004 the top 10 percent of income earners (with qualifying income of $105,647) got more than 43 percent of reported income, about the same share they held in 1930. Their share fell the most from 1940 to 1950, sliding further from 1950 to 1970, when it started an uphill climb, including a large increase during the 1980s, followed by continued but slower growth through 2000. The share of the top 10 percent then fell moderately over the next two years, before rising once more between 2002 and 2004 to get back to its level of 2000. Within those periods of greatest growth, it is clear that those in the top one-tenth of 1 percent (with qualifying income of $1,962,998) made out the best, as they more than doubled their share during the 1980s and continued to improve it greatly through the 1990s. These findings not only reinforce the picture of growing income inequality drawn by the analyses cited earlier; they also illustrate the disproportionate gains realized by those at the very top of the income spectrum. The rich did indeed get richer.

Another analysis, also using IRS data, reinforces the picture of growing inequality just drawn. Ian Dew-Becker and Robert J. Gordon found that the relative share of wage and salary income received by the top 10 percent of income earners increased by 11.1 percentage points between 1966 and 2001, and the share of the bottom 90 percent correspondingly *fell* by 11.1 percentage points.

Table 9.2

Top Income Shares: Selected Years, 1920–2004

	Top 10%	Top 1%	Top 0.1%
1920	38.10	14.46	5.37
1930	43.07	16.42	6.40
1940	44.43	15.73	5.57
1950	33.87	11.36	3.53
1960	31.66	8.36	2.10
1970	32.62	7.80	1.94
1980	32.87	8.18	2.23
1985	34.25	9.09	2.91
1990	38.84	12.98	4.90
1995	40.54	13.53	4.98
2000	43.11	16.49	7.13
2004	43.11	16.08	6.81

Source: Thomas Piketty and Emmanuel Saez, "Income Inequality in the United States, 1913–1998," *The Quarterly Journal of Economics*, vol. CXVIII, issue 1 (February 2003). Updates available September 2006 at http://elsa.berkeley.edu/~saez/.

Note: Income defined as annual gross income, excluding capital gains and government transfer payments.

Within that shift, the top 1 percent increased its share by 6.7 percentage points, whereas the share of the bottom 50 percent declined by 4.7 percentage points. Looking at the real-dollar *gains* of income groups, the top 1 percent got 16.3 percent of the real-dollar growth of wage and salary income between 1966 and 2001 compared to 11.9 percent for the bottom half of income earners. The top one-tenth of 1 percent alone pocketed 6.8 percent of the income growth.[8]

Assessing the real-dollar gains of income groups during 1997–2001, what the authors refer to as "the period of productivity revival," the top 1 percent captured 23.9 percent compared to only 12.7 percent for the bottom 50 percent. Income inequality clearly widened, as those at the very top reaped a growingly disproportionate share of productivity-driven income growth.[9]

Collaborating researchers from MIT, Harvard University, and the Brookings Institution extended the above analyses by closely examining wage growth *within* the bottom 90 percent of wage and salary earners. Although their research confirmed the divergent wage gains won by the top income earners, they found that wage and salary inequality toward the bottom of the distribution stabilized since the late 1980s, largely a product of growth in the bottom quartile (25 percent) that outpaced the rate of growth in the middle two quartiles. Those at the top of the distribution made out the best, followed by those at the bottom, with those in the middle faring the worst, creating what the authors label a "polarization" of the U.S. labor market.

The authors turn to changing patterns of demand in the labor market in offering an explanation for the disparity. Technological advances and the higher premium placed on knowledge power have worked to the advantage of those at the top end of the wage and salary distribution while squeezing those in the middle, whose formerly higher-prized skills have been depreciated by innovations in automation and information processing. Rising demand for workers in what the authors brand as "non-routine manual tasks" pushed up the wages of those whose jobs are the least affected by technological change.[10]

In spite of growing income inequality and the squeeze on middle-income earners, consumer spending continued to rise as a percentage of disposable income (DI). Credit buoyed spending, as consumers increasingly took advantage of expanding credit opportunities. As inequality increased, the supply of easy credit grew. Credit-card debt as a percentage of DI more than tripled from 1984 through 2004.[11]

Taxation's Effects on Income Inequality in the United States

The IRS's latest release of individual income tax data, for 2004, allows us to compare the share of federal income taxes paid by different income groups compared to their share of reported adjusted gross income (AGI). The top 1 percent of income earners received 19 percent of AGI in 2004 (compared to 16 percent of gross income, not adjusted for tax purposes, as shown in Table 9.2). In contrast, the entire bottom half of income earners received 13 percent of AGI, illustrating the highly unequal distribution of income that exists in the United States. In 2004 tax filers minimally needed $328,049 to fall within the top 1 percent of AGI, whereas an AGI of $30,122 or less kept one in the bottom 50 percent. The top 1 percent carried a much heavier tax burden than did the bottom 50 percent, paying 37 percent of total federal income taxes collected in that year compared to only 3 percent paid by the bottom half of income earners. The top 1 percent paid federal income taxes at an average tax rate of 23 percent compared to an average tax rate of only 3 percent paid by the bottom half.[12]

Yet we also want to know the extent to which taxation has altered the distribution of income over time. To accomplish that we need to compare the distribution of after-tax income with the distribution of pre-tax income among different income groups, assessing the percentage change in income realized by each group over a given number of years. Fortunately, the Congressional Budget Office (CBO) has compiled data that allow us to make that comparison. The CBO data cover the period from 1979 through 2000 and therefore do not take into account the effects of the large 2001 and 2003 tax reductions, popularly referred to as the Bush tax cuts, which we will examine later. The CBO used data from both the Census Bureau and the IRS to analyze changes in income distribution, relying on IRS data

Table 9.3

Change in Average Pre-Tax and After-Tax Income by Income Group, 1979–2000 (using constant 2000 dollars)

Income Group	Pre-Tax Income		After-Tax Income	
	Dollar Change	Percent Change	Dollar Change	Percent Change
Lowest Fifth	900	6.6	1,100	8.7
Second Fifth	3,500	11.7	3,400	13.3
Middle Fifth	5,600	12.5	5,500	15.1
Fourth Fifth	14,000	23.1	11,500	24.1
Highest Fifth	80,700	69.7	57,400	68.3
81st–95th Percentile	31,300	36.5	23,400	35.9
96th–99th Percentile	76,900	53.6	55,000	53.1
Top 1 Percent	836,600	184.2	576,400	201.3

Source: Robert Greenstein and Isaac Shapiro, "The New, Definitive CBO Data on Income and Tax Trends" (Washington, DC: Center on Budget and Policy Priorities, September 23, 2003).

to probe more finely the distribution within the top 20 percent of income earners, including those in the top 1 percent.

The CBO data incorporate income not included by the Census Bureau, most significantly capital gains and income resulting from the Earned Income Tax Credit (EITC) claimed by low-income working Americans, along with the income value of in-kind assistance in the form of food stamps, public housing and rental assistance, and publicly funded health care for the needy. On the tax side, the CBO data include both federal income taxes and payroll taxes (Social Security and Medicare).

Table 9.3 compares change in income before and after the payment of federal taxes. The highest fifth of income earners realized the biggest real-dollar income gain among all of the income quintiles over the twenty-one years, while those lower down the income categories did progressively less well. Breaking down the dollar gains within the top 20 percent, it is clear that the top 1 percent did the best by far, realizing an average income gain of $836,600 in 2000 dollars—more than tenfold the increase averaged by those in the ninety-sixth to ninety-ninth percentile. Although it is true that all income categories improved their lot from 1979 through 2000, both the size of the dollar increase and percentage gain varied enormously, heavily skewed in favor of upper-income earners.

Tax policy reduced the dollar gain for all but those in the lowest quintile who benefited from the Earned Income Tax Credit, reflecting the tax system's

Table 9.4

Shares of After-Tax Income by Income Group: Selected Years, 1979–2000 (%)

Income Category	1979	1989	2000	Percentage Point Change in Shares, 1979–2000
Lowest Fifth	6.8	5.1	4.9	−1.9
Second Fifth	12.3	10.8	9.7	−2.6
Middle Fifth	16.5	15.7	14.6	−1.9
Fourth Fifth	22.3	21.9	20.2	−2.1
Highest Fifth	42.4	47.6	51.3	8.9
81st–95th Percentile	24.3	24.6	23.8	−0.5
96th–99th Percentile	10.6	11.7	12.0	1.4
Top 1 Percent	7.5	11.3	15.5	8.0

Source: Robert Greenstein and Isaac Shapiro, "The New, Definitive CBO Data on Income and Tax Trends" (Washington, DC: Center on Budget and Policy Priorities, September 23, 2003).

overall progressive nature. But if we look at the relative percentage point change in *shares* of after-tax income, the top 1 percent increased their share by eight percentage points, followed by those in the next-highest 4 percent, who enjoyed a 1.4 percentage point increase. In relative terms, those at the very top widened their advantage. (See Table 9.4.)

The Bush Tax Cuts

Congress, at President George W. Bush's strong urging, passed two major tax-cut acts during Bush's first term in office. The contexts for the two initiatives differed significantly, however. The first, enacted in June 2001, had its roots in the 2000 presidential campaign in which both candidates promised to champion large tax cuts. The federal budget ended with a $236 billion surplus at the close of FY 2000, the third straight year of budget surplus and the largest of the three. A good part of the campaign centered on what should be done with the surplus, which budget prognosticators saw growing nearly unbounded during the remainder of the decade. With five years of strong economic growth on record and worker productivity riding a wave of strong growth, the candidates, the media, and leading economists pointed optimistically to what they saw as the durability of the "new economy" transformed by technological advances. In that environment, Republican candidate Bush proposed a $1.31 trillion tax-reduction package through 2010 while Democratic candidate Al Gore supported net tax cuts of $480 billion over the period. Of the two, Gore called for spending $426 billion more of the projected surplus than did Bush—mostly on domestic programs—and for putting more of the surplus into the euphemistic "lockbox" reserved for Social Security. The candidates also differed on how the tax cuts should be targeted. Gore favored cuts targeted toward middle-income earners, whereas upper-income earners would reap the biggest share of the Bush tax cuts.[13]

In April 2001, just five months after the presidential election, the CBO upped the forecasted federal budget surplus, projecting it to grow from $304 billion at the end of FY 2002 to $833 billion at the close of FY 2011, totaling a whopping $5.6 trillion over the ten-year period. Those heady days in the spring of 2001 reinforced Bush's resolve to deliver on his campaign promise to give a substantial part of the surplus back to taxpayers through income tax cuts.

In signing the tax-cut legislation, President Bush put the moment in historical perspective, remarking:

> Across-the-board tax relief does not happen often in Washington, D.C. In fact, since World War II, it has happened only twice: President Kennedy's tax cut in the 1960s and President Reagan's cuts in the 1980s. And now it's happening for a third time, and it's about time.[14]

Branding the initiative as the "first major policy achievement of a new era," he added:

> Tax relief expands individual freedom. The money we return, or don't take in the first place, can be saved for a child's education, spent on family needs, invested in a home or in a business or mutual fund, or used to reduce personal debt. The message we send today, it's up to the American people; it's the American people's choice. We recognize loud and clear the surplus is not the government's money. The surplus is the people's money, and we ought to trust them with their own money.[15]

President Bush's message, wrapped in classical liberal ideology, echoed President Ronald Reagan's expressed sentiments underlying the former president's support for earlier tax cuts. Both presidents structured their supply-side tax cuts to give the largest after-tax savings to those who would most likely save them—those with high incomes who pay the most income tax in the first place.

The tax legislation passed by Congress and signed into law by President Bush on June 7, 2001, phases in a series of tax cuts from 2002 through December 31, 2010, after which the act is repealed in its entirety (unless extended by Congress), returning the tax code to the way it was before enactment. The new law reduces taxes by $1.35 trillion over the nine years. Most of the reduction, $843 billion, results from changes in individual income tax brackets and rates. The lowest rate dropped from 15 percent to 10 percent, retroactive to January 1, 2001. The other rate reductions—from 28 percent to 25 percent, from 31 percent to 28 percent, from 36 percent to 33 percent, and from a top effective rate of 39.6 percent to 35 percent—were fully phased in by 2006. Congress also included several other provisions in the legislation, notably increases in the child tax credit and in the standard deduction for married couples filing jointly (who before the change could take a lower deduction than that available to an unmarried couple living together), a phaseout of the estate tax, liberalization of limits governing tax-deferred retirement savings, and favorable tax treatment for educational expenses.

Congress passed its second major tax-cut legislation of Bush's first term on May 23, 2003. The nation's economic context had changed by then. The economy fell into recession in 2001, and economic recovery got off to a slow start, yielding a net loss of jobs until well into 2003. By the end of FY 2002, the four-year string of federal budget surpluses had turned into a $158 billion deficit and was well on its way to a $375 billion deficit at the end of FY 2003. This time the president and Congress justified the tax-cut package as a fiscal tool of economic recovery, as symbolized by the act's title: the Jobs and Growth Tax Relief Reconciliation Act (JGTRRA) of 2003. At a cost of an additional $400 billion through 2008, the act expanded the 10 percent and 15 percent tax brackets and accelerated the effective dates for rate changes approved in the 2001 legislation; markedly reduced tax rates on capital gains and dividends (from treating them as ordinary income subject to the graduated tax-rate structure to new rates of 15 percent for most tax filers and 5 percent for taxpayers of moderate income); and increased the exemption of income counting toward the Alternative Minimum Tax (AMT), which Congress had earlier enacted to ensure that taxpayers pay their fair share of taxes by limiting the aggregate tax-reducing effects of deductions, tax-exempt interest, accelerated depreciation of property, nonreimbursed business expenses, and other forms of tax sheltering. Congress included the last provision to limit the number of taxpayers who would become subject to the AMT, as its reaches increasingly extended into the ranks of the middle class.

In 2004 Congress passed the Working Families Tax Relief Act (WFTRA), which extended several expiring provisions of the 2001 and 2003 tax-cut acts, including the $1,000 child tax credit, the elimination of the marriage penalty, and the 10 percent bracket. It also once again increased the AMT exemption.

The Distributive Effects of the Bush Tax Cuts

The Bush tax cuts did indeed reduce effective tax rates for taxpayers in all income categories. In that sense, all taxpayers benefited from the cuts. As

Table 9.5

Effects of the Bush Tax Cuts on Effective Federal Tax Rates

Cash Income Category	Effective Federal Tax Rates (in percent)		
	Pre-Bush Tax Changes	Current Law	Percentage Point Change
Bottom Quintile	3.5	3.2	−0.3
Second Quintile	9.1	7.2	−1.9
Middle Quintile	16.4	14.2	−2.2
Fourth Quintile	20.3	18.4	−1.9
Top Quintile	27.3	24.7	−2.6
Top 10 Percent	28.8	26.1	−2.7
Top 1 Percent	32.7	29.6	−3.1

Source: Leonard E. Burman, "The Impact of Tax Reform on Low- and Middle-Income Households," *Testimony Submitted to the House Committee on Ways and Means,* June 8, 2005, 14.

Note: Tax cuts include the tax-cut acts of 2001 (EGTRRA), 2003 (JGTRRA), and 2004 (WFTRA).

Table 9.5 illustrates, however, some benefited more than others, and gains are largely skewed in favor of those with higher incomes. The Tax Policy Center, a joint enterprise of the Urban Institute and the Brookings Institution, estimates that the effective federal tax rate paid on income and payroll taxes in 2005 by the top 1 percent of income earners fell by 3.1 percentage points compared to tax law prior to the Bush cuts and that it fell by 2.7 percentage points for the top 10 percent. At the other end of the distribution, the bottom 20 percent, the rate dropped by two-tenths of one percentage point, and it dropped by 1.9 percentage points for the second quintile. Despite the greater rate reduction benefiting those at the top of the income range, certain features of the tax cut combined to greatly limit the tax exposure of those in the bottom two income quintiles. Liberalization of the EITC, the addition of the 10 percent bracket, and the broadening of the 15 percent bracket, along with the child tax credit, created a new reality in which the bottom 40 percent of households receive more in refundable tax credits than they pay in taxes, on the average. The bottom fifth alone receives tax credits worth 5.5 percent of income.[16]

Even though upper-income earners enjoyed the largest percentage-point drop in effective federal tax rates, those at the top paid the lion's share of federal taxes. Those in the top 10 percent income category paid 57 percent of all federal taxes, excluding customs duties and excise taxes, in 2005. Looking only at the individual income tax, the top 10 percent contributed 73 percent of collected revenue. The top 1 percent paid 27 percent of all federal taxes but 38 percent of the individual income tax.[17] (See Table 9.6.) It should not

Table 9.6

Estimated Distribution of Federal Taxes by Cash Income Category, 2005

Cash Income Category	Share of	
	Individual Income Tax*	Federal Taxes**
Bottom Quintile	−1.4	0.4
Second Quintile	−1.9	2.2
Middle Quintile	3.1	7.8
Fourth Quintile	13.2	17.5
Top Quintile	87.0	72.0
Top 10 Percent	73.2	56.5
Top 1 Percent	38.3	26.6

Source: Leonard E. Burman, "The Impact of Tax Reform on Low- and Middle-Income Households," *Testimony Submitted to the House Committee on Ways and Means,* June 8, 2005, 13.

Notes:

*Negative shares reflect tax credits exceeding tax obligation.

**Excludes custom duties and excise taxes.

be all that surprising, then, that those in the top 1 percent would get a sizable share of tax-cut savings, most of which are generated by reductions in the individual income tax.

Departing from tax model–derived estimates for 2005, the most recent *actual* income tax data, released by the IRS in September 2006, shows the top 1 percent of taxpayers paying 37 percent of federal individual income tax, very close to the Tax Policy Center's estimates for 2005. The IRS data also show that the bottom 50 percent of federal taxpayers paid a surprisingly small 3 percent of federal individual income tax in 2004.[18]

Based on analysis by the Institute on Taxation and Economic Policy, employing its microsimulation tax model, the top 1 percent of income-earning households would receive a 30 percent share of the total Bush tax cut in 2006. In comparison, the bottom 60 percent would get a 15 percent share of the tax cut while paying 10 percent of all federal taxes but only less than 1 percent of the individual income tax after tax credits.[19] By 2010, with the tax cuts fully implemented, the top 1 percent would significantly expand its share to 51 percent, while the share received by the bottom 60 percent would grow by less than one percentage point.[20]

A separate analysis, conducted by the Tax Policy Center, using its microsimulation model, forecast that tax filers in the top 1 percent income category would realize an average $54,182 tax cut in 2010 compared to $699 for those in the middle quintile (who benefit much less from the EITC than those in the bottom two quintiles). That large disparity would occur even though the Tax

Policy Center's model estimates that the share of income tax paid by the top 1 percent would increase by 2010 by about a percentage point but would fall by a near-equivalent degree for the middle quintile, reflecting differences in the projected rate of growth in income for the two groups.[21]

Public Awareness of Rising Inequality in the United States

The flurry of reports from such organizations as the CBO, the Tax Policy Center, and the Institute on Taxation and Economic Policy, which showed income inequality increasing in the United States, caught the attention of the editorial boards of three major U.S. newspapers: the *Los Angeles Times*, the *Wall Street Journal*, and the *New York Times*, all of which launched series on aspects of growing income inequality and its effects on social mobility. The *Los Angeles Times'* series, titled "The New Deal," was the first to go to press, with its first article appearing on October 10, 2004. The *Wall Street Journal* followed on May 13, 2005, with the first article in its series titled "Moving Up—American Dream or American Myth?" Two days later, the *New York Times* published the first installment of its series, "Class Matters." These initiatives were prompted not only by the growing attention given to recent empirical analyses of income inequality in the United States but also by a new wave of scholarly publications comparing income inequality and social mobility in the United States with that existing in other advanced industrial nations.

Comparative analyses of income inequality tend to use data compiled by the Luxembourg Income Study (LIS), a nonprofit cooperative research endeavor based at the University of Luxembourg, which receives most of its financial support from the national science and social science foundations of its thirty member countries. Researchers and LIS staff members have devoted considerable effort toward harmonizing household income survey data provided by the various nations' statistical information offices. A plethora of affiliated researchers drawn from academia and government agencies have produced hundreds of research papers since the project's fledgling beginning in 1983.

Although summarizing their findings is not an easy task, research papers over the past ten years or so have found a general pattern of rising income inequality in advanced, industrial nations. Using both the Gini coefficient and the ratio of the top 10 percent of household income to the bottom 10 percent as the most commonly employed measures of income inequality, research findings place the United States at or near the top of inequality scales, with its rank varying only modestly depending on the years of analysis selected. On both measures of income inequality, the United States can typically be found at the top of a cluster of English-speaking nations that have the greatest income inequality, including the United Kingdom, Ireland, Australia, and Canada, followed by clusters of decreasing inequality found in Southern Europe, Central Europe, and Northern Europe.[22] However, when looking at *change* in inequality over time, the United States falls from its top rung to a position somewhere between the top third and the top half of countries included in the LIS database. One analysis of LIS data, which examined change between 1989 and 2000, found the United States to rank seventh out of the seventeen countries analyzed, with inequality growing the fastest in Belgium, Finland, and Sweden, all of which started from a much more equal position compared to the United States. Nonetheless, the same study found the United States to have the highest income inequality in both 1989 and 2000.[23]

This comparative research also demonstrates that the United States makes less use of tax policy and transfer payments to reduce market-generated income inequality than do most nations. Studies consistently place the United States at or near the bottom of European and other industrial nations in the degree to which government policy makers utilize fiscal redistribution to reduce income inequality. In one well-publicized study, originally published as an LIS working paper, only Switzerland, among the thirteen nations examined, made less use overall of fiscal redistribution than did the United States. Focusing on redistribution resulting from transfer payments alone, the United States ranked dead last.[24] Another study, using data from the Organisation for Economic Co-operation and Development (OECD), placed the United States last in the cash value of government transfer payments as a proportion of disposable household income.[25]

Several studies of comparative public opinion on government's role vis-à-vis income inequality use survey data collected through the auspices of the International Social Survey Program (ISSP), which began as a cooperative effort of German and U.S. universities and now involves organizations from forty-one countries. The strength of ISSP's public opinion research is that it has employed common questions over time about inequality and government redistribution, thus capturing opinion change in the consistent set of countries included in the surveys. Key questions during the 1980s and 1990s ask respondents to register their opinion regarding the extent to which they agree or disagree with the statement that "differences in income in [their country] are too large," followed by their level of agreement with the statement that "it is the responsibility of the government to reduce the differences in income between people with high incomes and those with low incomes." Using response data drawn from eight countries (five European countries plus Australia, Canada, and the United States), researchers compared changes in public opinion on these issues with the extent to which income inequality had grown, narrowed, or remained about the same during the 1980s and 1990s.

They found income inequality highest overall across time in the United States and the United Kingdom and lowest in the Scandinavian nations. Public support for government redistribution was consistently the lowest in the United States, changing very little between 1984 and 1999.[26]

While stressing the value of personal responsibility and hard work as key to seizing opportunity, Americans are leery of government intervention to redistribute the returns that the market gives them. Said differently, Americans prefer market justice to political justice.[27] They view the market economy as responsive to individual wants and believe that it produces outcomes consistent with the principle of earned deserts, or just deserts: that people get from the market about what they deserve given what they put into it and that they control their own destiny in market transactions. As Benjamin Page and Robert Shapiro conclude, based on their fifty-year study of public opinion on policy preferences, "Surveys since the 1930s have shown that the explicit idea of income redistributing elicits very limited enthusiasm among the American public. Most Americans are content with the distributional effects of private markets."[28] The long-time work of sociologists James Kluegel and Eliot Smith on American public opinion comes to a similar conclusion. They report that Americans believe that everyone should count equally in moral terms and in the eyes of the law but prefer equality of opportunity and individual effort over equality of results.[29] Here again, Americans can be contrasted with Europeans. The Roper Center for Public Opinion Research reports that only about one-third of Americans believe that government should redistribute wealth compared to almost two-thirds of Europeans.[30]

The Myth of the American Dream and the Expectation of Upward Mobility

Americans believe in the myth of the American dream, a term that was not in popular use until the early twentieth century. Bonded with the values of personal freedom and equality of opportunity, it embodies the expectation that people can advance their economic and social fortunes through dedication and hard work. They just need to seize the opportunity afforded by the American system to compete to become unequal, as John Manley ironically puts it.[31]

President Bill Clinton captured the essence of the American dream in a 1993 address to the Democratic Leadership Council:

> The American dream that we were all raised on is a simple but powerful one—if you work hard and play by the rules you should be given a chance to go as far as your God-given abilities will take you.[32]

Unlike the lore popularized by Horatio Alger's stories in the late nineteenth century, of poor boys who rose from rags to riches in big-city America, surveys of contemporary public opinion consistently show that most Americans do not equate the American dream with becoming rich. Nonetheless, a 2003 Gallup poll surprisingly showed that 31 percent of respondents thought it somewhat likely or very likely that they would indeed become rich at some point in their lives and that percentage rose to an astounding 51 percent for young adults between eighteen and twenty-nine years of age.[33] Americans, however, most commonly associate the American dream with living in freedom, owning a home, and attaining financial security.[34] When asked in a 2004 poll if they themselves are living the American dream as they see it, 63 percent said they are, while 34 percent answered that they are not; however, 52 percent of those replying in the negative responded that they believe it is still within their reach.[35] A 2006 survey paints basically the same picture. Of those responding that they are not realizing the American dream, 51 percent believe that it is still attainable.[36] And the American public sees initiative seizing opportunity as the path to success. Comparing levels of agreement in 1994 and 2004 to the proposition that "everyone has it in their own power to succeed," the Pew Research Center reports that the percentage agreeing dropped by only one percentage point, from 79 percent to 78 percent—still a sizable majority.[37]

Although the myth of the American dream is still compelling, how does it square with the reality of upward mobility in the United States? How likely is it for Americans to move up the economic and social ladder? To answer this query it is necessary to move beyond comparisons of income distributions at different points in time, which tell us whether inequality in those distributions has changed over the period studied. Comparisons of Gini coefficients or quintile shares of income over time, as employed earlier in this chapter, do indeed provide measures of changing inequality from point A to point B, but they cannot tell us whether income *mobility* rose, fell, or remained about the same. For that it is necessary to discern how the income of individual families has changed over time. We want to know whether individual families remain within the same income category at points B and C that they started out in at point A or whether they rose or fell across categories. In other words, we want to determine the extent to which individual families have experienced upward or downward income mobility.

No U.S. government agency provides data on individual families' changing income over time. Fortunately, though, the University of Michigan's Survey Research Center began collecting individual family-centered income data in 1968 and continues to do so today. Their panel data allow researchers to examine changes in income mobility from decade to decade. The results of one research team's highly publicized findings show that income mobility increased modestly during the 1970s and 1980s but decreased slightly during the 1990s, the decade during which income inequality rose the fastest of the three. At the same time, that higher increase in income inequality found in the 1990s exerts a methodological effect of pushing quintile boundaries farther apart, thus creating a higher hurdle for moving up or down a quintile.[38]

The Fate of the Middle Class

With growing income inequality, how has the middle class fared? To answer this question, we first must have a sense of who constitutes the middle class. Public opinion polls consistently show that a vast majority of Americans, upward of 90 percent, identify themselves as members of the broad middle class. In 2005 it took $126,090 to be included in the ninetieth percentile of annual household income. Do we want to stretch middle-class income that far? Is median household income of $46,326 in 2005 synonymous with middle-class standing? Most people would agree that it falls somewhere within the range of middle-class income but see the income band wider at both ends. Using divisions of household income provided by the Census Bureau, a range of $35,000 to $99,999, in 2005 dollars, might strike one as a reasonable approximation of middle-class income, even though some might take issue with the upper limit. Using that range, the percentage distribution of households with middle-class incomes fell over the twenty-five years between 1980 and 2005, from 47.9 percent to 44.4 percent, as Table 9.7 illustrates. During those same years, households earning $100,000 or more grew from 7.7 percent of the distribution to 17.2 percent. Households earning less than $35,000 shrank from 44.4 percent to 38.4 percent. The middle class did indeed shrink, but the lowest income category shrank even more. At the other end of the income spectrum, households earning $100,000 or more increased their share by 124 percent, rising by 9.5 percentage points.

Lowering the upper boundary of the middle-class range to $74,999 produces a similar result. The middle class's share shrank even more, by 4.9 percentage points compared to 3.5 percentage points using the higher upper limit, and the share of those earning more than $75,000 rose by 10.9 percentage points. The bottom category's share, as above, fell by 6 percentage points. Using both upper limits, the middle class did indeed shrink, not by swelling the ranks of the less-well-off but by adding to the ranks of the richer.[39]

If the analysis is restricted to the recent past, from 2000 to 2005, the picture changes somewhat. Although the middle class shrank marginally using both middle-income ranges, the percentage of households in the lowest income category increased. The upper-income category, with its floor set at $75,000,

Table 9.7

Percentage Distribution of Households by Annual Income Category
(1980, 2000, and 2005)

	1980	2000	2005
Under $35,000	44.4	37.3	38.4
$35,000–$74,999	38.2	33.6	33.3
$75,000 and above	17.4	29.1	28.3
Under $35,000	44.4	37.3	38.4
$35,000–$99,999	47.9	45.5	44.4
$100,000 and above	7.7	17.2	17.2

Source: Census Bureau, U.S. Department of Commerce, *Income, Poverty, and Health Insurance Coverage: 2005*, August 2006, Table A-1.

also declined but remained constant when the floor is changed to $100,000. In contrast to the twenty-five-year time span, the ranks of upper-income households did not grow as the middle class declined. The ranks of the lower-earning households grew instead, using constant 2005 dollars. Yet care needs to be exercised in generalizing from such a short time frame.

But beyond income, how has the middle class done in the first decade of the twenty-first century? To answer that inquiry, we have to first ask another question: Along what important dimensions? Several dimensions of well-being are most apparent and are related to the American dream: owning a home, having health insurance, possessing the ability to send one's children to college, accumulating savings for contingencies, and attaining financial security in retirement. The problem is that there are no available data that consistently tie these dimensions explicitly to the middle class, as defined previously.

At the end of 2005, 69 percent of households in the United States owned their own homes, up from 67.5 percent in 2000 and 65.5 percent in 1980.[40] Houses were less affordable in 2005 than in 2000 but much more affordable than in 1980. According to the National Association of Realtors, the median-income household at the end of 2005 had 109.5 percent of the income needed to qualify for a loan (an affordability index value of 109.5) to buy a median existing-price home with a 20 percent down payment. In 2000 that household had 133.4 percent of the required income, putting it in a far more favorable financial position.[41] Declining real median income, sharply rising housing prices, and rising interest rates after June 2003 are largely responsible for the decrease in affordability. Despite the drop, housing in 2005 was much more affordable than it was twenty-five years earlier, when the affordability index averaged only 79.9.[42]

Yet a certain precariousness in home ownership existed in 2005 that was not present in 1980, and it worsened in 2006. Although increased affordability contributed to expanded home ownership, so did the greater willingness of lenders to make home loans to less-qualified borrowers. The growing use of sub-prime loans made to the most financially marginal borrowers carried elevated interest rates, increasing the earnings of lenders but putting added pressures on income-strapped borrowers. Lenders also introduced and expanded mortgage options that made it easier for borrowers to get into homes and make payments early in the loan term. Examples include the use of low introductory rates; sliding-scale payment-option mortgages, which offer lower payments initially but higher payments later on; and so-called balloon payments that require a lump-size payment due at the end of the loan period, typically many times larger than the scheduled monthly payment. Interest-only loans constitute another increasingly common device—for which borrowers pay only the interest due for a fixed period of time, typically five to seven years, but fail to reduce the principal over that term, then are obliged to repay the balance owed, refinance, or begin making payments that include both interest and principal reduction. Sub-prime loans made up about one-fifth of all loans originated in 2006, up from only 6 percent four years earlier.[43]

Borrowers who avail themselves of options that lower payments on the front end of a mortgage but make little or no dent in the principal run the risk in a declining housing market of owning a home whose value falls short of the balance owed. Those with adjustable rate mortgages that increase payments later in the loan's life, or that require large balloon payments at the end of the loan period, face elevated payments that they cannot afford.

In sum, not only have thrift institutions been increasingly willing to make it easier for less-qualified borrowers to acquire mortgages and afford payments in the short run; they have also upped the risk of default. While more and more Americans have come to acquire their piece of the American dream, home ownership for an increasing number has become shaky. Defaults on loans have risen, and an increasing number of borrowers can be expected to be squeezed financially to honor the terms of their mortgages.[44]

On the health-care front, Americans have become less financially secure. In 2005, 59.5 percent of Americans had health insurance provided by their employer, down from 63.6 percent five years earlier. Within that population of working Americans, 78.5 percent of families earning middle incomes (between 200 and 399 percent of federal poverty standards) had employer-provided health insurance, still down from 82.4 percent in 2001. Employees in families with incomes at or above 400 percent of the poverty level fared even better, with 92.2 percent having employer-provided insurance, down only slightly from 92.9 percent in 2001. Working families with incomes between 100 and 199 percent of poverty experienced greater health insecurity, with only 51.7 percent getting health insurance from their employers in 2005, down by seven percentage points from 2001.[45]

Nearly 15 percent of employees had no employer-provided health insurance in 2005, up from 12.5 percent in 2001. Middle- and upper-income workers were not much affected; the decline was greatest for the working poor and near-poor. The working poor have gotten squeezed at both ends: they have been the most likely to lose employer-provided health insurance and they often earn too much to be eligible for publicly financed Medicaid.[46]

Those workers fortunate to have employer-provided health insurance still faced rising out-of-pocket costs. They paid on average about 26 percent of the cost of premiums in 2005, down from 27 percent in 2000, giving them some modest relief. However, premium increases outstripped general inflation by an average factor of almost four to one, rising between 8.2 percent and 13.9 percent annually from 2000 through 2005. In 2005 workers paid an average of $226 per month as their share of premium costs, up significantly from $135 in 2000.[47]

As with health care, the cost of a college education has increased at a rate well beyond general inflation. In the 2005–2006 academic year, tuition, fees, and room and board at a private four-year college cost $29,026, up 31 percent from 2000 to 2001—a 17 percent increase above inflation. Although the average composite cost to attend a public four-year college in the 2005–2006 academic year was considerably cheaper, at $12,127, it rose from 2000–2001 at an even faster rate of 44 percent, or 28 percent in inflation-adjusted dollars. Most students, however, do not pay these published prices; they pay net costs after taking into account the value of grants and tax benefits, reducing the average cost of attending a private college in 2005–2006 by about a third and a public college by about 27 percent. Costs still increased well above inflation on a net basis, rising by 15 percent in constant dollars for private colleges and by 17 percent for public colleges between the 2000–2001 and 2005–2006 academic years.[48]

The pressure exerted on family budgets by rising college costs came at the same time that personal saving continued its fall, turning negative in 2005—the first year on record that the spending of Americans exceeded their disposable personal income. The recent decline in personal saving is nothing new. It has been sliding over the past twenty-five years. In 1980 Americans saved more than 10 percent of their after-tax income. By 2000 the saving rate had dropped to 2.4 percent, falling farther to -0.4 percent in 2005.

Americans are spending beyond their means, increasingly relying on their growing number of credit cards as the preferred instrument to finance their overspending. In 2005 the revolving debt of the average American household reached $7,569, up by 30 percent from $5,823 in 2000.[49] An ethic of "I want it now consumption" has clearly replaced the earlier treasured ethic of saving for the future.

While savings have plummeted and debt has grown, Americans also increasingly look toward less secure retirement. The traditional mainstay of retirement security, **defined-benefit pensions** provided by private-sector employers, has eroded significantly over the recent past. Traditional defined-benefit pensions in the private sector have represented a social contract of sorts, just as Social Security has. In essence, employers promised employees a fixed monthly income in retirement based on the length of employees' time on the job and their earnings. Longer work and higher earned income translated into higher retirement income. With the number of private-sector defined-benefit plans reaching a peak of 112,000 in 1985, the growing number of covered workers had a stable base of retirement income supplemented by Social Security. At that time, defined-benefit plans covered about one-third of all American workers. By 2004 only about 30,000 such plans remained.[50] Some have been eliminated altogether, using the assets to purchase annuities from private vendors that cover promised benefits for existing workers; others have been converted to **defined-contribution plans**, in which employers typically match employee contributions into 401(k)-type retirement vehicles, transferring risk from employers to their employees; and still others have defaulted, for which a federal government agency, the Pension Benefit Guaranty Corporation (PBGC), assumes responsibility to pay employee retirement benefits but at significantly reduced levels. The PBGC receives no general tax revenue support and relies on premiums paid by companies that offer defined-benefit plans. It does not insure employers offering defined-contribution plans. In FY 2004 the PBGC paid out $3 billion in reduced benefits to retirees whose employers fell into default.[51]

Just as employees' pension benefits have shrunk, so have employer-provided health benefits for retirees. In 1993, 40 percent of moderately large employers, those with 500 or more employees, offered health benefits for their workers who retired at normal retirement age. By 2004 that percentage fell by half—down to 20 percent.[52] Others that have continued to provide health insurance have raised the premiums that retirees pay for coverage, tightened eligibility, reduced benefits, or instituted some combination of these options. Some employers have established caps on how much they are willing to spend on health benefits for retirees. With this latter approach, as costs rise, retirees are left with picking up the difference.[53]

In this environment of shrinking private-sector pension and health-care benefits, both Social Security and Medicare will be called upon to do more.

As a wave of baby-boomer retirements begins in 2011, both programs will face mounting fiscal pressures, as discussed in chapter 8.

The Economy, Government, and Well-Being

The U.S. economy has performed well since rising out of the deep recession of 1981–82, with real GDP growth in the United States outpacing that of the Euro area and Japan over the next nearly twenty-five years. Yet the income generated by that growth was not equally distributed; in fact, income inequality rose. Only the top quintile of income earners increased their share of household income between 1980 and 2005. Those at the very top realized the greatest gains. Tax policy, especially the large federal income tax cuts of 1981, 2001, and 2003, disproportionately benefited upper-income taxpayers, those who pay the lion's share of income taxes in the first place. Expansions of the Earned Income Tax Credit during both the Clinton and George W. Bush administrations, along with expansion of the child tax credit, have put cash in the pockets of working low-income Americans. Those in the bottom two quintiles of income earners pay no federal income tax overall and they get a payment back from their tax filing. (See Table 9.6.)

It is those in the middle of the income range who have been squeezed. They have seen their share of market income shrink and have benefited the least from changes in federal tax policy. Furthermore, they have experienced the greatest insecurity in retaining health insurance and paying rising premium costs and in keeping private pension coverage. The rising price of housing in the middle of the first decade of the new century increased middle-income homeowners' home equity from which they could borrow to maintain or increase their spending. Rising home prices at the same time made homeowners feel wealthier and fostered increased spending, to the detriment of saving.

President Bill Clinton often remarked that government has an obligation to help people help themselves. But that dictum starts with people helping themselves. And an important way for people to help themselves is to live more within their means and put aside savings to meet future needs and contingencies. That is what Tom Brokaw's "Greatest Generation" did.[54] Government, though, can provide incentives to induce people to save, and it has done just that by creating and liberalizing tax-deferred saving plans, most prominently 401(k) (for employees of private-sector businesses) and 403(b) (for employees of educational institutions and nonprofit organizations), along with individual retirement accounts (IRAs) and college saving plans. Recognizing that the market has allocated income in favor of upper-income earners, especially those at the top, government could target income tax cuts to give greater benefit to middle-income taxpayers. Given the middle class's precarious financial situation, its members would likely spend the additional after-tax income on discretionary items or use it to retire debt and improve their financial position instead of saving it. That is the essence of individual freedom. Moreover, to the extent that they spend it, they contribute to aggregate demand and give the economy a demand-side boost. It is saving, however, that gives parents the wherewithal to send their children to college, that finances down payments on home purchases, that contributes to retirement security, and that makes the United States less dependent on the savings of foreigners.

Glossary

Appropriation— The authority to spend or obligate public funds.

Authorization— A legislative act that provides authority for the establishment or continuation of a governmental program. A program must be authorized before funds can be appropriated in its support and obligations can be incurred.

Balanced Budget— A budget in which revenues equal or exceed expenditures.

Balance of Payments— A summary of quarterly economic transactions of the United States with foreigners, including governments, organizations, and individuals. It includes trade in goods and services, receipts and payments of income, capital transfers, and transactions in U.S.-owned and foreign-owned financial assets.

Block Grants— Lump sum payments for grants-in-aid to states. With very few stipulations attached, they allow states to decide how best to spend the money.

Budget Authority— The legal authority to commit or spend public funds, whether in the form of an appropriation or the authority to borrow or enter into contractual obligations.

Budget Deficit— A condition in which spending exceeds revenues for a given budgetary period.

Budget Surplus— A condition in which revenues exceed spending for a given budgetary period.

Business Cycle— The trajectory of a national economy, in which it experiences periods of growth and contraction. Technically, the period of time it takes a national economy to rise from trough (low point) to peak and then to fall to the next trough.

Capital Budget— A budget for capital investment. State and local governments use the capital budget to segregate capital investments from operating expenditures. The federal government has no separate capital budget.

Capital Gain (Loss)— The increase or decrease in the selling price of an asset since the time it was purchased.

Concurrent Budget Resolution— An act of Congress not requiring presidential approval that establishes aggregate binding ceilings for revenues, budget authority, and outlays, yielding a projected surplus or deficit. It also includes estimates of budget authority and outlays for each budget function constituting the federal budget.

Constant Dollars— Dollars converted to the monetary value of a reference year, adjusted to the purchasing power of the dollar in that year.

Currency Exchange Rate— The rate at which one currency can be exchanged for another. It is the most widely accepted standard for comparing national economic output.

Current Account— A part of the balance of payments calculation. It includes the net sales from goods and services, income payments and income receipts, and net unilateral transfers from abroad.

Current Dollars— The current-year value of the dollar, unadjusted for changes in the dollar's purchasing power over time.

Deficit Spending— Spending beyond current revenue constraints. It is a tool of fiscal policy employed by the national government to increase aggregate demand in times of economic malaise.

Defined-Benefit Pensions— Plans in which employers promise employees a fixed monthly income in retirement based on the length of the employees' time on the job and their earnings.

Defined-Contribution Pensions— Plans in which employers typically match employee contributions into 401(k)-type retirement vehicles, transferring risk from employers to their employees.

Deflation— A decline in the overall price structure.

Deregulation— The process by which the government reduces or eliminates regulatory constraints on businesses and individuals to facilitate the efficient operation of markets.

Discount Rate— The rate of interest charged to depository institutions that borrow directly from the Federal Reserve.

Discretionary Spending— Spending over which budget makers have discretion, within limits set by law.

Disinflation— A decline in inflation, not a drop in overall price structure.

Disposable Personal Income— The amount of personal income left to individuals after they have paid taxes due. This is the amount available for spending or saving.

Dividends— After-tax profits that corporations pay out to their stockholders.

Domestic Content Requirement— Stipulation that a certain percentage of a final product be manufactured or assembled in the home country.

Emission Credits— Credits earned by firms employing pollution-abatement controls that reduce pollution emissions below required levels, which can subsequently be sold to firms that fail to meet emission requirements but use the acquired credits to avoid sanctions.

Entitlement— A requirement in federal law, applied to certain programs, that individuals who meet eligibility requirements for federal assistance have a legal right to that assistance, regardless of the amounts appropriated in support of the program.

Executive Budget— The chief executive's budget recommendations for a governmental jurisdiction.

Federal Funds Rate (FFR)— The rate of interest, set by the Federal Reserve through its open market transactions, that lending institutions charge one another for overnight loans.

Federal Grants-in-Aid— Federal financial assistance to state or local governments in support of federal programs.

Fiscal Policy— Economic policy that incorporates tax and spending decisions to expand or contract economic demand. Congress, typically at the behest of the president, increases spending or cuts taxes to increase demand and raises taxes or reduces spending to dampen demand.

Foreign Direct Investment— The ownership or control by individuals or corporations in one country of 10 percent or more of the voting securities of a corporation in another country or the equivalent interest in an unincorporated enterprise.

Foreign Portfolio Investment— The ownership or control of less than 10 percent of a private company's voting securities, along with foreign holdings of company or government bonds.

Gross Domestic Product (GDP)— The aggregate value of all goods and services produced within a country during a given period.

Gross National Product (GNP)— The total value of all goods and services produced by a country's citizens during a given period.

Holding Company— A corporation that owns companies outright or holds a controlling interest in their stock.

Impoundment— Executive action to prevent appropriated funds from being obligated or spent.

Inflation— A rise in the overall price structure.

Inflation Targeting— A practice in which a central bank announces inflation targets that it wishes to achieve in the near term and uses them to guide changes in interest rates.

Misery Index— The combined rate of unemployment and inflation.

Monetary Policy— Economic policy that deals with the availability and cost of loanable funds. Unlike fiscal policy, the authority for monetary policy has been vested in an independent government agency, the Federal Reserve.

Monopoly— Conditions that greatly restrict competition through collusion or ultimately by a single firm dominating the market.

National Debt— The total of borrowed money the government has yet to repay. It is the result of cumulative budget deficits.

National Health Service— A national system of universal health care in which public employees provide medical care in publicly owned offices and hospitals. This approach has been adopted in the United Kingdom, Italy, Spain, and various other European nations.

Negative Externalities— A condition in the economy in which the actions of private participants impose costs on others who fail to be compensated for them.

Neocorporatism— An economic strategy in which representatives of government, business, and labor voluntarily come together to shape national industrial strategy and manage conflict among the sectors' participants.

Outlays— Actual expenditures in a given fiscal year, which can include payment of obligations incurred in a prior year as well as the current year.

Peak Associations— Organizations at the national level to which individual unions and corporations are willing to yield significant authority to represent their interests.

Phillips Curve— The theorized inverse relationship, identified by economist A.W. Phillips, between unemployment and inflation. Stated simply, as unemployment declines, wages increase, precipitating a corresponding rise in the prices of goods and services.

Positive Externalities— A condition in the economy in which the actions of private participants confer benefits on others, who fail to pay for the benefits derived.

Progressive Taxation— A tax that increases as ability to pay increases. This is most typically associated with the income tax, where rates increase as income rises.

Proportional Taxation— A tax that applies the same rate to all levels of income.

Purchasing Power Parity— A method of comparing currency value that adjusts exchange rates to reflect differences in the purchasing power of currencies in their own countries.

Quotas— Limits on the amount of imported goods allowed into a country.

Recession— A condition in which the real (inflation-adjusted) gross domestic product declines for at least two consecutive quarters.

Reconciliation— The process by which Congress enacts legislation to modify authorizations or appropriations to comply with the limits included in the concurrent budget resolution.

Regulatory Authority— The power exercised by government agencies to command individuals and organizations to behave in certain ways. This authority in the federal government is vested in government agencies by acts of Congress or, under certain circumstances, by executive action of the president.

Reserve Requirement— A policy instrument of the Federal Reserve Board imposed on depository institutions requiring that they hold a certain percentage of their deposits—typically between 8 and 14 percent—in reserve, either in vault cash or as balances in Federal Reserve banks.

Sacrifice ratio— The extent to which unemployment has to increase to bring inflation down by one percentage point.

Sequestration— A presidential order to withhold federal budget authority in excess of the deficit level permitted for a given year.

Stagflation— A term used to describe a period of concomitant high price inflation and high unemployment.

Structural Unemployment— The degree to which unemployment is inevitable. This condition results from the unwillingness or inability of workers to find jobs, as well as changes in the composition and requirements of the economy.

Sum-Sufficient Appropriation— An appropriation in which the amounts in the schedule represent estimated outlays, but the actual draw on the treasury is a product of the costs of providing financial assistance or services to all those who meet statutorily prescribed eligibility requirements. A term used at the state level, comparable to entitlement at the federal level.

Tariffs— Taxes on imported goods, which raise the effective price of those goods to consumers, making them less price competitive and thereby biasing the options of consumers away from imported goods.

Tax Abatements— Incentives offered by local, state, and national governments to corporations in an attempt to attract new and expanded development within their jurisdictions. They can consist of reduced tax rates, deferrals of tax liability, or outright exemption from taxation.

Tax Expenditures— Foregone revenues that would otherwise have been collected had special provisions not been included in income tax codes.

Trade Balance— The dollar-value difference between exports and imports of goods and services. When a country imports more than it exports, it runs a trade deficit. The converse condition constitutes a trade surplus.

Transfer Payment— Direct payment of benefits to individuals who meet eligibility requirements to receive those benefits. Welfare (Temporary Assistance for Needy Families [TANF]), unemployment compensation, veterans' benefits, and Social Security constitute major transfer payments.

Worker Productivity— A measure of ouput divided by the number of hours worked.

Notes

Chapter 1. An Introduction to America's Political Economy

1. Bureau of Labor Statistics, U.S. Department of Labor, www.bls.gov.

2. Lawrence Lund, *Factors in Corporate Locational Decision* (New York: The Conference Board, 1979); Roger W. Schmenner, *Making Business Location Decisions* (Englewood Cliffs, NJ: Prentice-Hall, 1982); Michael Kieschnick, "Taxes and Growth: Business Incentives and Economic Development," in *State Taxation Policy*, ed. Michael Barker (Durham, NC: Duke University Press, 1983), 155–280; Richard H. Mattoon, *Economic Perspectives* 17, no. 3 (May/June 1993), 11–23; and Roger W. Schmenner, "The Location Decisions of New Services," in *New Service Development*, ed. James Fitzsimmons and Mona Fitzsimmons (Thousand Oaks, CA: Sage, 1999), 216–34.

3. *Budget of the United States Government*, FY 2007, *Historical Tables*, Tables 9.6 and 12.2.

4. Ibid., Tables 9.2 and 9.4.

5. Ibid., Table 9.8.

6. Charles W. Anderson, *Statecraft: An Introduction to Political Choice and Judgment* (New York: John Wiley & Sons, 1977), 17–22.

7. John Locke, "The Second Treatise of Government," in *Two Treatises of Government*, 3d ed., ed. Peter Laslett (New York: Cambridge University Press, 1988), 265–429.

8. John Stuart Mill, *On Liberty* (New York: Liberal Arts Press, 1958).

9. Adam Smith, *An Inquiry into the Nature and Causes of the Wealth of Nations* (New York: Modern Library, 1937).

10. Graham K. Wilson, *Business and Politics: A Comparative Introduction*, 3d ed. (New York: Chatham House Publishers, 2003), 111.

11. Ibid., 111–12. See Wilson's book for an excellent comparative introduction to business and politics.

12. Bureau of Labor Statistics, U.S. Department of Labor, *Union Members in 2006*, ftp://ftp.bls.gov/pub/news.release/union2.txt; Richard Lehne, *Government and Business* (New York: Chatham House Publishers, 2001), 50.

13. David Vogel, "Why American Businessmen Distrust Their State," *British Journal of Political Science* 11 (1981): 15.

14. John Maynard Keynes, *The General Theory of Employment, Interest and Money* (New York: Harcourt, Brace, 1964).

15. A.W. Phillips, "The Relation Between Unemployment and the Rate of Change of Money Wage Rates in the United Kingdom, 1861–1957," *Economica* 25 (November 1957): 263–99.

16. Robert E. Lane, "Market Justice, Political Justice," *American Political Science Review* 80 (June 1986): 383–402.

17. Pew Research Center, December 2004.

18. Pew Research Center, *Mapping the Political Landscape 2005*, 81.

19. The Gallup Organization, April/May 1998.

20. The Gallup Organization, January 2001.

21. Washington Post–Harvard University–Kaiser Foundation Poll, August 1998.

22. Pew Research Center, November 1997.

23. National Public Radio–Kaiser Foundation–Harvard University Kennedy School, January/February 2001.

24. Steve Farker et al., "Now That I'm Here: What Immigrants Have to Say About Life in the U.S. Today," January 2003, www.publicagenda.org/specials/immigration/executivesummary_now_that_im_here.pdf.

25. American Enterprise Institute, "Taking Stock of Business: Public Opinion After the Corporate Scandals," *AIE Public Opinion Studies*, May 26, 2006, 16.

26. Pew Research Center, *Mapping the Political Landscape 2005*, 82–83.

27. Charles E. Lindblom, "The Market as Prison," *The Journal of Politics* 44 (May 1982): 324–36.

28. Charles E. Lindblom, *Politics and Markets* (New York: Basic Books, 1977), 172.

Chapter 2. Measuring Economic Performance

1. Two resources provide helpful introductions to how the Bureau of Economic Analysis in the U.S. Department of Commerce organizes the complex sets of national income and product accounts. See *An Introduction to National Economic Accounting* (Springfield, VA: National Technical Information Service, U.S. Department of Commerce, March 1985) and Norman Frumkin, *Tracking America's Economy*, 4th ed. (Armonk, NY: M.E. Sharpe, 2004).

2. Bureau of Economic Analysis, U.S. Department of Commerce, *News Release: Gross Domestic Product*, March 29, 2007, Table 9.

3. Paul Krugman, *The Age of Diminished Expectations* (Cambridge, MA: The MIT Press, 1994), 22.

4. *Remarks by Governor Ben S. Bernanke at the Peter McColough Roundtable Series on International Economics, Council on Foreign Relations*, University of Arkansas at Little Rock, February 24, 2005.

5. Jonathan Skinner and Douglas Staiger, "Technology Adoption from Hybrid Corn to Beta Blockers," *National Bureau of Economic Research Working Paper 11251*, March 2005.

6. Raffaella Sadun and John Van Reenen, "Information Technology and Productivity: It Ain't What You Do, It's the Way You Do It," *London School of Economics and Political Science EDS Paper 002*, October 2005.

7. Bureau of Labor Statistics, U.S. Department of Labor.

8. Bureau of Economic Analysis, U.S. Department of Commerce, *News Release: Gross Domestic Product*, March 29, 2007, Table 1.

9. A.W. Phillips, "The Relationship Between Unemployment and the Rate of Change of Money Wage Rates in the United Kingdom, 1861–1957," *Economica* 25 (November 1957): 263–99.

10. Carl E. Walsh, "The National Rate, NAIRU, and Monetary Policy," *FRBSF Economic Newsletter*, September 18, 1998.

11. Norman Frumkin, *Tracking America's Economy*, 4th ed., 47.

12. Laurence Bell and N. Gregory Mankiw, "The NAIRU in Theory and Practice," *National Bureau of Economic Research Working Paper 8940*, May 2002.

13. Donald L. Kohn, "Inflation Modeling: A Policymakers' Perspective," *Paper Presented at the Quantitative Evidence on Price Determination Conference*, Washington, DC, September 29, 2005.

Chapter 3. Monetary Policy Making

1. This section on monetary policy draws on information and analysis found in *U.S. Monetary Policy: An Introduction* (San Francisco: The Federal Reserve Bank of San Francisco, 2004).

2. Before 1980, only banks that were members of the Federal Reserve System were subject to reserve requirements. However, the Monetary Control Act of 1980 extended the requirement to all depository institutions.

3. Kelly H. Chang, *Appointing Central Bankers* (Cambridge, United Kingdom: Cambridge University Press, 2003), 130–37; Donald F. Kettle, *Leadership at the Fed* (New Haven: Yale University Press, 1986), 42–55.

4. *Remarks by Laurence H. Meyer, Member of the Board of Governors of the Federal Reserve System at the University of Wisconsin, LaCrosse, Wisconsin*, October 24, 2000.

5. *Remarks by Alan Greenspan, Chairman of the Board of Governors of the Federal Reserve System, at a Symposium Sponsored by the Federal Reserve Bank of Kansas City, Jackson Hole, Wyoming*, August 26, 2005.

6. *Remarks by Laurence H. Meyer*, October 24, 2000.

7. *Remarks by Edward M. Gramlich, Member of the Board of Governors of the Federal Reserve System, at the Euromoney Inflation Conference, Paris*, May 26, 2005.

8. Cristina D. Romer and David H. Romer, "The Evolution of Economic Understanding and Postwar Stabilization Policy," *Rethinking Stabilization Policy: A Symposium Sponsored by the Federal Reserve Bank of Kansas City, Jackson Hole, Wyoming*, August 29–31, 2002.

9. Glenn Rudebusch, "Interest Rates and Monetary Policy," *FRBSF Economic Letter*, no. 97–18 (June 13, 1997).

10. Alan Greenspan, *Testimony Before the Subcommittee on Domestic and International Monetary Policy of the House Committee on Banking and Financial Services*, July 22, 1997.

11. Ibid., 7.

12. Dean Foust, "Alan Greenspan's Brave New World," *Business Week*, July 14, 1997: 45–50.

13. Federal Reserve Bank of New York, *Fedpoint*, June 2003, www.ny.frb.org/aboutthefed/fedpoint/fed48.html.

14. Quoted in *Business Week*, July 7, 1997: 48.

15. Alan Binder, "The Speed Limit: Fact and Fancy in the Growth Debate," *The American Prospect* 34 (September–October 1997): 57–62.

16. Robert Eisner, *The Misunderstood Economy* (Cambridge, MA: Harvard Business School Press, 1995), 145–213; Lester Thurow, "The Crusade That's Killing Prosperity," *The American Prospect* 25 (March–April 1996): 54–59; James K. Galbraith, "The Surrender of Economic Policy," *The American Prospect* 25

(March–April 1996): 60–67; James K. Galbraith, "Test the Limit," *The American Prospect* 34 (September–October 1997), 66–67; and Barry Bluestone and Bennett Harrison, "Why We Can Grow Faster," *The American Prospect* 34 (September–October 1997): 63–70.

17. Lester Thurow, "The Crusade That's Killing Prosperity": 59.

18. *Remarks by Ben S. Bernanke, Member of the Board of Governors of the Federal Reserve System Before the National Economists Club*, Washington, DC, November 21, 2002.

19. Alan S. Binder and Ricardo Reis, "Understanding the Greenspan Standard," prepared for the Federal Reserve Bank of Kansas City symposium, *The Greenspan Era: Lessons for the Future*, Jackson Hole, WY, August 25–27, 2005.

20. *The Economist* 378, no. 8460 (January 14, 2006): 67.

21. The National Association of Realtors, www.realtor.org/Research.

22. Sue Kirchhoff, "Bubble or Not, High Home Prices Can Hurt," *USA Today*, May 10, 2005, www.usatoday.com/money/perfi/housing/2005–05–10-housing-cover_x.htm

23. Ben S. Bernanke and Mark Gertler, "Should Central Banks Respond to Movements in Asset Prices," *The American Economic Review* 91, no. 2 (May 2001): 253–57; and Ben S. Bernanke and Mark Gertler, "Monetary Policy and Asset Price Volatility," prepared for the Federal Reserve Bank of Kansas City symposium, *New Challenges for Monetary Policy*, Jackson Hole, Wyoming, August 26–28, 1999.

24. Ben S. Bernanke and Mark Gertler, "Should Central Banks Respond to Movements in Asset Prices": 253.

25. Donald Kettl, *Leadership at the Fed* (New Haven, CT: Yale University Press, 1986), 93.

26. Thomas Havrilesky, *The Pressures on American Monetary Policy*, 2d ed. (Boston: Kluwer Academic Publishers, 1995), 65.

27. William Greider, *Secrets of the Temple: How the Federal Reserve Runs the Country* (New York: Simon and Schuster, 1987), 217.

28. Ibid., 357.

29. Quoted in ibid., 379.

30. Clyde H. Farnsworth, "Brady Warns That Fed Could Delay Recovery," *New York Times*, June 2, 1992; and Richard H. Timberlake, *Monetary Policy in the United States: An Intellectual and Institutional History*, 390–401.

31. www.Eisenhowerinstitute.org/programs/livinghistory/SaulnierOutline.htm.

32. *Remarks by Laurence H. Meyer*, October 24, 2000.

33. John T. Woolley, "The Politics of Monetary Policy: A Critical Review," *Journal of Public Policy* 14 (1994): 57–85.

34. John T. Woolley, *Monetary Politics* (New York: Cambridge University Press, 1984), 144–52.

35. Ibid., 150.

36. Ibid., 143.

37. *Statistical Abstract of the United States*, 1987, 395.

38. Bureau of Labor Statistics, Employment, Hours, and Earnings from the Current Employment Survey, www.bls.gov.

Chapter 4. Fiscal Policy Making

1. Stephen L. Robertson, "The Executive Office of the President: White House Office," in *Cabinets and Counselors: The President and the Executive Branch*, 2d

ed., ed. W. Craig Bledsoe et al. (Washington, DC: Congressional Quarterly, Inc., 1997), 3.

2. Herbert Stein, *The Fiscal Revolution in America* (Washington, DC: The AEI Press, 1996), 108–20.

3. Herbert Stein, *Presidential Economics*, 3d ed. (Washington, DC: The AEI Press, 1994), 34–46.

4. Roger Porter, "Economic Advice to the President, from Eisenhower to Reagan," *Political Science Quarterly 98* (Fall 1983): 403–26; and Edwin C. Hargrove and Samuel A. Moorley, eds., *The President and the Council of Economic Advisors: Interviews with CEA Chairmen* (Boulder, CO: Westview Press, 1984).

5. James J. Gosling, *Budgetary Politics in American Governments*, 4th ed. (New York: Routledge, 2006), 118–21.

6. Jeffrey E. Cohen, *Politics and Economic Policy in the United States* (Boston: Houghton Mifflin Co., 1997), 144–45.

7. Aaron Wildavsky, *The Politics of the Budgetary Process* (Boston: Little, Brown, 1964), 58.

8. Office of Management and Budget, *The Budget of the United States Government*, Fiscal Years 1961 and 1975.

9. Committee on the Budget, United States Senate, *Congressional Budget Reform* (Washington, DC: Government Printing Office, 1976), 8.

10. Herbert Stein, *The Fiscal Revolution in America*, 49–63.

11. Ibid., 170–75.

12. Marc Allan Eisner, *The State in the American Political Economy* (Englewood Cliffs, NJ: Prentice-Hall, 1995), 246–49; and Daniel C. Diller and Dean J. Peterson, "Chief Economist," in *Powers of the Presidency*, 2d ed. (Washington, DC: Congressional Quarterly, Inc., 1997), 248.

13. Herbert Stein, *The Fiscal Revolution in America*, 314.

14. Ibid., 299–308.

15. Ibid., 329.

16. Arthur F. Burns and Paul A. Samuelson, *Full Employment, Guideposts and Economic Stability* (Washington, DC: American Enterprise Institute for Public Policy Research, 1967), 86–88.

17. Herbert Stein, *Presidential Economics*, 89–101.

18. Council of Economic Advisers, *Economic Report of the President*, 1963, xxiv.

19. Ibid., 74.

20. Herbert Stein, *Presidential Economics*, 107.

21. Ibid., 111–12; and *Economic Report of the President*, 1966, 38.

22. Marc Allan Eisner, *The State in the American Political Economy*, 254.

23. Norman C. Thomas and Joseph A. Pika, *The Politics of the Presidency*, 4th ed. (Washington, DC: Congressional Quarterly Press, 1996), 40–42.

24. Marc Allan Eisner, *The State in the American Political Economy*, 256.

25. Paul Krugman, *Peddling Prosperity* (New York: W.W. Norton, 1994), 126.

26. The Concord Coalition, "The Surplus Field of Dreams," *Issue Brief*, October 11, 2000.

27. *Remarks by the President in Tax Cut Bill Signing Ceremony*, Office of the Press Secretary, The White House, June 7, 2001.

28. Ibid.

29. *President Signs Jobs and Growth Tax Reconciliation Act of 2003*, Office of the Press Secretary, The White House, May 28, 2003.

Chapter 5. Deficits and Debt

1. James J. Gosling, *Budgetary Politics in American Governments*, 4th ed. (New York: Routledge, 2006), 93.

2. *Budget of the United States Government, FY 2008, Analytical Perspectives*, 235.

3. *The Budget of the United States Government, FY 2000, Historical Tables*, Table 1.1, 19–20.

4. Council of Economic Advisers, *Economic Report of the President*, February 1999, 331.

5. Robert L. Bartley, *The Seven Fat Years and How to Do It Again* (New York: The Free Press, 1992).

6. Allen Schick, *The Federal Budget: Politics, Policy, Process* (Washington, DC: The Brookings Institution, 1995), 4–6.

7. Social Security Administration, *A Summary of the 2006 Annual Social Security and Medicare Trust Fund Reports*, www.ssa.gov/OACT/TRSUM/trsummary.html.

8. Congressional Budget Office, *The Budget and Economic Outlook: Fiscal Years 2008 to 2017*, January 2007, 50.

9. *Budget of the United States Government, FY 2008, Historical Tables*, 52–53.

10. Robert Eisner, *The Misunderstood Economy: What Counts and How to Count It* (Boston: Harvard Business School Press, 1994), 101.

11. Brian Riedl, "Why America's Debt Burden Is Declining," *Backgrounder No. 1820* (Washington, DC: Heritage Foundation, February 7, 2005), 3–4.

12. Eric Engen and Glenn Hubbard, "Federal Government Debt and Interest Rates," *Institute Working Paper No. 105* (Washington, DC: American Enterprise Institute, June 2, 2004), 1.

13. Paul Krugman, *The Age of Diminished Expectations* (Cambridge, MA: The MIT Press, 1994), 51–52.

14. Benjamin M. Friedman, "U.S. Fiscal Policy in the 1980s: Consequences of Large Budget Deficits at Full Employment," in *Debt and the Twin Deficits Debate*, ed. James M. Rock (Mountain View, CA: Mayfield Publishing Co., 1991), 149.

15. Paul Krugman, *The Age of Diminished Expectations*, 54.

16. Benjamin M. Friedman, "U.S. Fiscal Policy in the 1980s: Consequences of Large Budget Deficits at Full Employment," 163–164; and Robert Eisner, *The Misunderstood Economy: What Counts and How to Count It*, 41.

17. Robert Eisner, "Deficits for Us and Our Grandchildren," in *Debt and the Twin Deficits Debate*, ed. James M. Rock, 82.

18. Ibid.

19. Robert Heilbroner and Peter Bernstein, *The Debt and the Deficit*, 71–81.

20. Paul Krugman, *The Age of Diminished Expectations*, 91–93.

21. Robert Eisner, *The Misunderstood Economy: What Counts and How to Count It*, 196–99.

22. David Alan Aschauer, "Is Public Expenditure Productive," *Journal of Monetary Economics* 23 (March 1989): 177–200; and Robert Eisner, "Extended Measures of National Income and Product Account," *Journal of Economic Literature* 26 (December 1988): 1611–84.

23. Robert Eisner, "Deficits for Us and Our Grandchildren," 85.

24. Karen M. Paget, "The Balanced Budget Trap," *The American Prospect* 29 (December 1996): 21–29.

25. Reported in *Congressional Quarterly Weekly Report* 53, no. 2 (January 14, 1995): 144.

26. Richard Kogan, *The New Pay-As-You-Go Rule* (Washington, D.C.: Center on Budget and Policy Priorities), January 12, 2007.

Chapter 6. America in the Global Economy

1. Council of Economic Advisers, *Economic Report of the President*, 2006, 156.

2. Ronald I. McKinnon, "Government Deficits and the Deindustrialization of America," *The Economists' Voice* 1, Issue 3 (2004), www.bepress.com/ev.

3. "Survey of the World Economy," *The Economist* 376, no. 8445 (September 24, 2005): 4.

4. "Special Report: Asia and the World Economy," *The Economist* 381, no. 8500 (October 31, 2006): 80.

5. Ben S. Bernanke, "The Global Saving Glut and the U.S. Current Account Deficit," *The Homer Jones Lecture, St. Louis, Missouri*, April 14, 2005.

6. Raymond J. Mataloni Jr., "U.S. Multinational Companies: Operations in 2003," *Survey of Current Business*, July 2005: 13.

7. *The Economist* 379, no. 8471 (April 1, 2006): 60.

8. *Economic Report of the President*, 2006, 150.

9. Ibid.; and Jeffrey E. Cohen, *Politics and Economic Policy in the United States* (Boston: Houghton Mifflin Company, 1997), 320.

10. *Economic Report of the President*, 2006, 150–51.

11. The World Trade Organization, *The WTO in Brief*, 2005.

12. See Stephen Cohen et al., *The Fundamentals of U.S. Foreign Trade Policy* (Boulder, CO: Westview Press, 1996).

13. Robert E. Lane, "Market Justice, Political Justice," *American Political Science Review* 80 (June 1986): 383–402.

14. David Ricardo, *On the Principles of Political Economy and Taxation*, in *The Works and Correspondence of David Ricardo*, ed. Piero Straffa (Cambridge, MA: Cambridge University Press, 1966).

15. For a comprehensive illustration of this point, see Chalmers Johnson, *MITI and the Japanese Miracle* (Stanford, CA: Stanford University Press, 1982).

16. The provisions highlighted in this table are drawn from discussions found in Linda M. Aguilar, "NAFTA: A Review of the Issues," *Economic Perspectives* 17, no. 1 (July/February 1993): 12–20.

17. Robert Lawrence, "Emerging Regional Arrangements: Building Blocks or Stumbling Blocks," in *Finance and the International Economy*, ed. Richard O' Brien (New York: Oxford University Press, 1991), 22–35.

18. Office of the United States Trade Representative, *Trade Facts*, March 2006, www.ustr.gov.

19. Office of the United States Trade Representative, *NAFTA at Eight*, May 2002, www.ustr.gov.

20. Jennifer L. Koncz and Daniel R. Yorgason, "Direct Investment Positions for 2004," *Survey of Current Business*, July 2005: 41, 44.

21. James K. Jackson, "U.S. Direct Investment Abroad: Trends and Current Issues," *CRS Report for Congress*, April 29, 2005.

22. William L. Zeile, "Merchandise Trade of U.S. Affiliates of Foreign Companies," *Survey of Current Business*, October 1993: 63.

23. Bureau of Economic Analysis, U.S. Department of Commerce, *Summary Estimates for Multinational Companies: Employment, Sales, and Capital Expenditures for 2004*, April 10, 2006.

24. *Economic Report of the President*, 2006, 161.

25. Thomas Palley, "The Economics of Outsourcing: How Should Policy Respond?" *FPIP Policy Report*, March 2, 2006.

26. Ibid.

27. Diana Farrell and Jaeson Rosenfeld, *U.S. Offshoring: Rethinking the Response*, McKinsey and Company, December 2005; and John C. McCarthy, *Near-Term Growth of Offshoring Accelerating*, Forrester Research, Inc., May 14, 2004.

28. Ralph Kozlow, "Globalization, Offshoring, and Multinational Companies: What Are the Questions, and How Well Are We Doing in Answering Them?" paper presented at the 2006 Annual Meeting of the American Economic Association, Boston, MA, January 6, 2006, 8–9.

29. Includes Germany, France, Italy, Spain, Netherlands, Belgium, Austria, Finland, Greece, Portugal, Ireland, and Luxembourg.

30. International Monetary Fund, *World Economic Outlook*, April 2006, www.imf. org/Pubs/FT/weo/2006/01/index.htm.

31. See Paul Krugman, *The Age of Diminished Expectations* (Cambridge, MA: The MIT Press), 50–58.

Chapter 7. Government Regulation and Deregulation

1. Milton Friedman, *Free to Choose* (Chicago: University of Chicago Press, 1980), 5.

2. This insight comes from John G. Francis, in his *The Politics of Regulation: A Comparative Perspective* (Cambridge, MA: Blackwell Publishers, 1993), 11–17.

3. This discussion draws on Marc Allan Eisner's historical analysis in *The State in the American Political Economy* (Englewood Cliffs, NJ: Prentice-Hall, 1995).

4. Eisner, *The State in the American Political Economy*, 99.

5. Marc Allan Eisner, *Regulatory Politics in Transition* (Baltimore: Johns Hopkins University Press, 1993), 47–72.

6. *Wabash, St. Louis & Pacific Railway Co. v. Illinois*, 118 U.S. 557 (1986), cited in Eisner, *The State in the American Political Economy*, 113.

7. Jeffrey E. Cohen, *Politics and Economic Policy in the United States* (Boston: Houghton Mifflin Co., 1997), 264.

8. Lynn Hargis, "PUCHA for Dummies," *Public Citizen*, September 2003, www. citizen.org.

9. Donald V. Harper, *Transportation in America: Users, Carriers, Government*, 2d ed. (Englewood Cliffs, NJ: Prentice-Hall, 1982), 468.

10. William Lilley III and James Miller III, "The New Social Regulation," *The Public Interest* 47 (Spring 1977): 52–53.

11. Steven Kelman, "Occupational Safety and Health Administration," in *The Politics of Regulation*, ed. James Q. Wilson (New York: Basic Books, 1980), 236–66.

12. This section incorporates and selectively revises material written by the author and included in Dennis L. Dresang and James J. Gosling, *Politics and Policy in American States and Communities*, 6th ed. (New York: Pearson Longman, 2008), 506–18. It appears with permission of the publisher.

13. Kenneth J. Meier, *Regulation: Politics, Bureaucracy, and Economics* (New York: St. Martin's Press, 1985), 141–43.

14. This analysis largely comes from Kenneth J. Meier in his *Regulation: Politics, Bureaucracy, and Economics*, 143–44, although it is supplemented by the insights of Alfred Marcus in his chapter "Environmental Protection Agency," appearing in *The Politics of Regulation*, ed. James Q. Wilson, 267–303, and those of Charles O. Jones in his *Clean Air* (Pittsburgh: Pittsburgh University Press, 1975), 191–93.

15. Norman J. Vig and Michael E. Kraft, "Environmental Policy from the Seventies to the Eighties," in *Environmental Policy in the 1980s: Reagan's New Agenda*, eds. Norman J. Vig and Michael E. Kraft (Washington, DC: Congressional Quarterly Press, 1984), 17.

16. The Council on Environmental Quality, *Environmental Quality*, 1981 (Washington, DC: Government Printing Office, 1981), 33, 243, 246.

17. Helen M. Ingram and Dean E. Mann, "Preserving the Clean Water Act: The Appearance of Environmental Victory," in *Environmental Policy in the 1980s: Reagan's New Agenda*, 255–256.

18. Ibid.

19. *Environmental Quality*, 1980 (Washington, DC: The Council on Environmental Quality, 1980), iv.

20. Michael E. Kraft, "A New Environmental Policy Agenda: The 1980 Presidential Campaign and Its Aftermath," in *Environmental Policy in the 1980s: Reagan's New Agenda*, 29–50.

21. Norman J. Vig, "The President and the Environment: Revolution or Retreat," in *Environmental Policy in the 1980s: Reagan's New Agenda*, 87.

22. Ibid.

23. Susan Welch et al., *American Government*, 4th ed. (St. Paul, MN: West Publishing, 1992), 578.

24. R. Shep Melnick, "Pollution Deadlines and the Coalition for Failure," in *Environmental Politics*, eds. Michael S. Greve and Fred L. Smith (New York: Praeger, 1993) 89–104.

25. *Oral Testimony of Fred Hanson, Deputy Administrator, Environmental Protection Agency, Before the Subcommittee on Commercial and Administrative Law, Committee on the Judiciary, U.S. House of Representatives*, July 20, 1997; and Jackie Cummins Radcliffe and Jeff Dale, "Defining Dirty Air," *State Legislatures* 23, no. 5 (May 1997): 20–25.

26. Tom Arrandale, "The Selling of the Garbage Glut," *Governing* (April 1993): 28–32.

27. National Conference of State Legislatures, *Air Quality*, April 27, 2000.www.ncsl.org/programs/esnr/cleanair.htm; and Sierra Club, *Clean Air Program*, www.sierraclub.org/cleanair/standards.asp.

28. *White Paper on the Clear Skies Initiative and the Current Clean Air Act* (Washington, DC: U.S. Environmental Protection Agency, 2002).

29. James E. McCarthy, "Clean Air Act Issues in the 109th Congress," *CRS Issue Brief for Congress*, updated May 3, 2006, www.ncseonline.org/NLE/CRSreports/06apr/IB10137.pdf.

30. National Resources Defense Council, Rewriting the Rules (2005 Special Edition), www.nrdc.org/legislation/rollbacks/execsum.asp.

31. James E. McCarthy, "Clean Air Act Issues in the 109th Congress."

32. This discussion of the deregulation of commercial transportation relies on

the work of Charles F. Bonser et al., *Policy Choice and Public Action* (Upper Saddle River, NJ: Prentice-Hall, 1996), 217–40; and Martha Derthick and Paul Quirk, *The Politics of Deregulation* (Washington, DC: The Brookings Institution, 1985), especially chapters 1, 2, and 7.

33. Charles F. Bonser et al., *Policy Choice and Public Action*, 235.

34. John E. Robson, "Airline Deregulation: Twenty Years of Success and Counting," *Regulation* 21 (1988): 17–22; Adam D. Thierer, "Twentieth Year of Airline Deregulation: Cause for Celebration, Not Re-regulation," *The Heritage Foundation Backgrounder* (October 28, 1997); and Steven A. Morrison and Clifford Winston, *The Evolution of the Airline Industry* (Washington, DC: The Brookings Institution, 1995), 6–19.

35. Paul Teske et al., *Deregulating Freight Transportation: Delivering the Goods* (Washington, DC: The AEI Press, 1995); and Clifford Winston et al., *The Economic Effects of Surface Freight Regulation* (Washington, DC: The Brookings Institution, 1990).

36. Cohen, *Politics and Economic Policy in the United States*, 274.

37. Martha Derthick and Paul Quirk, *The Politics of Deregulation*, 238–45.

38. John W. Kingdon, *Agendas, Alternatives, and Public Policies*, 2d ed. (New York: HarperCollins, 1995).

39. A concept contributed by Herbert Simon that gets at the way decision makers simplify choice by screening out cues that are inconsistent with a restricted set of options in harmony with ingrained predispositions, or givens. See his *Administrative Behavior* (New York: Macmillan, 1958).

40. Jon Healey, "Information Network: Congress Tries to Merge Public Goals with Industry Interests," *The Information Arena: Making Communications Policy for the Next Generation, Congressional Quarterly Special Report* 52, Supplement to no. 19 (May 14, 1994): 11.

41. Dick W. Oluffs III, *The Making of Telecommunications Policy* (Boulder, CO: Lynne Rienner Publishers, 1999), 35.

42. The FCC's *Execunet* decision (*MCI Telecommunications Corporation v. FCC*), 1979.

43. Dick W. Oluffs III, *The Making of Telecommunications Policy*, 53.

44. Ibid., 55; and Elizabeth E. Bailey, "The Evolving Politics of Telecommunications Regulation," in *A Communications Cornucopia*, ed. Roger G. Noll and Monroe E. Price (Washington, DC: The Brookings Institution, 1968), 390–92.

45. Elizabeth E. Bailey, "The Evolving Politics of Telecommunications Regulation," 392.

46. Dick W. Oluffs III, *The Making of Telecommunications Policy*, 102.

47. Ibid., 102–3.

48. Dan Carney, "Congress Fires Its First Shot in Information Revolution," *Congressional Quarterly Weekly Report* 54, no. 5 (February 3, 1996): 289–94; and Jon Healey, "Telecommunications Highlights," *Congressional Quarterly Weekly Report* 54, no. 7 (February 17, 1996): 406–20.

49. *Remarks by the President in Signing Ceremony for the Telecommunications Act Conference Report*, February 8, 1996.

50. Robert D. Boerner, "Reach Out, But Not Too Far," *State Legislatures* 24, no. 5 (May 1998), 32–33; and Lisa Moskowitz, "Telecom Update: Baby Bells Fight Improved Net Service, *PCWorld online*, July 22, 1997, www.idg.net/idg_frames/english/content.cgi?vc=docid_0–73009.html.

51. David Masci, "Telecoms' Unfinished Business," *Congressional Quarterly Special Report* 57, Supplement to no. 19.

52. As reported in Thomas Hazlett and Coleman Bazelon, "Regulated Unbundling of Telecommunications Networks: A Stepping Stone to Facilities-Based Competition?" unpublished draft, September 20, 2005.

53. 540 US 398 (2004).

54. 359 F3d 554 (2004).

55. For a fuller discussion of these decisions and their impact, see Thomas W. Hazlett, "Rivalrous Telecommunications Networks with and without Mandatory Sharing," *AEI-Brookings Joint Center for Regulatory Studies Working Paper 05–07*, March 2005; and Scott Wallsten, "Broadband and Unbundling Regulations in OECD Countries," *AEI-Brookings Joint Center for Regulatory Studies Working Paper 6–16*, June 2006.

56. Richard E. Balzhiser, "Technology to Play Hand in Future Power Market," *Forum for Applied Research and Public Policy* 12, no. 3 (Fall 1997): 24.

57. Ibid., 25. Thanks go to Brigham Daniels for helping me to appreciate technology's contributions to electric-power deregulation.

58. Adam D. Thierer, "Energizing America: A Blueprint for Deregulating the Electricity Market," *Backgrounder*, no. 1100 (The Heritage Foundation, January 23, 1997c), 5–7.

59. "Electric Industry Restructuring: Issues and Opportunities for the States," *NGA Issue Brief* (February 2, 1997), 1; and Eric Hurst, "21st Century Will Transform Power Industry," *Forum for Applied Research and Public Policy* 12, no. 3 (Fall 1997): 7–8.

60. Pamela S. Easter, "A Spotlight on Electric Deregulation," *Public Management* (February 1997): 11.

61. National Conference of State Legislatures, *Energy Newsletter* 2, no. 1 (March 2006): 2.

62. Jeffrey E. Cohen, *Politics and Economic Policy in the United States*, 275–77.

63. Ibid., 278–80.

64. Susan E. Dudley and Angela Antonelli, "Congress and the Clinton OMB: Unwilling Partners in Regulatory Oversight?" *Regulation* 20, no. 4 (Fall 1997): 17–18.

65. Alan Freedman, "GOP's Secret Weapon Against Regulations: Finesse," *Congressional Quarterly Weekly Report* 56, no. 35 (September 5, 1998): 2314–20.

66. David Kohn, "Foes Say Bush Plan Would Create Debating Society over Science," *Baltimore Sun*, December 19, 2003: 3.

Chapter 8. Government and Social Provisioning

1. Louis Hartz, *The Classical Tradition in America* (New York: Harcourt, Brace, 1955).

2. Andrew Kohut and Bruce Stokes, "Two Americas, One American," *Pew Research Center Backgrounder*, June 6, 2006, www.pewresearch.org/pubs/29/two-americans-one-america.

3. Roper Center for Public Policy Research, *Public Perspective* 9, no. 2 (February/March 1998): 32.

4. Meg Bostrom, *Achieving the American Dream: A Meta-Analysis of Public Opinion Concerning Poverty, Upward Mobility, and Related Issues* (New York: Ford Foundation, 2001), 14.

5. National Public Radio, *Poverty in America*, based on the results of an NPR–Kaiser Foundation–Harvard University Kennedy School Poll, January/February 2001.

6. Pew Research Center for the People & the Press, 2004.

7. Peter Whiteford and Edward Whitehouse, "Pension Challenge and Pension Reforms in OECD Countries," *Oxford Review of Economic Policy* 22, no. 1 (2006): 87 and Economic Policy Institute, *Social Security Facts at a Glance*, May 2005, www.epinet.org/content.cfm/issueguide_socialsecurityfacts.

8. Census Bureau, U.S. Department of Commerce, *Income, Poverty, and Health Insurance Coverage in the United States: 2005*, August 2006, 46–58.

9. U.S. Census Bureau News Release, CB97–155 (April 8, 1997).

10. *Income, Poverty, and Health Insurance Coverage in the United States: 2005*, 46.

11. Hispanics were included within the category of whites in 1959, whereas they are excluded in 2005.

12. *Income, Poverty, and Health Insurance Coverage in the United States: 2005*, 49, 51.

13. Ibid., 14.

14. Ibid., 49.

15. *Federal Register* 71, no. 15 (January 24, 2006): 3848–49.

16. This section incorporates and selectively revises material written by the author and included in Dennis L. Dresang and James J. Gosling, *Politics and Policy in American States and Communities*, 6th ed. (New York: Pearson Longman, 2008): 475–80.

17. Jeffrey L. Katz, "Long-Term Challenges Temper Cheers for Welfare Successes," *Congressional Quarterly Weekly Report* 55, no. 42 (October 25, 1997): 2605.

18. Council of Economic Advisers, *Explaining the Decline in Welfare Receipt, 1993–1996*, May 9, 1997.

19. Office of the Press Secretary, *Statement by the President*, August 22, 1996.

20. Christopher R. Conte, "Will Workfare Work?" *Governing* 9, no. 7 (April 1996): 20.

21. Rebecca M. Blank, "Was Welfare Reform Successful?" *Economists' Voice*, March 2006, www.bepress.com/ev.

22. Joint Economic Committee, U.S. Congress, "Handbook of Public Income Transfer Payments and Training for Low Income Populations," in *A Decade of Federal Antipoverty Programs*, ed. Robert H. Haveman (New York: Academic Press, 1977), 123–89; Irene Laurie, "Work Requirements in Income-Conditional Transfer Programs," *Social Security Review* 52 (December 1978): 551–66.

23. Census Bureau, U.S. Department of Commerce, *Current Population Survey 2004, Annual Social and Economic Supplement*, August 2005, Table PINC-08; Elise Golan and Mark Nord, "How Government Assistance Affects Income," *Food Review* (January–April 1998): 6.

24. Lawrence Mead, *The New Politics of Poverty* (New York: Basic Books, 1992), 8.

25. Ibid., 15.

26. Charles Murray, *Losing Ground* (New York: Basic Books, 1984).

27. Mary Jo Bane, "Welfare as We Might Know It," *American Prospect*, no. 30 (January–February 1997): 47–55.

28. Christopher Jencks, "The Hidden Paradox of Welfare Reform," *American Prospect*, no. 32 (May–June 1997): 33–40.

29. Frances Fox Piven and Richard A. Cloward, "The Contemporary Relief Debate," in *The Mean Season: The Attack on the Welfare State*, 45–108.

30. Social Security Administration, July 28, 2006, www.socialsecurity.gov/pubs/11125.html.

31. Census Bureau, *Income, Poverty, and Health Insurance Coverage in the United States: 2004*, 16.

32. Elise Gould, "The Chronic Problem of Declining Health Care Coverage," *Economic Policy Issue Brief*, no. 202 (September 16, 2004): 3.

33. Center for Medicare and Medicaid Services, U.S. Department of Health and Human Services, *Medicaid-at-a-Glance* 2005.

34. This discussion of the Medicaid program incorporates and selectively revises material written by the author and included in Dennis L. Dresang and James J. Gosling, *Politics and Policy in American States and Communities*, 6th ed. (New York: Pearson Longman, 2008), 486–87. It appears with permission of the publisher.

35. Simone Grimmeisen and Heinz Rothgang, "The Changing Role of the State in Europe's Health Care Systems," paper presented at the ASPAnet Conference, Oxford University, London, September 9–11, 2004.

36. U.S. Department of Agriculture, *Food Stamp Program Annual Summary*, www.fns.usda.gov/pd/fssummar.htm.

37. U.S. Department of Agriculture, *Current Monthly Summary of FNS Programs*, www.fns.usda.gov/pd/currentsum.htm.

38. This discussion incorporates and selectively revises material written by the author and appearing in James J. Gosling, *Understanding, Informing, and Appraising Public Policy* (New York: Pearson Longman, 2004), 136. It appears with permission of the publisher.

39. Gavin McCrone and David Mark Stephens, "Housing Policy in a European Perspective," *Housing Research* 129 (October 1994).

40. Robert W. Burchell and David Lstokin, "Influence on United States Housing Policy," *Housing Policy Debate* 6 (1995): 598.

41. Barbara Sard and Will Fischer, *House VA-HUD Appropriations Bill Would Jeopardize Access to Housing Vouchers for Low-Income Families* (Washington, DC: Center for Budget and Policy Priorities, November 22, 2002), 1.

42. The Joint Center for Housing Studies, *The State of the Nation's Housing* (Cambridge, MA: Harvard University, 2002), 24.

43. Social Security Administration, *Social Security Basic Facts*, July 20, 2006, www.ssa.gov/pressoffice/basicfact.htm.

44. Christian Weller and Edward N. Wolff, *Retirement Income: The Crucial Role of Social Security* (Washington, DC: Economic Policy Institute, 2005), 1.

45. Social Security Administration, *A Summary of the 2006 Annual Social Security and Medicare Trust Fund Reports*, www.ssa.gov/OACT/TRSUM/trsummary.html.

46. Social Security Administration, *2006 OASDI Trustees Report*, Figure II.D3, www.ssa.gov/OACT/TR/TR06/tr06.pdf.

47. Six members, four of them by virtue of their administrative position in government (the secretaries of the Treasury, Labor, and Health and Human Services and the commissioner of Social Security), along with two public members.

48. Social Security Administration, *A Summary of the 2006 Annual Social Security and Medicare Trust Fund Reports*.

49. Joseph F. Quinn and Olivia S. Mitchell, "Social Security on the Table," *American Prospect*, no. 26 (May–June 1996): 77.

Chapter 9. Distributing the Benefits of Economic Growth: Rising Income Inequality and the Middle-Class Squeeze

1. Adam Smith, *The Wealth of Nations*, ed. Edwin Cannan (Chicago: The University of Chicago Press, 1976), 2:18.

2. Heather Boushey and Christian E. Weller, "Inequality and Household Economic Hardship in the United States of America," *DSEA Working Paper No. 18*, April 2006, 2.

3. The G-7 nations include Canada, France, Germany, Great Britain, Italy, Japan, and the United States.

4. *The Economist* 380, no. 8495 (September 16, 2006): 12–14.

5. Ibid., 14–15.

6. Center on Budget and Policy Priorities, *Poverty Remains Higher, and Median Income for Non-Elderly Is Lower Than When Recession Hit Bottom*, September 1, 2006.

7. Calculated income shares for 1913–98 are included in Thomas Piketty and Emmanuel Saez, "Income Inequality in the United States, 1913–1998," *The Quarterly Journal of Economics*, vol. CXVIII, issue 1 (February 2003), and updated calculations through 2004 were made available in September 2006 at http://elsa.berkeley.edu/~saez/, compliments of Emmanuel Saez.

8. Ian Dew-Becker and Robert J. Gordon, "Where Did the Productivity Growth Go?: Inflation Dynamics and the Distribution of Income," *National Bureau of Economic Research Working Paper 11842*, December 2005, Table 7.

9. Ibid., Figure 8.

10. David H. Autor, Lawrence F. Katz, and Melissa S. Kearney, "The Polarization of the U.S. Labor Market," *National Bureau of Economic Research Draft Working Paper*, January 2006.

11. Heather Boushey and Christian E. Weller, "Inequality and Household Economic Hardship in the United States of America," 14.

12. Gerald Prante, "Summary of Latest Federal Individual Income Tax Data," *Tax Foundation Fiscal Fact No. 66*, September 25, 2006, www.taxfoundation.org/publications/printer/250.html.

13. The Concord Coalition, "The Surplus Field of Dreams," *Issue Brief*, October 11, 2000.

14. *Remarks by the President in Tax Cut Bill Signing Ceremony*, Office of the Press Secretary, The White House, June 7, 2001.

15. Ibid.

16. Leonard E. Burman, "The Impact of Tax Reform on Low- and Middle-Income Households," *Testimony Submitted to the House Committee on Ways and Means*, June 8, 2005, 2.

17. Ibid., 13.

18. Gerald Prante, "Summary of Latest Federal Individual Income Tax Data."

19. Ibid.; and Citizens for Tax Justice, *The Bush Tax Cuts Enacted Through 2006*, June 22, 2006, 2.

20. Citizens for Tax Justice, *The Bush Tax Cuts Through 2006*, 2.

21. William G. Gale and Peter R. Orszag, "Bush Administration Policy: Distributional Effects," *Tax Notes* (September 27, 2004): 1561.

22. Andrea Brandolini and Timothy M. Smeeding, "Inequality: International Evidence," unpublished paper, June 2006.

23. Timothy M. Smeeding, "Public Policy, Economic Inequality, and Poverty: The United States in Comparative Perspective," *Social Science Quarterly, Supplement to Volume 86* (2005): 955–83.

24. Vincent A. Mahler and David K. Jesuit, "Fiscal Redistribution in the Developed Countries: New Insights From the Luxembourg Income Study," *Socio-Economic Review* 4 (2006): 490.

25. Marco Mira d'Ercole, "Income Inequality and Poverty in OECD Countries: How Does Japan Compare?" *Japanese Journal of Social Security Policy* 5 (June 2006): 9.

26. Lane Kenworthy and Leslie McCall, "Inequality, Public Opinion, and Redistribution," unpublished paper, August 2005.

27. Robert E. Lane, "Market Justice, Political Justice," *American Political Science Review* 80 (June 1986): 383–402.

28. Benjamin I. Page and Robert Y. Shapiro, *The Rational Public: Fifty Years of Trends in America's Policy Preferences* (Chicago: The University of Chicago Press, 1992), 128.

29. James Kluegel and Eliot R. Smith, *Beliefs About Inequality: Americans' Views of What Is and What Ought to Be* (New York: Aldine Publishing, 1986).

30. Roper Center for Public Opinion Research, *Public Perspective* 9, no. 2 (February/March 1998): 32.

31. John F. Manley, "American Liberalism and the Democratic Dream: Transcending the American Dream, *Policy Studies Review* 10 (1990): 90.

32. President Bill Clinton, *Address to Democratic Leadership Council*, November 13, 1993.

33. The Gallup Organization, January 20–23, 2003.

34. Lake Research Partners, *The American Dream Survey*, August 14–20, 2006; Widmeyer Research and Polling, *New American Dream, July 2004*; National League of Cities, *The American Dream in 2004*, September 2004; and *Harris Poll #27*, June 12, 2002.

35. *The American Dream in 2004*.

36. *The American Dream Survey*.

37. Pew Research Center, December 2004.

38. Katharine Bradbury and Jane Katz, "Are Lifetime Incomes Growing More Unequal?: Looking at New Evidence on Family Income Mobility," *Federal Reserve Bank of Boston Regional Review* (Quarter 4, 2002): 5.

39. Note that the Census Bureau data are for household income, whereas the Bradbury and Katz study uses University of Michigan panel data for family income—the two of which are not directly comparable.

40. www.census.gov/hhes/www/housing/hvs/historic/histt14.html.

41. www.realtor.org/Research.nsf/files/Rel06Q2F.pdf/$FILE/Rel06Q2F.pdf.

42. Data for 1980 provided by Thomas J. Doyle, National Association of Realtors, October 25, 2006.

43. *The Economist* 382, no. 8517 (March 10, 2007).

44. *Remarks by Susan Schmidt Bies, Member of the Board of Governors of the Federal Reserve System, at the National Credit Union Administration's 2007 Risk Mitigation Summit*, January 11, 2007.

45. Lisa Clemens-Cope, Bowen Garrett, and Catherine Hoffman, "Changes in Employees Health Insurance Coverage, 2001–2005," *Kaiser Commission on Medicaid and the Uninsured Issue Paper*, October 2006, 8.

46. Ibid., 2.

47. Kaiser Family Foundation, *Trends and Indicators in the Changing Health Care Marketplace*, 2006, Exhibit 3.5.

48. The College Board, *Trends in College Pricing, 2005*, 11, 15.

49. Federal Reserve Board, *Consumer Credit*, October 27, 2006, www.federalreserve.gov/releases/g19/hist/cc_hist_sa.html.

50. Pension Benefit Guarantee Corporation, *An Analysis of Frozen Defined Benefit Plans*, December 21, 2005, 1–2.

51. Employee Benefit Research Institute, "Basics of the Pension Benefit Guarantee Corporation (PBGC)," *Facts from ERBI*, July 2005, 3.

52. Employee Benefit Research Institute, "The Impact of the Erosion of Retiree Health Benefits on Workers and Retirees," *ERBI Issue Brief*, no. 279 (March 2005): 7.

53. Ibid., 6.

54. Tom Brokaw, *The Greatest Generation* (New York: Random House, 2000).

Index

About the Author

James J. Gosling has taught at the University of Wisconsin-Madison and the University of Utah. His recent books include *Politics and Policy in American States and Communities* (with Dennis L. Dresang), Sixth Edition (Pearson Longman, 2008); *Budgetary Politics in American Governments*, Fourth Edition (Routledge, 2006), and *Understanding, Informing, and Appraising Public Policy* (Pearson Longman, 2004).